Imbert de Saint-Amand

Marie Louise and the decadence of the Empire

Imbert de Saint-Amand

Marie Louise and the decadence of the Empire

ISBN/EAN: 9783337274221

Printed in Europe, USA, Canada, Australia, Japan

Cover: Foto ©ninafisch / pixelio.de

More available books at **www.hansebooks.com**

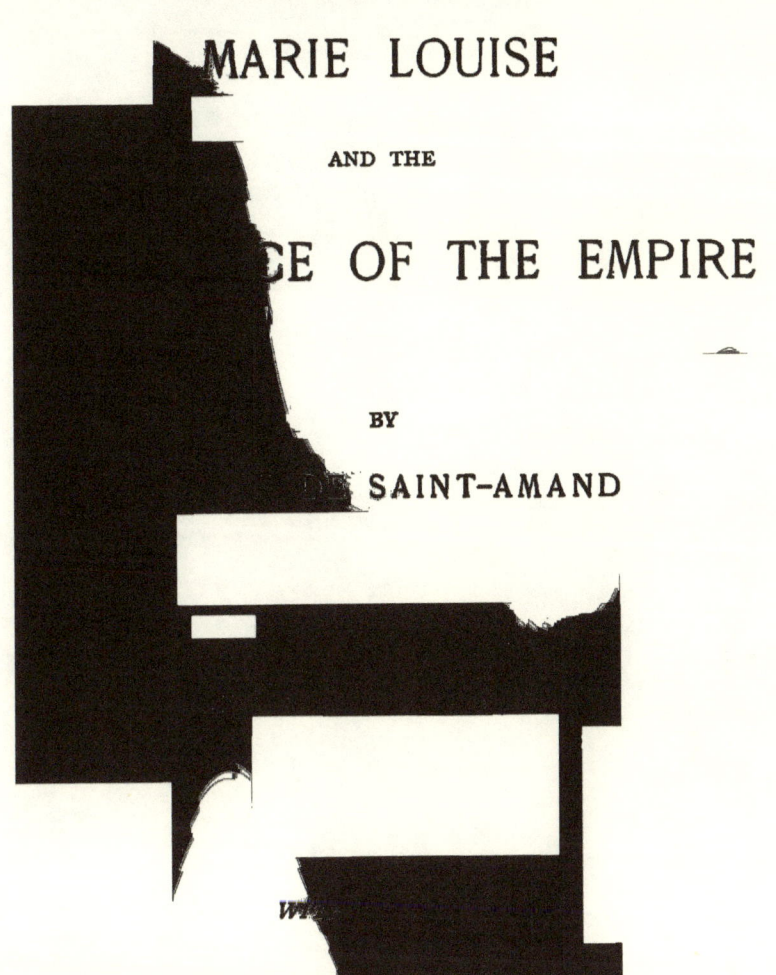

MARIE LOUISE

AND THE

...E OF THE EMPIRE

BY

...SAINT-AMAND

NEW YORK
CHARLES SCRIBNER...
1890

CONTENTS.

MARIE LOUISE

AND

THE DECADENCE OF THE EMPIRE

MARIE LOUISE

THE DECADENCE OF THE EMPIRE.

I.

MARIE LOUISE AT SAINT CLOUD.

MARIE LOUISE, after her triumphal progress to Prague, reached the Palace of Saint Cloud on her return July 18, 1812, and her arrival was announced by the cannon of the Invalides. This paragraph appeared in the *Moniteur* of the 21st: "Paris, July 21st. A vast crowd took advantage of the beautiful weather yesterday to visit Saint Cloud and the neighboring country. At six in the afternoon the Empress drove through the park in a barouche. When Her Majesty and the King of Rome appeared, warm cheers broke out on all sides, and accompanied Her Majesty all the way." Sunday, July 26, the Empress received, after mass at the palace, in the Apollo Gallery, the great bodies of state and persons who had been presented at court; then going into the ball-room, she gave audience, with her accustomed grace, to the princes who held high positions, the

1

ministers, the high officers of the Empire, the Grand
Eagles of the Legion of Honor, and the Diplomatic
Body.

Marie Louise was not Regent: Napoleon reigned
and governed from the heart of Russia. An auditor
of the Council of State carried to him every week the
reports and propositions of the ministers. The Ministers of Police wrote to him every day; and the
Emperor also received confidential notes from people
who, although they held no official position, were
commissioned to write to him on questions of internal policy, on the state of public sentiment, and
even on literary subjects. From a distance of seven
hundred leagues he directed his vast empire, with its
one hundred and thirty departments, reaching from
the Tiber to the mouths of the Elbe and the Scheldt,
exactly as if he had been in his capital.

It was not the Empress, but the Archchancellor
Cambacérès, who presided at the meetings of the ministers. "Marie Louise," says the Baron of Méneval,
"had charge of nothing but the court presentations.
Every Sunday she went to mass, at which any one
who had been presented was allowed to be present.
After mass she passed through the gallery before the
chapel, speaking to all who were there : she also
received on formal occasions. Her timidity was
always noticeable, and her attempts to overcome it
often gave her an air of awkwardness. Every evening she received men and women whose names were
on the list of invited guests. The Emperor drew up

this list, and took pains to choose such as the Empress would like; so she always on such occasions felt perfectly at ease, and did the honors freely and gracefully. She played billiards with such persons as she chose: whist-tables were set, as a matter of form, in the drawing-room she was in, and the evening ended with singing or acting."

Yet, in spite of all the homage of her attentive and obsequious courtiers, Marie Louise was sad. Far from her husband, her counsellor and protector, this woman of twenty felt lonely and homesick. When the Emperor was away, she felt like a foreigner in France, and longed for the country in which she had grown up. Her first impression on seeing Saint Cloud without Napoleon had been very painful. "May Heaven grant him a speedy return!" she wrote to her father. "For this separation I find most painful, and I have not courage enough to keep from complaining." To all the pomp and splendors that surrounded her, to the river flowing at her feet, to the great capital she saw in the distance, to the venerable trees in the park of Saint Cloud, to the beautiful view glowing under the brilliant sun, she might have said with the poet: —

"You miss one person, and all is empty."

Every evening when she was enjoying the coolness of that lovely garden, her thoughts turned with melancholy to the rash husband who was forever defying fortune. Why, she would ask with a sigh, does he not take his wife and son with him? Would he not be as happy in this beautiful park as in the wild steppes of Russia? Had he not fought battles enough, faced enough dangers, gathered all the laurels he needed? Was the empire which reached from the Eternal City to the Hanseatic towns too small for the ambition of the younger son of a poor Corsican family? Should he not be satisfied with the control of such an empire? And had not the King of Italy, the Protector of the Confederation of the Rhine, the Mediator of the Swiss Confederation, the son-in-law of the Emperor of Austria, and the father of the King of Rome, the right to rest? The unbroken calm that prevailed in the young Empress's peaceful retreat presented a marked contrast with the terrible convulsions that were agitating the other side of Europe. But Marie Louise was often beset with gloomy presentiments; when lost in revery she seemed, amid the silence of the gardens, to be listening to the distant echoes of a terrible war. It was in vain that her courtiers continually told her that Napoleon could not be beaten; her good sense said that no man in the world was invincible or immortal.

She tried to forget her gloomy thoughts in her affection for the little King of Rome. "My boy is very well," she wrote, August 9; "every day he becomes handsomer and stronger; he can already walk alone; he has fifteen teeth, but he has not begun to talk." Marie Louise found much comfort in her active correspondence with her husband and her father, who, much to her satisfaction, seemed closely united and much attached to each other.

August 15, 1812, the Emperor's birthday was celebrated with its usual splendor, and the Empress made a visit to the Tuileries. An enormous crowd greeted her with enthusiasm. No bad news had yet come from the seat of war, and every one expected that the wonders of Austerlitz, Jena, and Wagram were about to be repeated by this grand army, the largest and finest that France had ever sent forth. Absolute confidence prevailed, not among wise and thoughtful people, — for they already dreaded the future, — but among the multitude, who regarded Napoleon as a supernatural being, a sort of demigod.

A few weeks later, the conqueror's glory was to suffer a terrible blow, but in Paris, August 15, 1812, it was without a shadow. Early in the morning the firing of cannon announced the opening of the celebration. At noon the Empress-Queen surrounded by her ladies and officers in waiting received at the Tuileries, in the Throne Room, the princes holding high offices, the cardinals, the high officers of the Crown, the Grand Eagles of the Legion of Honor, the Princes of the Confederation of the Rhine, and every one who had admission to court. Napoleon was very anxious that no details should be omitted in his absence. Then the Diplomatic Body was introduced to the audience with the usual formalities. When it was over, the Empress betook herself to the chapel of the palace to hear mass, which was said by her First Almoner, Count Ferdinand de Rohan: it was followed by a Te Deum. That evening Paër's opera, *Numa*, was given in the palace theatre, and when it was over, Marie Louise made her appearance on the balcony of the Hall of the Marshals, and was greeted with rapturous applause from the garden and terraces. From the balcony she listened to an out-door concert. Then there were fireworks on the Place de la Concorde, after which the Empress returned to Saint Cloud.

The Grand Army also celebrated the Emperor's birthday, and desired to fire on the remote banks of the Dnieper some salvos in Napoleon's honor. All the marshals went with their staffs to present the compliments to their sovereign. At that moment the cannon sounded in sign of joy, and when the Emperor complained of the waste of precious ammunition, the marshals, with ingenious flattery, answered that the powder that was used had been captured from the Russians at the battle of Krasnoë. Alas! neither he nor his soldiers had any suspicion of the terrible disasters that were to befall them three months later at that very spot. But yet they were depressed: the original faults of the fatal expedition had begun to show themselves. Desertions were very frequent; the heat, as excessive as was to be the cold, had reached 90° F. The army was growing wearied of this region of plains and marshes into which it was plunging imprudently, without getting

sight of the enemy; of this war in which it found
everything destroyed before it; of the alarming solitudes, the vile roads, the wooden towns which a
single torch had sufficed to set ablaze. Already abandoned by Turkey and Sweden, from which aid had
been expected, too timid to restore Poland in spite of
all the heroism it displayed, losing an illusion every
day after he crossed the Niemen, Napoleon, who no
longer had the health or the ardor of his earlier days,
could not say again what he had said at the beginning of the campaign: " A more favorable combination of circumstances could not occur. I feel that it
is leading me on." The conqueror was indeed led
on, but by fate to the abyss. Possibly he already
regretted that he had not remained at Saint Cloud,
in that charming spot where his wife would have celebrated his birthday with such affection, and he might
have celebrated that of the King of Rome. How
many tears, how much bloodshed, he would have
saved! Less than three years later Blücher was to
establish his headquarters in this same Palace of Saint
Cloud, which, as well as all the Imperial palaces and
all his grandeur, wealth, and glory, Napoleon might,
with a little wisdom, so easily have preserved. The
tailors of the enemy's army set up their workshops
in the theatre. Prussian soldiers caught goldfish in
the large basin under the palace windows. Blücher
slept with his dogs in the chamber of Marie Louise,
turning that abode of luxury into a kennel and a
smoking-room. July 12, 1815, he invited Prince

Metternich to dinner in the dining-room of the palace, and when after it he was walking with the Austrian minister through the Apollo Gallery, he said, "What a fool a man must be, who when he has all these fine things at home, has to run off to Moscow!"

II.

NAPOLEON was impatiently awaiting the battle which should throw open to him the road to Moscow. September 6, 1812, the sun shone on thousands of helmets, bayonets, and cannon on the heights of Borodino, and the Emperor, who had bivouacked the previous night on the left bank of the Kolocza, in the midst of his guard, had the satisfaction of seeing the Russians in position and determined to fight. At nine o'clock in the morning a civilian arrived before his tent. He had travelled eight hundred leagues; and all the way from Saint Cloud, his starting-place, to the Imperial headquarters, he had found the road full of soldiers, marching alone or in companies; the wounded returning home, prisoners going to the rear, artillery trains, vehicles of every sort; in short, an unending crowd: France, Germany, Italy, Poland, and yet other nations, seemed to be meeting on this narrow way. Napoleon received this new arrival with warmth. It was the Baron of Bausset, Prefect of the Palace, who brought him news from the Empress Marie Louise, and a portrait of the King of

9

Rome, the masterpiece of the great artist Gérard.
This portrait was packed in a box which filled the
whole top of the carriage. M. de Bausset thought
that in view of the decisive and long-expected battle
that was to be fought the next day, the Emperor
would not care to have the box opened; but he was
much mistaken. Napoleon forgot all other occupations in his desire to gaze upon his son's features.
The child's gentle face presented a great contrast
to the formidable preparations for the obstinate and
bloody struggle of the morrow. Then he placed the
picture before his tent, and summoned the officers of
his household to share with them his paternal joy.
"Gentlemen," he said to them, "you may be sure
that if my son were fifteen years old, he would be
here, among so many brave men, and not in a picture." A moment later he added, "It is an admirable portrait." All day long the painting remained
before the father's tent, and the soldiers of the Old
Guard were never tired of looking at it.

No day, indeed, was ever calmer than the one
before that great battle. Not a shot was fired, as if
hostilities had ceased by agreement. Why should
needless harm be wrought? Was not the next day
to decide everything? In the night the laughter of
the French, who are always merry, even in the face
of death, and the hymns of the Russians, who had
been invoking the celestial sword of Saint Michael the
Archangel, had at last been silenced in sleep. Both
armies were peacefully sleeping around the great fires

that they had lit against the cold and the dampness of a penetrating rain which had fallen in the evening. Napoleon did not sleep; the sudden change of the weather affected him; he was feverish and troubled with a dry cough. Worn out in body and mind, he in vain tried to quench his consuming thirst. One of his aides heard him speaking about the emptiness of glory. "What is war?" asked the winner of so many battles. "A barbarous business; its whole art is nothing but being the stronger at a given point." Then he added, "A great day is approaching. It will be a terrible battle." And terrible it was to be. Napoleon was to be victorious, but victorious without capturing any cannon, any flags; victorious, but with forty-seven of his generals and thirty-seven of his colonels killed or wounded; victorious, but the defeated were also to remain on the battle-field, and the enormous number of ninety thousand men, what would be the whole population of a large city, were to be stretched on the earth, wounded or dead.

Napoleon was not himself. Through fear of the future he did not dare to call on the Imperial Guard, who would have made the victory decisive. "Every one about him," says the General de Ségur, "gazed at him with astonishment. Previously in hot combats he had displayed a calm activity; but now it was a dull calm, an inactive, flaccid gentleness. Some thought it was the prostration that follows intense emotion; others that he was tired of everything, even of the glow of the battle. Many have noticed that

this calm persistency, this coolness which great men
exhibit on momentous occasions, turns with time into
indifference and sluggishness, when their fervor is
dulled by age. The most zealous explained his im-
mobility as due to the necessity of avoiding excessive
change of place, when in command of a long line,
lest it should be impossible to communicate with the
commander-in-chief." Alas! why had he not stayed
at Saint Cloud?

The victory itself was silent and sombre. In the
face of this huge slaughter, the generals ceased to
flatter him. During the contest, Marshal Ney, indignant that Napoleon refused to make use of the Guard,
exclaimed angrily: "What's the Emperor doing in
the rear of the army? That is the place for defeat, not
for success. If he doesn't want to fight himself, and
is no longer general, and wants to be Emperor everywhere, let him go back to the Tuileries, and let us
command in his place!" When Napoleon returned
to his tent, a deep melancholy was added to his physical sufferings. There is nothing gloomier than war
when one is ill. As he himself said, "Health is
indispensable in time of war; nothing can take its
place." The Emperor, who had known how to conquer, was unable to take advantage of his victory.
He stayed for three days at Mojaïsk, the victim of
a severe fever, and was compelled by the loss of his
voice, to write, instead of dictating, his orders. At
last, September 12, he was well enough to go to the
front in his carriage. He was but two days from
Moscow.

Moscow! it was the magic name, the proud name which amid their perils and sufferings the soldiers kept repeating to give themselves courage. Moscow they looked forward to as an oasis after the blood-stained desert. So, September 14, at two in the afternoon, when the French army reached the Mountain of the Salute (so called because there the Russians cross themselves and prostrate themselves at the sight of their holy city from its summit), and thence looked down on the many-colored city sparkling in the sun, with its two hundred and ninety-five churches, its terraces, its steeples with golden balls, its fifteen hundred castles, its vast gardens, its colossal Kremlin, their surprise, delight, and enthusiasm exceeded all description. Every soldier forgot his past sufferings; every heart glowed with military pride, patriotism, and the glow of conquest, and all burst into rapturous applause. At the height of his power Napoleon cried out, " There's the famous city at last ! " Then he added, " And high time, too ! "

Nevertheless, as if warned by a secret voice of the abyss that was about to open before him, the conqueror, with something very unlike his usual audacity, did not at first establish himself in Moscow. He merely entered a little way, then, turning round, he stopped at an inn in one of the suburbs of the city, Dragomilof, and spent the night there. The next day, September 15, since all seemed calm, he conquered the presentiments of the previous evening, and made a triumphant entry into the Moscovite capital. He had imagined that the keys of the city would be respectfully brought to him by delegates of the population, and that he would make a grand entrance into Moscow, as he had already done into Berlin and Vienna, amid a vast crowd which should feel for him as much admiration as awe. It was a great mistake: the city was deserted, and the soldiers were the sole spectators of their own glory. The footfalls of the cavalry horses alone broke the disturbing and solemn silence of the great city, which seemed dead. Five-sixths of the inhabitants had disappeared, and those who remained had hidden themselves. The streets and public places were solitudes. Thousands of blackbirds, crows, and rooks were fluttering about the belfries of this strange city, which wore a more Asiatic than European aspect.

By the side of the stone bridge over the Moskowa stands the Kremlin of the Ruricks and Romanoffs, with its staircase outside, the long, straight stairway called the Red Staircase, with the terrace running along outside of the Hall of the Czars, with its palace of Peter I. to the left, with the arsenal and two huge bronze mortars, and two gigantic cannon at each side of the main door,—the Kremlin with the church of Ivan the Great, the church with its lofty tower, its gilt domes, and its legendary cross. Napoleon was exultant, and in an outburst of pride he said: "At last I am in Moscow! I am in the old Palace of the Czars! I am in the Kremlin!" And he ascended to the top of the tower of Ivan the

Great, and thence looked down haughtily upon his conquest, through which wound the Moskowa. It was a solemn and mighty moment, — the culminating moment of an incomparable pyramid of glory and colossal power.

Let us pause here a moment. In a few moments Providence was to give the signal for this giant's fall, and the death agony of the immense empire, an agony which was to last two years, was about to begin. Fire had already broken out in different parts of the city, but they were supposed to be unimportant accidents, the results of the soldiers' carelessness. That evening Napoleon went to sleep in the Kremlin, and possibly dreamed of glory and greatness. Certainly before he closed his eyes he did not foresee the terrible catastrophe which was about to break forth. Meanwhile the fire was spreading in every direction before the equinoctial winds; they ran for the fire engines, but there were none, and the truth became clear. The governor, Rostopchin, had commanded convicts to set fire to the sacred city as if it were the meanest village on the Smolensk road. It was a terrible sight: drunken men were running about with torches, uttering horrid cries; savage women, fierce criminals, were hurrying through the flames, which they fed with wood dipped in pitch.

Napoleon still slept, and no one dared to wake him. At last the light of the sun and the fire aroused him, and he rushed to the window, exclaiming: "So that's the way they make war! The civilization of Petersburg has deceived us. They are nothing but Tartars."

The danger was ever growing; blazing cinders were falling upon the tow gunswabs which were spread out on the ground in front of the Kremlin, and threatened to set them on fire. There were four hundred caissons of ammunition in the courtyard; the arsenal was full of powder; the Emperor and his guard were sure to be blown up if a single one of the cinders had fallen on a single caisson. The merest spark might change the fate of the world: on such slender threads hang the fates of conquerors and of empires! There was the sorest anguish; it was rumored that the Kremlin was ruined, and that Napoleon and his fortune were about to disappear in a sea of fire. The fury of the fire grew wilder; it roared and surged like waves in a storm. The incendiaries were shot wherever found, and their bodies were thrown into the flames they had themselves lit. The city was a mere shell of crumbling ruin; the air was full of smoke and ashes. The windows of the Kremlin were melted and fell in fragments. His officers ran to Napoleon and earnestly addressed him: "Leave, Sire, leave, we beseech you."

At first the conqueror refused to leave his prey, but his persistence was vain: the fire was stronger. Conquered by the conflagration, he yielded and left the place. It was a terrible moment, prophetic of all that destiny would compel him to abandon. He hurried down the great northern staircase, famous for the massacre of the Strelitzes, but there he was hemmed in by a sea of flames which blocked every exit. What was to be done ? Napoleon could neither advance nor retreat. Fortunately there was descried a gate opening on the Moskowa, and through this narrow passage the fugitive escaped from the Kremlin. But his danger had only begun ; now he had to plunge into the city, which was all a fiery furnace. A narrow, winding street, already afire; was to be seen, and into that the Emperor plunged. All about him roofs were falling, arches crumbling,, beams crashing down : it was like one of the circles of Dante's Inferno. A few staunch friends proposed to the Emperor to cover him from head to foot with their cloaks and to carry him to safety in their arms ; he refused, and hastened on over the glowing cinders. His gray overcoat was burned in many places ; his hair was singed. At last, as if by miracle, he made his escape from the accursed city, and that evening he found quarters, a league away, on the Saint Petersburg road, in the castle of Petrovski, the summer-house of one of the Emperor Alexander's chamberlains.

When Napoleon awoke the next day, September 17, he looked at Moscow : the horizon was all aglow ; the fire, so far from going out, was burning with redoubled violence. He exclaimed sadly, " This betokens great misfortunes ! " Yet he did not lose heart; he wished to defy fortune again, and with greater audacity. Since one of Russia's two capitals

was burned, he wished to march on the other; but
his lieutenants murmured: "What! no rest? Are
we to march again? To push on to the north? To
go to meet the winter, as if it would not come soon
enough?" When the Emperor took counsel with
them, they all dissuaded him from this course. One
day at Saint Helena he said, "If it had been the
month of August, we should have marched on Saint
Petersburg." In the middle of September it was too
late.

The burning of Moscow lasted through the 17th
and the 18th; the 19th it slackened; the 20th it
stopped. Since the Kremlin had escaped, Napoleon
went back thither, imagining that his presence in the
city of the Czars, even if it were in ashes, would
augment his glory, and that the Emperor Alexander
would decide to sue for peace.

At the Kremlin Napoleon occupied a vast but
nearly unfurnished apartment; he had there his little
iron camp-bed, which he always carried with him to
the castles in which he slept in his campaigns. His
windows looked out on the Moskowa. Being struck
by the vast number of crows and ravens that were
cawing about, he said, impatiently, "Heavens! are
these birds of evil going to follow me everywhere?"
He found consolation in looking at the portrait of
the King of Rome, which he had placed in his bedroom. Marshal Davout wrote to his wife, September
22: "I have seen the portrait of the King of Rome.
I can say nothing about the likeness, for I have never

seen the young Prince, but the painting seemed to me admirable. The Emperor seemed to examine the portrait with a great deal of pleasure, with much more, indeed, than one would have thought possible amid so many cares."

The Emperor's court at the Kremlin consisted of the principal officers of the army. There were also present Count Daru, Secretary of State; the Count of Turenne, Chamberlain and Keeper of the Wardrobe; the Barons of Saluces and of Lambertye, equerries. Couriers took eighteen days to come from Paris, and there was not a day in which news from France failed to reach the Kremlin. Besides the couriers, mail-coaches plied between Paris and the imperial headquarters. Moreover, every week an auditor of the Council of State brought the work of the Ministers and carried it back to Paris, when it had been signed by the Emperor. There was also the usual active correspondence with the European courts.

Illusions still prevailed. Marshal Davout, that man of iron, wrote from Moscow, October 10, to his wife: "All the fatigues of the campaign have disappeared; the faces of the men are cheerful; their bearing is excellent. The position of the French army is such that if the Russians desire any chance to escape complete destruction, they must long for peace and try all means to secure it." October 4, still maintaining his heroic illusions, the Marshal wrote again: "All our dangers are over, and I have

no doubt that the enemy, if he wishes to escape the
risk of total destruction, will open his eyes and sue
for peace. They have burned a large part of Moscow, but there are enough houses left to quarter the
army, and enough supplies to feed it. The enemy
have ruined their empire for ages to come by this
atrocious act, which will harm only them. We have
repaired our losses and rested since our arrival much
more fully than could have been expected. Every
day we grow stronger in every respect."

The soldiers had found rich booty in the cellars
of the houses that had been burned, — wine, *liqueurs*,
clothes, furs, — and had recovered their usual gaiety,
forgetful of the past and careless of the future. A
company of French comedians, under the direction
of an actress, Madame Burray, was acting in the
pretty little theatre of the Posniakoff Mansion, which
the flames had spared. The first play given was the
Sports of Love and Chance. This frivolity presented
a curious contrast with events more terrible than any
tragedy. "There was no cabal," says the Baron of
Bausset, "either in the audience, which was composed
of soldiers, or on the stage, where there was no odious
rivalry. The pit was filled with soldiers, and the two
rows of boxes occupied by officers of every branch of
the service. The orchestra was very good; it consisted of the band of the Guards. There were eleven
performances. Napoleon was never present; but the
Prefect of the Palace had found another entertain-
ment for the Emperor. Among the strangers who

had remained in Moscow was an excellent tenor, named Tarquinio, whom he had sing Italian airs in the Kremlin. It was not a light matter," adds M. de Bausset, " to have been able, amid all the ruins that surrounded us, to organize so speedily a court concert and a town theatre."

Napoleon also thought of sending to Paris for the company of the Théâtre Français, and he was within an ace óf sending them an order to start from Paris for Moscow, for he meant to pass the winter there; moreover, every one in Paris, even Marie Louise, thought that was his intention.

At the first review, on the grand Place of the Kremlin, of the regiments already decimated, but still, through their ingenuity and devotion, presenting a martial, almost a faultless air, the Emperor said to his aide-de-camp, " Well, my dear Narbonne, what do you say about such a fine army manœuvring under such a bright sun?" " I say, Sire;" was the reply, " that it is already rested and can start for its winter quarters in Lithuania or, in Poland, and leave to the Russians their capital in the state to which they have brought it." Napoleon cast a long glance at his troops, but said nothing.

He still lulled himself with vain hopes of some arrangement with the Czar. He said to a Russian, M. de Jakowleff: " This war is embittered by a desperation which is due neither to Alexander nor me. Your Emperor is deceived, and the English are inflicting on Russia a blow which will bleed for a long time. Since Smolensk I have passed through nothing but burning towns and villages. Your patriotism is mere madness. Peter the Great himself would call you barbarians; and what would he say if he were to breathe the ashes of Moscow? Rostopchin's madness costs you more than ten battles. Besides, what has this fire profited you? Are there not enough houses left for my generals? Do not my soldiers find abundant stores in your cellars? But, once more, I didn't come to your capital to settle down there. I should have halted at the gates, I should have quartered my army in the suburbs, I should have declared Moscow a neutral town, if Alexander had said a word. That word I waited for several hours; I desired it. The slightest step would have shown to me that Alexander still felt in the bottom of his heart some trace of attachment to me. Then we should have promptly made peace without outside interference. He would have said to me, as he did at Tilsit, that he had been cruelly deceived about me, and everything would have been quickly forgotten. Instead of that, you see where we are! How much blood has been shed, what evils encompass us, from not understanding each other!"

Napoleon's great mistake lay in thinking that Moscow was like Berlin and Vienna. He had counted on a war in accordance with the rules, and he found a savage war. He was like a duellist who should expect a small sword and faces a club. This is expressed by Count Leo Tolstoi, in his *War and*

Peace, — a book in which all the passions of 1812 are revived: " After Smolensk," he says, " a war began to which none of the usual traditions could be applied. The burning of the towns and villages, the retreating after the battles, the continual attack of marauders, the guerilla warfare, were all outside of the usual rules. Napoleon, who halted at Moscow in the correct attitude of a duellist, felt this more than any one, and he never ceased blaming Kutusoff and the Emperor Alexander; but in spite of his complaints and the mortification of certain high personages at seeing the country fight in this way, the national club arose in a threatening fashion, and without troubling itself about the good taste or the rules, smote and crushed the French, until by sheer dint of brutal and ponderous strength it had completely repulsed the invasion!" And the Russian nobleman, excited by the memory of this patriotic hatred, adds: " Happy the people who, instead of offering the handle of their sword to the generous victor, grasp the first club within reach, without stopping to think of what others would do in the same case, and who do not lay it down before wrath and vengeance have given place in their hearts to contempt and pity!"

Napoleon kept waiting for a message of peace, but no message came. " What shall I do?" he asked of Count Daru. "Stay here," replied the faithful officer; "turn Moscow into an entrenched camp and spend the winter here." " That is bold advice," resumed the Emperor. "But what would they say at Paris? France would not become accustomed to my absence, and Prussia and Austria would take advantage of it." Was it indeed possible to remain motionless for six months two hundred leagues from Wilna, three hundred from Dantzic, seven hundred from Paris, with the prospect of being hemmed in, not merely by the snows of winter, but by all the forces of Russia?

His genius, once so swift in forming plans and so audacious in carrying them out, was no longer itself; he hesitated, fumbled, changed his mind. At one moment he decided to push on, then to remain stationary, then to retreat. He was no longer the man whose slightest word seemed the decree of fate; he ceased to be the all-powerful master who had made fortune his slave. How often he had blundered! No one of his courtiers could again call him infallible. He had made a mistake in venturing into the north before he had completed the subjection of Spain; in failing to secure, before starting, an alliance with Sweden and Turkey; in beginning the war too early, in view of the political conditions, too late, in view of the time of year; in not following his victory on the Moskowa, and in yielding to an excess of prudence after an excess of rashness; and in prolonging a fatal delay at Moscow. "Don't I know," he said, "that Moscow has no military value? Moscow is not a military position; it is only a political position. I am thought to be a general there, when in fact I am an emperor." Then he went on to say that a sovereign ought never to acknowledge a fault; that he would thereby only lose reputation and glory; that he should push on, and his persistency would insure success. His common-sense told him that he ought to have known that the terrible winter would not await his permission to fall upon him; that all his guns, were they as numerous as the waves of the sea or the stars in the sky, would be of no avail against the storms and the snowdrifts: Napoleon knew all this, but to withdraw, to retreat, would be to lose his reputation as an infallible and invincible man. What would France, what would England say? What would be the verdict of posterity? Time slipped by, and the bright autumn weather only nourished his illusions.

The Emperor, held fast in the Kremlin by an irresistible force, became more and more undecided. General de Ségur describes him as he was at that time, languid, sitting long over his meals, which formerly were simple and brief, lying down for hours at a time, and, novel in hand, waiting for the conclusion of his own terrible career. "Having reached the height of his glory, he doubtless foresaw that this first step backward would be the signal of its decay ; hence he remained motionless, lingering yet for a few moments upon this summit." He would not own it to himself, that, like an aëronaut who has risen to too great a height, he had to descend or die. What was his employment during the last hours of his stay in the

City of the Czars?   He discussed the merit of the
new verses he had received from Paris, and spent
three evenings in drawing up the regulations of the
Comédie Française.   In the morning of October 15,
he took a puerile pleasure in dating this decree from
Moscow.   That evening, in the drawing-room which
he occupied at the Kremlin, just beneath the Czarina's
apartments, when the candles were lit, and a huge fire
was blazing in the fireplace adorned with marble and
gold, he spoke with satisfaction of the decree that he
had that morning signed, in order to get in this frivolous distraction some relief from the secret anguish
which rent his soul without betraying itself upon his
face.   Then he strode up and down the room, talking
freely about art, literature, Corneille, and Talma.

Nevertheless, time pressed.   October 13, there fell
a slight frost, without in the least disturbing the fine
weather, indicating to all that the time had come for
a final decision: if Moscow was to be abandoned, there
was not a moment to lose.   October 18, a beautiful
morning, just when the Emperor was reviewing Marshal Ney's corps, the sound of cannon was heard in
the direction of the outpost of the King of Naples;
the Russians had resumed hostilities without even
proclaiming a truce.   There could no longer be any
question of negotiations for peace.   Napoleon hesitated no longer.   Moscow was to be abandoned the
next day.

The illusions prevailed up to the last moment.
October 17, two days before the retreat began, Mar-

shal Davout wrote to his wife : " The Emperor has never made a finer campaign. In three months he has conquered the enemy's capital, and defeated the large armies which they cannot form anew. It was high time to make this campaign; the preparations of the Russians were very formidable, and if we had not met them when we did, they might have had great advantages. Now they have only cavalry left : their infantry amounts to nothing; for an ignorant, untrained militia cannot be counted. Whatever may be the hostile spirit of the government and the influence of the English, it is probable that in a few months, when their fervor is exhausted, they will become conscious of their misfortunes, and will be anxious for peace as the sole means of safety."

Before leaving, Napoleon desired to carry away, as a memorial of his brief conquest, the huge golden cross surmounting the steeple of Saint Ivan the Great. He meant to place it above the dome of the Invalides in Paris. But it was not easy to detach it from the Russian monument; and while the workmen were busy at this work of destruction, amid the cawing of innumerable crows, Napoleon exclaimed, " Doesn't it seem as if these crows were defending the cross ? "

October 19, Moscow was full of movement from early dawn; the hour of departure had struck. It was an exodus like those in ancient times when whole nations were emigrating. The files were interminable; there were a hundred thousand soldiers; besides them, forty thousand men and women of all ages; numberless vehicles of every sort followed; handsome barouches, heavy carts, heavily loaded ammunition wagons, wheelbarrows laden with booty, more than five hundred and fifty cannon, two thousand artillery wagons: the men were sturdy and healthy, the women anxious, the horses lean and exhausted. Every language was spoken in this motley cohort; there were countless trophies won from the enemy, — Russian, Persian, and Turkish flags, and the huge cross, the cross of Saint Ivan, so heavy that it had to be abandoned on the way, as a cumbersome burden. Was it an army or a vast caravan, this strange medley of the most dissimilar things? In the broad avenue of Kalouga, by which they left Moscow, eight wagons drove abreast; and though this vast mass was not interrupted for a moment, the exodus which began in the early morning had not ended by evening. A bright sun, in a cloudless sky, lit up the first day of this retreat, the most lamentable known to history; and when they reached the Mountain of the Salute which, a few weeks before, they had ascended with so much joy, the fugitives turned a last look upon Moscow and its ruins.

III.

EVER since the month of October, uneasiness had begun to spread in France; contradictory rumors were in circulation. Some said that the Emperor had met with serious disasters; others that, not content with conquering Russia, he designed to conquer India. It was generally expected that he would spend the winter at Moscow, and this prospect did not inspire confidence. Although he announced a victory, that of the Moskowa, the 18th bulletin of the Grand Army, which was printed in the *Moniteur* of September 27, produced a gloomy impression. It was felt that it was not one of those decisive battles, like Austerlitz, Jena, or Wagram, which terminate a war by a crushing blow.

From the Imperial headquarters at Mojaïsk, September 10, 1812, Napoleon had addressed to the archbishops and bishops of his empire a circular letter, in which he said: "The passage of the Niemen and the Dnieper; the battles of Mohilof, Potolsk, Ostrono, Smolensk, and finally the battle of the Moskowa, all call upon us to render thanks to the God of

29

our armies. It is hence our desire that, on receipt
of these presents, you make arrangements with the
proper persons. Collect my people in the churches
to offer their prayers in conformity with the rites
and ceremonies of the Church in such circumstances.
This letter being intended only for this purpose, I
pray God to hold you in his keeping." In the *Moniteur* we read: "To-day, Sunday, October 4, 1812,
Her Majesty the Empress and Queen went to the
Palace of the Tuileries; she heard mass in the
chapel, and was present at the *Te Deum* sung in
honor of the victories of His Majesty the Emperor
and King. After the mass there was a reception.
After the reception Her Majesty returned to the
Palace of Saint Cloud. A *Te Deum* was sung the
same day in the cathedral."

In spite of this commanded thanksgiving, much
uneasiness prevailed. The continuance of this vast
war, to which no end could be seen, excited general
alarm. Every one said it was to be a second edition
of the Spanish war. Banking, commerce, and industry were suffering severely. Many families were
already in mourning. "In Paris," says the Duke of
Rovigo, in his Memoirs, "every one had a map of
Russia, in which were stuck pins at all the places
mentioned in the bulletins. Everywhere information was anxiously sought about an army in which
every one had a brother, a son, or a friend."

The burning of Moscow produced a general feeling of alarm; the confident calmness of the official

language satisfied no one. The 22d bulletin of the Grand Army, dated September 27, and published in the *Moniteur* of October 14, was yet noteworthy for its tone of calm and optimism. " Consul-General Lesseps," it said, " has been appointed superintendent of the province of Moscow. He has organized a city council and many committees, all composed of the inhabitants. The fires are completely extinguished. Every day there are discovered stores of sugar, skins, and clothes. The enemy's army appears to be retiring on Kalouga and Tula. Tula contains the largest manufactory of arms in Russia. Our advance guard is on the Pakra. The Emperor is quartered in the Imperial Palace of the Kremlin. In the Kremlin there have been discovered many ornaments used for the coronation of the Emperors, and all the flags captured from the Turks in the last hundred years. The weather is like that of the end of October in Paris. It rains a little, and there are occasional white frosts. It is asserted that the Moskowa, and the rivers of the country, do not freeze before the middle of November. The greater part of the army is cantoned at Moscow and is resting from its fatigues."

Judging from his bulletins, Napoleon was as tranquil and happy in the Palace of the Czars as in his Imperial country places of Saint Cloud, Compiègne, or. Fontainebleau, and one would have said that the winter was never coming. But the auditors of the Council of State who returned to Paris from Moscow with the portfolio, who had seen the terrible ravages of the

fire, who knew the enormous losses which the army
had already suffered, and had seen the Emperor's
embarrassment and indecision, were only too fearful
of the approaching disasters, and their alarm spread
rapidly in official circles and in the Parisian drawing-
rooms, though everywhere else perfect peace prevailed.
The capital and the provinces uttered no murmur.
Napoleon, at a distance of seven hundred leagues
from his empire, was feared and obeyed as if he had
been on the spot, and the numberless wheels of the
government turned with perfect regularity.

Marie Louise was living in perfect quiet in the
Palace of Saint Cloud, when, in the night of October
22, there broke out the most unexpected and strange
conspiracy.   There happened to be at that time in a
private hospital in Paris, kept by Dr. Dubuisson, in
a house to the left of the Faubourg Saint Antoine,
near the Barrière du Trône, a former general of
Moreau's army, who passed for a fanatical Republican, and in 1807 had been accused of secret plot-
ting against the Emperor; but being regarded rather
as a lunatic than as a real conspirator, he had at first
been confined in the Conciergerie, but afterwards had
been transferred to a private hospital.   His name was
Charles François de Malet, and he was born at Dôle,
June 28, 1754.   In spite of his reputation as an
ardent Republican, he was descended, on both his
father's and his mother's side, from the old nobility
of Franche Comté, and under the old régime he
had served among the musketeers in the King's

household. His attitude as a prisoner was not stoical. He had written, July 3, 1810, to the Duke of Rovigo, Minister of Police: "My Lord, I am detained for having repeated a few possibly indiscreet, but yet in no way really reprehensible remarks, which became serious only through the perfidious way in which they were interpreted. The first ground which I bring forward, in trying to persuade Your Excellency to put an end to a long and undeserved detention, is the zeal and devotion which I have at all times shown in His Majesty's service, as is set forth in a memorial wherein, without mention of my former service, I speak only of those I have rendered to His Majesty since the establishment of the Empire." Thus the pretended Brutus bowed before the Cæsar, but hated him all the while. He was convinced that the Imperial Colossus had feet of clay, and in the month of October he thought the time ripe for carrying out the fantastic plan which had haunted him for many years. The means that he devised at the first glance seem childish, and it is surprising that they could have succeeded for even an hour.

To pretend that the Emperor had died in Russia October 8; to make this falsehood the keynote of the conspiracy; to invent an alleged report of an alleged extraordinary session, pretended to have been held in the evening of October 22; to invent likewise a decree of the Senate abolishing the Imperial government, appointing a provisional government, and setting General Malet at the head of the Post of

Paris of the first military division; to escape secretly
from Dr. Dubuisson's private hospital; to have two
silent companions, one disguised as an aide-de-camp,
the other as Commissary of Police; to go to the Popincourt barracks; there to read the false decree to the
commander of the 10th cohort; by means of forged
orders to take this band as an armed force; to go to
the Prison de la Force and set free Generals Lahorie
and Guidal, who were confined there for political reasons, to make them his accomplices, without saying
anything to them about it before they were set free,
and then with the aid of the 10th cohort to proceed
to arrest the Duke of Rovigo, Minister of Police, the
Duke of Feltre, Minister of War, M. Pasquier, Prefect
of Police, General Hulin, Commander of the Post of
Paris; to have prepared at the Hôtel de Ville the
quarters destined for the provisional government; to
do all this in the night between the 22d and the 23d
of October, and in the morning of the 23d to proclaim
the Revolution, — such was the outline of the plot.

At first General Malet took into his confidence
only three persons, — a Royalist abbé, named Lafon,
who was in the private hospital with him, and helped
him prepare the forged orders; and two young men,
Rateau, a corporal of the Guard of Paris, and Bon-
treux, a law student: the first was to take the part
of the aide; the other, that of Commissary of Police.
October 22, 1812, at about ten in the evening, the
general made his escape from Dr. Dubuisson's house
and went to the rooms of a Spanish priest, in the

Place Royale, to put on his uniform, which he had instructed his wife to send thither. Here he found the two young men, who dressed themselves for the part they had to play. It was raining in torrents, and to pass the time they ate a supper and brewed a punch. It was half-past three in the morning when the general and his two acolytes began their expedition. They went first to the Popincourt barracks where the 10th cohort was quartered. No one was allowed to enter the barracks at night; so Malet pretended that he wanted to see only Colonel Soulier, in command of the 10th cohort. He was conducted to the colonel's quarters, which were outside of the barracks. He had him waked up, and pretending that he was not General Malet, but General Lamotte, — for this whole affair was one mass of lies, — he said to the commander of the 10th cohort, "I see that you have not heard the news ; we have had the misfortune to lose our Emperor." On hearing this, Colonel Soulier, a good and brave man, though of a credulous nature, burst into tears. " The government has been changed," went on the pseudo-General Lamotte, "and here is an order which General Malet gave me to hand to you a moment ago." This order commanded that the cohort should fall into line, ready for action ; that it should be informed of the state of affairs, and be placed under the orders of the alleged General Lamotte.

The colonel obeyed without questioning; he called out his men, and had read to them the forged decree of the Senate, and they marched out, twelve hundred men strong, under the command of Malet, who called himself General Lamotte. Only one company remained in the barracks. It was to accompany Colonel Soulier to the Hôtel de Ville, to prepare the rooms destined for the provisional government. The colonel was moreover promoted to the post of brigadier-general, and received an order on the Treasury for one hundred thousand francs.

Malet was delighted with the success of his first step. The second was to go to the Prison de la Force to set free Generals Guidal and Lahorie, and to get them to join in his undertaking, of which they had not yet heard a word. He passed through the rue Saint Antoine at the head of the 10th cohort, and when he reached the prison, he had the doors opened without difficulty, embraced the two generals, announced to them the Emperor's death, and told them what they would have to do. " There is not a moment to be ,lost," he said to them. " Here are your instructions : take these troops and carry them out. I need only a half-company to seize the government. Then we shall meet at the Hôtel de Ville." General Lahorie was charged with the arrest of the Prefect of Police ; he was, besides, with the aid of General Guidal, to proceed to arrest the Ministers of War and of Police. As for General Malet, he reserved for himself the most difficult task, — the arrest of the Commander of Paris, General Hulin.

Everything passed in accordance with the conspirators' wishes. M. Pasquier, the Prefect of Police,
was a gentle and inoffensive man; he had already
got up and was at work in his office when they came
to arrest him, and he submitted to his arrest with the
best grace in the world, got into the cab, and was
driven to the Prison de la Force together with his
first assistant. Savary, the Duke of Rovigo, Minister
of Police, made a little more resistance, but seeing
that his life was threatened, he yielded. He describes his arrest in his curious Memoirs. General
Lahorie, formerly chief of staff of the Army of the
Rhine, had been his comrade in the first Revolutionary campaigns, and knew him intimately. "You are
under arrest," Lahorie said to him; "congratulate
yourself on falling into my hands; no harm shall
come to you." Savary did not understand. Lahorie
went on, "The Emperor was killed, October 8,
under the walls of Moscow." "What stuff you are
talking!" answered the Duke of Rovigo. "I have a
letter from him of that very day. I can show it to
you." A few moments later, General Guidal came
in, sword in hand, and he placed the point on
Savary's breast, who exclaimed, "Have you come
here to disgrace yourself by a cowardly assassination?" "No," replied Guidal; "I am not going to
kill you, but you must come with me." "Very well!
yes; but let me put on my clothes." "I'll have
them brought here." Savary, who before General
Guidal came, had tried in vain to undeceive the

soldiers, dressed as slowly as possible, in order to gain time. Then he was driven in a cab with Guidal to the Prison de la Force, accompanied by a few soldiers of the 10th cohort.

On the way, as he was passing along the Quai des Lunettes, an idea occurred to him : he devised a way of escaping ; he quietly opened the carriage door, and when he got near the clock-tower, he sprang out and ran towards the Palais de Justice. But he was at once pursued with cries of " Stop him ! stop him ! " and soon caught. He was brought back to the carriage, and a few minutes later was behind lock and key in the Prison de la Force.

At the Prefecture of the Seine, that is to say, at the Hôtel de Ville, everything proceeded as smoothly as General Malet could have wished. Count Frochot, Prefect of the Seine, had spent the night in the country, and was not to return to Paris till the morning. He was not at the Hôtel de Ville when Colonel Soulier arrived there at the head of a part of the 10th cohort and announced the Emperor's death, and that he was going to take possession of the rooms destined for the provisional government. An official of the Prefecture was at once sent off for the Prefect. The bearer of this message met him in the rue du Faubourg Saint Antoine on his way to Paris, unconscious of what was going on, and handed the note inviting him to come as soon as possible, and ending with these words, " *Fuit imperator.*" As soon as he reached the Hôtel de Ville, he found Colonel Soulier there, and was shown the forged orders. Resistance seemed impossible, and making no objection, he had the rooms prepared for the meeting of the provisional government.

In three points, then, — the Ministry of Police, the Prefecture of Police, and the Prefecture of the Seine, — General Malet's plan had been perfectly successful. The delay in the Duke of Rovigo's arrest made a delay which prevented that of the Minister of War. It was in the Place Vendôme, the staff-office of the Post of Paris, that the conspiracy fell to pieces. Malet went there himself with a detachment of the 10th cohort. He broke into the room where General Hulin and his wife were sleeping, bade him get up, and said to him, "I have come to bring you sad news; the Emperor is dead. A decree of the Senate, dated yesterday, has abolished the Imperial government, and I have been ordered to take your place. I have an even more painful duty to perform: it is to place you temporarily under arrest." Then a voice issued from the alcove; it was that of Madame Hulin. "But, my dear," she said, "if this gentleman is to take your place, he must have some orders to show you." "True," exclaimed General Hulin; "where are your orders, sir?" "My orders?" replied Malet; "here they are!" and with his pistol he shot down Hulin, breaking his jawbone. Then he quietly descended the staircase and proceeded towards the door of the neighboring house, which was occupied by the staff; there he found Adjutant-General Doucet,

Commander Laborde, and a police inspector. This last recognized him, and said, "M. Malet, you have no permission to leave your house unless I go for you." Then turning to Adjutant-General Doucet, he added, "There's some mischief up; arrest him at once; I will go to the Ministry to see what this thing means." Malet was standing against the fireplace; seeing that the game was up, he seized a pistol which he had in his coat pocket, to blow out Doucet's brains; but this officer had seen the motion in the looking-glass, and suddenly sprang on the bold conspirator, escaping the shot. At the same moment Commander Laborde grasped him about the waist, shouting, "To arms!" Malet was flung to the ground and bound hand and foot. In this condition he was carried to the balcony, from which Colonel Doucet called out to the soldiers of the 10th cohort, that they had been deceived by an impostor. The conspiracy was over. By noon everything went on as usual; the Duke of Rovigo had established himself again in his ministry, and M. Pasquier had returned to the Prefecture of Police. The preparations at the Hôtel de Ville for the alleged provisional government vanished in the twinkling of an eye. It all seemed like a dream.

It is interesting to notice how General Malet proposed to treat the Empress. In an order which was not carried out, he had commanded General Deriot, Chief of Staff and Commander of the Stores of the National Guard, to occupy at once Sèvres, Ville d'Avray, and Saint Cloud; the intention was to provide for the Empress's safety. The order contained these words: "We have become responsible to the whole nation for the life of Marie Louise, both for the national honor and for the guarantee she gives us, so long as she is in our power, as to the conduct of the Emperor of Austria towards France. As soon as you shall have completed your arrangements, you will do well to go to Saint Cloud, to reassure this Princess with regard to the condition of things, until the government shall have done this through the regular channels of diplomacy."

As soon as the conspirators had been arrested, the Minister despatched the Horse Guards to Saint Cloud. They reached there on a gallop, and made a great clatter in the palace courtyard. Marie Louise was much surprised by this unexpected disturbance, and ran out on the balcony in her dressing-gown, with her hair flying. She had a moment of alarm, at least for her son if not for herself, and ordering under arms the infantry in the palace, commanded preparations for defence. Shortly word came from Paris that order was completely restored, and that there was absolutely no occasion for fear. Nevertheless, the affair left a painful impression on the Empress's mind; for she was already able to see the future treachery of her husband's officers.

The next day, October 24, 1812, the Parisians read in the *Moniteur* this statement, which was placarded on the walls of the Capitol: "Three ex-generals, Malet, Lahorie, and Guidal, deceived the National

Guards and led them against the Minister of Police,
the Prefect of Police, and the Commander of the post
of Paris, against whom they used violence.   They dis-
seminated the report of the Emperor's death.   These
ex-generals have been arrested ; they are convicted
of imposture; they will be brought to justice.   Perfect calm reigns in Paris ; there was no disturbance
except in the three buildings visited by these brig-
ands."

The cruel deception of which the Duke of Rovigo
had been the victim, was for the Parisians, who are
always malicious and sharp-tongued, an occasion for
numberless jests and jeers.   Friends and enemies of
the Empire alike laughed at it.   A Minister of Police
arrested, a Minister of Police humbugged, a Minister
of Police imprisoned, was a godsend to the merry-
makers !   Punning on the name of the prison to
which they had been carried, it was said that the
Minister and the Prefect of Police had made a "tour
de force."   Referring to the fact that the Minister's
wife, alarmed by her husband's nocturnal arrest, had
run out of her room in her chemise, they said that
" in the whole affair, the person who made the best
appearance was she."   The ladies, who were frequently
annoyed by the interference of the police, were avenged
by this adventure, and said, " They would do much
better to busy themselves with what goes on in the
barracks than with what goes on in our boudoirs."

Yet the affair was more sad than laughable.   The
Duke of Rovigo, in his Memoirs, thus sums the mat-

ter up: "Had it not been for the accident which
prevented the arrest of the Minister of War and
returned me to my duties, General Malet would have
been in control of a great many things in a very
short time, and in a country very susceptible to the
contagion of example. He would have had control
of the Treasury, which was then well filled, of the
posts and the telegraph, and there were in France a
hundred cohorts of the National Guard. He would
have learned by the couriers arriving from the army
the lamentable state of affairs there, and nothing
would have stood in the way of his seizing the
Emperor, if he had come alone, or of marching to
meet him, if he had come with troops." To these
pessimistic views the Duke of Rovigo adds these
words: "In spite of this, Malet would not long have
played the part of a second Cromwell, because the
deception would have been soon found out, and every-
body in France was tired of agitation. Probably he
would have been alone in carrying out his further
plans. But the danger that threatened the public
peace was a serious one; and it exposed a weak
point in our position which every one thought more
secure. A special cause of surprise was the readi-
ness with which the soldiers believed in the Emperor's death, without its occurring to a single officer
to seek confirmation of the statement, and above all,
without thinking of his son. . . . This was a painful thought, and those who did not like to deceive
themselves were compelled to think that trouble
was in the air."

What was not a subject of laughter was the rigid severity with which General Malet and his accomplices were treated, whose great fault had been excessive credulity. The trial, which took place before a military commission, began October 27. One of the judges said to Colonel Soulier, " I ask you how it could happen that a superior officer should lose his head when Malet came to him and told him, 'I bring you important news; the Emperor is dead.' On hearing that, a loyal officer ought to have all his presence of mind. It is just on occasions like that, it should be understood, that soldiers do not lose their heads, and that the Emperor is immortal. When the Emperor dies, one shouts, 'Long live the Emperor!'" When the presiding officer asked Malet who were his accomplices, he answered quickly, "All France; you yourself, sir, if I had succeeded." After the speech of the government advocate, he arose, and said, "A man who has assumed the defence of his country's rights does not need to plead; he triumphs or he dies." A delay was asked in favor of Colonel Soulier, who had wept on hearing the alleged death of the Emperor, but this delay was refused him. Within five days there were arrested, tried, and condemned, fourteen unhappy men; and of these, twelve, including Generals Malet, Guidal, and Lahorie, were shot.

Malet was the only one who deserved death; but let us rather quote from a conscientious and distinguished author, M. Albert Duruy, who, in the *Revue des Deux Mondes* for February 1, 1879, published an

article on Malet's conspiracy, both interesting and
novel. "Consider," he says, "those plumed and
bedizened personages, who vanished at the moment
of danger like the decorations of the opera, and when
seen again were doubly obsequious; consider, on the
other hand, those improvised judges, so contemptuous
of the rights of the defence and of the simplest rules
of justice, so eager to finish with the affair, and you
cannot escape a painful feeling. The viciousness of
excessive centralization makes its appearance in its
most odious form, and in view of this general confusion, it is easy to understand the successive crumbling
of the forms of government that followed. All, in
various degrees, rested on public officials; and in
critical moments there has always been a lack of the
energetic aid and solidity which should have been
looked for."

In foreign countries the article in the *Moniteur*,
announcing at once the conspiracy and its failure,
produced a great impression. November 4, 1812,
Count Otto, French Ambassador at Vienna, wrote to
the Duke of Bassano, Minister of Foreign Affairs,
who was then at Wilna: "My Lord, on receipt of the
article inserted in the article of the *Moniteur* of
October 24, concerning the criminal attempts of ex-
Generals Malet, Lahorie, and Guidal, the Emperor of
Austria hastened to send a courier to his august
daughter, to obtain news from her at the earliest
possible moment. Your Excellency will readily
believe that this article has produced the greatest

sensation here, and that the many enemies of France are already making numberless conjectures in regard to the consequences of a plot that has failed, but from which they nevertheless expect the greatest results. Inasmuch as it is a long time since we have had any direct news from our armies, some agitators pretend that our troops are really exterminated, and that His Majesty the Emperor is no longer living. Russia has especial advantages for disseminating in Europe false reports. A great many of its richest nobles, especially women, are to be found everywhere, living in the highest society, and attracting by their lavish expenditures a herd of parasites, who are ready to flatter them and to serve their purposes. It is to them that we must ascribe the wild rumors circulating in Europe. I notice, in fact, by my letters from Milan and Paris, that the false news, so common here, flood likewise those two capitals: I may even add that for everything concerning Spain, Paris and Milan take the initiative." It was in vain that Marie Louise wrote to her father, November 21, 1812: "I am not alarmed by the disorder which a few insane men have caused, for I know too well the good character of the people, and their devotion to the Emperor, to have a moment's fear"; the blow had told. Up to that time the French administration and excellent police had been regarded as the cornerstone of the Imperial government. From that moment, doubts were felt all over Europe concerning the solidity of the edifice, and people began to say that

France, instead of resting, as had been supposed, on a.firm rock, was perhaps over a volcano.

Thiers has represented Malet's conspiracy as a wholly Republican plot. We are inclined to believe that it was rather a Royalist conspiracy. This is the thesis which M. Albert Duruy has supported with original documents, and with arguments that to us seem convincing. He tries to prove, and we think on good grounds, that this affair was only, so to speak, the first sketch, the prologue, of the Royalist movement of 1814. The ideas, the passions, the language, were the same. Of the Republic there was not a word either in the false decree of the Senate or in the other forged papers. The name of King was not uttered; but it is evident that if he was not on the stage, he was at least just behind the scenes. Who were Malet's provisional government? General Moreau, President; Carnot, Vice-President; Count Frochot, Prefect of the Seine; the Duke Mathieu de Montmorency; the Count Alexis de Noailles; Generals Malet and Augereau, Vice-Admiral Truguet, Senators Volney, Garat, Lambrecht, Destutt-Tracy, and Messrs. Jacquemont and Florent-Guyot. Was it possible in 1812 to make Moreau, the future general of the Coalition, pass for a Republican? Could a Montmorency and a Noailles be counted as adherents of the Republic? Is there anything Republican in this sentence of the proclamation which the conspirator intended for the army: " Prove to the country that you were no more the soldiers of Bonaparte than

of Robespierre "? And what must we think of this
statement in the false decree of the Senate concerning "the despatch of a deputation to His Holiness,
Pius VII., to beg him, in the name of the nation, to
forget the evils he has suffered, and to invite him to
come to Paris, before returning to Rome "? To come
to Paris! and why? Possibly to crown the King,
after he had crowned the Emperor. And that other
clause in the forged decree, promising amnesty for all
military offences, even for desertion to foreign parts,
and inspiring the wholesale return of every *émigré*,
exile, and deserter: did not this do the work of the
Royalists? Moreover, who was Malet's principal
fellow-worker? An ecclesiastic, the Abbé Lafon.
He succeeded in escaping, and in a history of the
conspiracy wrote that General Malet was working,
with Messrs. de Puyvert and de Polignac, in behalf
of the re-establishment of the legitimate monarchy.
And was not General Guidal an avowed Royalist,
whose widow, in a letter written in 1816, recalled
his services to the King, Louis XVIII.? If Malet
had not been shot in 1812, who knows whether he
might not have been chosen Minister of War, two
years later, instead of General Dupont? Who knows
whether, from the Royalist point of view, his plot
might not have seemed a more meritorious action
than the capitulation of Baylen? Malet doubtless
thought that Jacobinism was more out of favor in
France than Royalty. This madman, this victim of
hallucinations, had, as it were, a vision of the future.

In the distance he had seen the throne of the Bourbons restored, the white flag once more hoisted. This pretended Democrat, this so-called Brutus, of whom Republicans have made themselves the most ardent apologists, was, we may be sure, only a would-be Monk.

IV.

OCTOBER 23, 1812, the day when General Malet's conspiracy broke out in Paris, what was happening in Russia to the Grand Army? On that day Napoleon was manœuvring about the little town of Maro-Jaroslawitz. He was deeply pained by being compelled to retreat, and had at first tried to give to his departure from Moscow the appearance of an advance; and instead of taking the Smolensk road, by which he had come, had taken that of Kalouga, by which he hoped to reach a fertile country where he might pass the winter in a mild climate.

Five days after the evacuation of Moscow he came across the army of Kutusoff, and the bloody battle of Maro-Jaroslawitz was fought. Prince Eugene covered himself with glory. Eighteen thousand Italians and Frenchmen, massed in a ravine, defeated fifty thousand Russians, posted over their heads and favored by all the advantages which a town possesses when built at the top of a steep slope. The next day, October 25, the battle-field presented an even more ghastly spectacle than that of the Moskowa.

50

The same day the Emperor was surprised by a band of Cossacks, near Gorodnia, and narrowly escaped being made prisoner.

The army was already the prey of the gloomiest forebodings, and yet the severe cold had not begun. The only way left was to take the shortest road to winter quarters in Poland, abandoning the march towards the south, proceeding to Mojaïsk, and thence taking the road to Smolensk, as rapidly as possible. Napoleon felt that this was a most alarming plan, but the fear of having to fight a second battle with Kutusoff, thus giving the final blow to the Grand Army, already so weakened; of having to abandon the wounded, too numerous to be transported; the sight of all these horrors; his reflections on his threatened capture by the Cossacks, — all these things made a deep impression on the Emperor and diminished the energy necessary for imposing his opinion. No one, not even he, believed any longer in his infallibility. It was October 26, after a council of war held in a barn at the village of Gorodnia, that he made the decision so painful to his pride and so fatal in its results: namely, to abandon the march towards the south and to return towards the north, taking as a fugitive the road by which he had come as conqueror. The whole march, since the evacuation of Moscow and the costly victory of Maro-Jaroslawitz, became useless. Seven precious, decisive days had thus been lost. Properly speaking, it was October 26 that the real retreat began.

In gloom and discouragement the army proceeded sadly, and yet the sky was clear; no snow had fallen. October 28 they reached Mojaïsk. When they saw again the battle-field of the Moskowa, lonely and desolate, silent and mournful, shorn of the terrible but poetic glow of combat, they were overwhelmed with painful emotion. The bare earth trampled and torn, the trees shattered by cannon-balls, the helmets, cuirasses, drums, littering the ground, the redoubt, which was the tomb of Caulaincourt and so many other heroes; besides the chill of death, the frost which had stiffened the corpses half eaten by wolves and vultures, all formed a terrible spectacle. The silence of the plains was broken only by the cries of birds of prey. Alas! what had been the result of this dreadful battle in which had been fired sixty thousand cannon-shots and fourteen hundred thousand musket cartridges, and ninety thousand men had been killed or wounded? What result had been obtained from all the powder burned, from all the blood shed? This was a bitter, inevitable thought, sure to dim the ardor and cool the enthusiasm of the hottest lovers of warfare. " Our hearts," says Baron Fain, " were filled with anguish at the sight of this plain where so many of our comrades had perished. They thought that they died for victory and peace. As we passed we stepped carefully, lest the earth should be too heavy on them beneath our retreating footsteps."

Napoleon himself, steeled as he was against emotion, shuddered with horror at the sight of this blood-stained field, and ordered that the soldiers should linger there as short a time as possible; for such a sight was for them an occasion of grief, and for himself one of self-reproach. The retreat continued, every day being more disastrous and more sanguinary than the one before.

November 6, the Emperor was on the heights of Mikalenska, near Dorogobush, on the road to Smolensk, when a courier, the first for ten days, arrived from Paris. Napoleon stopped to read the despatches which brought him the news of General Malet's conspiracy. He turned to Count Daru and said, " Well! if we had stayed at Moscow — " Then he went into a palisaded house, which had been a post-station, and reflected bitterly on the news he had just received. " What! " he said, with as much surprise as regret, " they did not think of my son, my wife, and the institutions of the Empire? " Then turning towards General Lariboisière, who had known personally the principal officers of Moreau's army, he added, " What did you think of General Lahorie? " Lariboisière answered, " He was an officer of the highest merit, who would have served you well, if they had not tried to ruin him in your estimation; he would have served you as General Eblé does, whom they tried to make you think ill of, and whose character and talents you are able to judge every day." " You are right," resumed the Emperor. " These fools, after letting themselves be deceived, are trying to make up for it by shooting men by the dozen."

November 6, the very day when Napoleon received the news of Malet's conspiracy, the weather suddenly changed for the worse. The sky, which had been clear for several days, was suddenly covered with frosty vapors. The thermometer fell to zero F. Four weeks before, the Russian peasants had said to the Frenchmen: " You don't know our climate. In a month the cold will freeze your nails off." The prophecy came true. When the English Commissioner Wilson complained of delay, the old Kutusoff only said, "Let the snow come." The snow did come; earth and sky were one white pall. Could the Emperor have been surprised at the appearance of his cruelest enemy, the winter? Did he expect to find in Russia the climate of Fontainebleau and Compiègne? Did not he write in the 16th bulletin of the Grand Army, dated Viazma, August 31, 1812, " The weather to-day is very fine, and we expect a continuance of pleasant weather until October 10, which will give us yet a campaign of forty days." And after he had written that, it was the 19th of October that he had chosen, not for the beginning of rest, but for opening the most dangerous and most terrible campaign that had ever been undertaken. When he saw the first snowflakes flying, must he not have regretted the thirty-five days he lingered at Moscow?

The great disasters began at this moment. High winds and severe frosts prevailed; a polar hurricane raged; the snow, driven by the tempest, drifted into

every ravine and hollow, hiding chasms into which
the men slipped; all the furies seemed let loose at
once to delay their march; the blasts cut short their
breath; the snow concealed an ambush at every step;
the ice prevented men and horses from proceeding;
the wind knew no respite; the nights were sixteen
hours long, and in them it was impossible to lie down,
even to sit down, and at the ghastly dawn, the drums
called to arms soldiers who knew no waking! Those
who escaped death looked more like phantoms than
like soldiers. Their thin summer clothing was frozen
on them. Their bleeding, shoeless feet they wrapped
in old rags. Their guns slipped from their numb
fingers. They had no more bread. They could
make no fires, for the wood of the trees was too
green to burn. Moreover, warmth meant death.
No sooner had they melted a little snow to mix with
it a spoonful of rye or flour, than the Cossacks were
upon them, hovering always about like swarms of
vultures, appearing and vanishing like spectres, slay-
ing the wounded, capturing or killing the stragglers.

"About the Emperor," says Baron Fain, an eye-witness of these horrors, "the courtiers' smiles vanished
from the lips that were most accustomed to wear
them; every face bore marks of distress. The brave
men, who wore no mask, were the only ones whose
expressions did not change when cold and sleepless-
ness left their harsh traces." The horses, uncalked,
slipt and fell, never to rise. The cavalry had to
march on foot; the artillery could not be drawn.

No one could keep on a horse. Napoleon himself walked, with difficulty, stick in hand. The edge of the ditches was lined with wretches, who, overcome with cold, succumbed to a sleep from which only the last trump will wake them.

Amid all these sufferings, one hope kept up the soldiers' spirits, — that of reaching Smolensk, where they expected to find in abundance reinforcements, supplies, clothes, and rest. They arrived there November 9, but to meet a cruel deception. The supplies they had expected were wanting. Starving and infuriated, the soldiers broke open the shops and pillaged them. Napoleon left Smolensk, November 14, at five in the morning: a longer stay would have been impossible. Kutusoff's army was not the only one to be feared; two other Russian armies, one commanded by Wittgenstein, the other by Tchitchakoff, threatened to block the retreat. Time was precious; not a moment was to be lost. Smolensk, which had been looked forward to as a promised land, was only one more illusion. The Grand Army, which, on leaving Moscow, had counted one hundred thousand men, had been reduced in twenty-five days to thirty-six thousand. They had to resume their march.

"The elements had declared against France," said Père Lacordaire, in his funeral oration over General Drouot. "Those heroic bands, which, from Lisbon to Moscow, from the Pyramids to Berlin, had met no conqueror, were surprised at last to feel their hearts

heavy, their arms uncertain. Providence had given
nature the signal, and these men, so often defiant of
fortune, were for the first time overcome with weakness. Military art and courage could no longer save
them; they needed another art, another courage:
they needed moral force, courage to endure and hope
forever." All possible disasters seemed to have met
at the same spot. Physical and moral tortures were
combined. Nature seemed anxious to determine just
how much men could suffer. Let us honor the brave
men who were able to survive such harrowing trials.
At Krasnoï, November 17, they had to fight a bloody
battle to keep open the path for their retreat. In
the heat of the action, the band of the grenadiers
of the Old Guard, those sturdy veterans who made
a rampart with their bodies about their Emperor,
played calmly the familiar holiday air, "Where is
one happier than in the bosom of one's family?"

The retreat became even more perilous; it seemed
as if nothing short of a miracle could save the whole
army, from Napoleon to the humblest soldier, from
extermination. An anecdote which we quote from
Villemain will show what feeling inspired these
heroes. One morning when the dim dawn faintly
lit the snowy field covered with the corpses of men
and horses, Napoleon, lowering the window of the
carriage in which he had spent the night, called his
aide-de-camp, the General de Narbonne. "What a
night, my dear General!" he said. "It was not
worse for our sentinels than it was for me, who spent

it in thinking, without closing my eyes. See that
they are relieved, and do you take this to revive you;
for courage alone can't keep a man warm with the
thermometer below zero." With those words the
Emperor had poured from a jug heated by an alcohol
lamp, into a gold cup, a mixture of boiling coffee
and chocolate. The general took the cup, but as he
was raising it to his lips, he saw a grenadier of the
Old Guard, on sentry duty, whose stern, worn face betrayed his sufferings only overcome by courage. "My
man," he said, "drink this; I command you." The
grenadier saluted, took the cup, and drained it with
one draught, then, as if overwhelmed with remorse,
he exclaimed: "General, how cold and hunger affect
a man! Ought I to have accepted that from you
when you had it at your own lips? I beg your pardon, and, on my word, I am thoroughly ashamed of
myself now that my stomach is warm." And he
respectfully handed the gold cup to the Count of
Narbonne. "No, no," answered the general, "keep
it!" Then the grenadier, saluting again, said: "No;
God forbid! I have never taken anything but my
pay and my rations when there have been any."
When the general insisted, the grenadier, who had
set the cup down on the snow, took it up and broke
off a bit as large as a twenty-franc piece. "Since you
order me," he said, "I will keep this Napoleon from
the gold cup. It shall be my medal; it will remind
me that I had the honor to be on guard behind the
Emperor's carriage, at this festivity, and to be
relieved by you, General."

Marshal Davout said with noble pride, "We were conquered by the winter, not by the Russians." The stoical endurance of the Grand Army has wrung admiration even from foreigners. What is more epical, more impressive than General de Ségur's description, which is almost a poem? Heinrich Heine, the author of the *Reisebilder*, said: "The heroes whom we admired in the *Iliad*, we find again in Ségur's poem. We see them deliberating, quarrelling, fighting as in old times before the Scæan gate. Although the helmet of the King of Naples was somewhat motley, his courage in action and his fearlessness are as great as in the son of Peleus; Prince Eugene appears before us like a gentle and brave Hector; Ney, like Ajax; Berthier is a Nestor; Davout, Daru, Caulaincourt, recall Menelaus, Ulysses, and Diomed."

Everything in Napoleon was colossal; his adversity as well as his prosperity. In his darkest days, shortly before the passage of the Beresina, he said to General Jomini, "When one has never known reverses, they will be as great as his good fortunes." The Emperor of legend, in good or evil fortune, ever impresses posterity as a gigantic sphinx. In this figure, which is rather a product of fable than a historic fact, there is an attraction which fascinates even his enemies. The fierce patriotism of Count Leo Tolstoi is pained by this. "Strangely and terribly enough," he says, "Napoleon is for the Russians themselves an object of admiration and enthusiasm;

in their eyes he is great, while Kutusoff, who from
the beginning to the end of 1812, from Borodino to
Wilna, persevered in one plan, never varying in word
or deed, an unprecedented example of the most absolute self-denial, seeing in what was happening about
him the future results, is represented by them as a
colorless being, deserving at the most of pity, a being
whom often they mention only with ill-disguised
shame."

As the retreat continued, the sufferings and disasters only grew. On reaching Orcha, November 19,
only about twenty-four thousand men under arms
and about twenty-five thousand stragglers were left;
that is to say, about one-eighth of the four hundred
thousand men who had crossed the Niemen. Two
new Russian armies, those of Wittgenstein and Tchitchakoff, were about to oppose the crossing of the
Beresina. The situation appeared absolutely desperate. Napoleon, feeling that all was lost, burned
all the documents that he had carried with him in
order to write his autobiography, — a distraction he had
purposed to give himself if he had spent the winter
at Moscow. He had the eagles of every corps brought,
and ordered them to be burned. He collected in two
battalions eighteen hundred dismounted cavalrymen
of the Imperial Guard, of whom only eleven hundred
and forty-four were supplied with muskets or car-
bines. Of all the cavalry that had left Moscow, only
a few mounted men were left. The Emperor collected
about him all the officers of this army who had saved

their horses, and transformed them into what he called his sacred battalion, in which generals of divisions served as simple captains.

When they had come before the Beresina, Napoleon was in the most critical position of his whole eventful career. Three Russian armies, amounting to a hundred and forty thousand men, barred every passage, and enclosed in an iron circle what had once been the Grand Army. To cross the river in such circumstances seemed impossible, yet Napoleon did not for an instant think of surrendering. His veterans said, " He will get us out of even this."

How was he to bridge the Beresina? Everything impeded the task: the marshy banks of the river, the half-frozen water, the pieces of ice carried by the current, the Russians on both sides in vastly superior numbers. But the chief engineer, General Eblé, had saved a caisson full of tires that had been thrown away, and these he had made into cramp-irons. This was the army's only chance for safety. The pontoon-makers were heroes who sacrificed themselves without a murmur. The whole night of the 25th of November they worked on without stopping, within range of the enemy's cannon and musketry, by the light of fires burning on the opposite bank. They worked in the same way all through the 26th. They were up to their necks in the icy stream; they hardly stopped long enough to swallow a little unsalted soup-meat. There were a hundred of them, and of this number but five returned to France : all the rest died from exhaustion and exposure. But they built the bridges and saved their Emperor. The 27th, thanks to their devotion, Napoleon was able to cross the river. When he reached the opposite bank, Napoleon exclaimed, "There's my star again!" He always persisted in thinking that his star was shining even when the skies were blackest. "At this moment," says Baron Fain, "one would have thought that a ray of sunlight pierced the snowy mist that encompassed us."

Napoleon had crossed, but what was to become of the army? The plan of the Russians was to attack it on the two banks while crossing, and to drive it into the river. The two bridges — one for the infantry, the other for the artillery and baggage — were torn by missiles. A terrible confusion prevailed. Men, women, and children, crushed, suffocated, were struggling beneath the feet of their companions, whom they grasped with their teeth and nails; shells were bursting; men were swearing, shouting, groaning; women were weeping; children crying; horses were plunging wildly; cannon-balls were ploughing through the surging mass! Never did the world behold a ghastlier sight; the reality surpassed Dante's most terrible visions; no dreamer ever conceived any such circles of iron, of ice, of fire!

Most unfortunate were those who had not time to cross, who, worn out by their fatigue and their suffering, until they had lost the feeling of self-preservation, lingered on the bank for a few moments' rest.

The Russians advanced, and it became necessary to
burn the bridges lest the Russians should make use of
them. Orders were given to set fire to them at seven
in the morning. General Eblé, out of humanity,
delayed until nine o'clock; but he had to obey then,
and the fire was set. Clouds of smoke enveloped the
two bridges, and the wretches who were on them
jumped into the water lest they should be hurled in
by their fall. From the crowd on the other shore,
making ready to cross, there rose a terrible cry of
anger and despair. Some sprang into the river,
others upon the blazing bridges. They perished in
the flames or the frost, victims of fire or cold, crushed
beneath the wheels of the wagons or the horses' feet,
or pierced by the bullets or cannon-balls of the two
posts. Those left on the shore — some eight or
ten thousand men, women, and children — were captured by the Cossacks, who put many to death; the
rest were sent to Siberia.

Thus, November 29, ended the crossing of the
Beresina, which had begun on the 20th. It was
a victory; but one dearly paid for! Napoleon was to
stay but seven days longer with his troops. From
the moment he had thus miraculously escaped from
the Caudine Forks, he had but one thought, — to
leave.

As in Egypt, he was suddenly seized with an
attack of homesickness. Always impatient and eager
in carrying out his plans, he desired to return to
Paris as he had desired to enter Moscow. The Tui-

leries became his goal, as the Kremlin had been. He
counted the days, hours, and minutes separating him
from the moment when he should ascend the steps of
the grand staircase of his palace. He had no remorse
in stealing away from the fragments of the Grand
Army, in going, like the Persian King whom Æschylus
set on the stage, a fugitive and alone, " with an empty
quiver." What could he do at the head of disbanded
troops, without their uniforms, wrapped up in rags?
What would Germany — still submissive, but quiver-
ing — say when it should see the ruler of the great
Empire in this plight? From Wilna or Königsberg
he would be seen by Europe only in the light of a
defeated man. From the Tuileries, on the other hand,
he would still make an immense impression: there
he would have with him his wife, his son, his Ministers, his Chamberlains, his flatterers. At his reviews
in the Carrousel, he would see superb regiments,
gorgeous uniforms; Malet's conspiracy would be of
some use to him; it would give him a chance to complain, to appear as an accuser instead of the accused,
to knit his brow like Olympian Zeus. And then if
he did not leave, other Malets might rise. When
that plot broke out, the disasters were yet unknown.
The Emperor was thought to be at Moscow, enjoying
an agreeable climate and preparing to spend a quiet
winter in the Palace of the Czars.

In Paris, not a word had been said about the
retreat; no one knew anything about the winter and
its snows. Could the truth long be hid? Would

every officer's letter have to be intercepted? Only one man could make the Parisians accept the fatal news, and that was the Emperor. If he were present, he said to himself, there would be no rebellion, no murmuring. He would be obeyed and silently; possibly he would be admired; and the great player, without delay or hesitation, prepared his vengeance in the face of a downtrodden Europe.

Once decided, Napoleon tolerated no discussion. At Smorgoni, in the evening of December 5, he summoned the King of Naples, Prince Eugene, and the marshals, and announced to them his departure. " I shall leave you," he said; " but it is to get three hundred thousand soldiers. We must make ready for a second campaign, since the first has not ended the war. . . . And why not? Our only conqueror is the cold, which came so early that it deceived even the natives. Schwarzenberg's counter-marches have done the rest. So the unheard-of audacity of an incendiary, an unprecedented winter, cowardly intrigues, stupid ambitions, a few faults, possibly treachery, and shameful mysteries which will come to light some day, have brought us to our present condition. Was ever a good chance disturbed by more unexpected accidents? The Russian campaign will none the less be the most glorious, the most difficult, and the most honorable known to modern history." Then he gave deserved praise to his principal lieutenants, and appeared more affable and kindly than usual. He confessed that every one, he himself like the rest, had blundered more than once in the campaign, and added, " If I had been born to the throne, if I were a Bourbon, it would have been easy for me to make no blunders." Then they sat down to table. After the supper the Emperor had Prince Eugene read the 29th and last bulletin, which was to produce so terrible an effect. The reading finished, he said, " I leave at once for Paris with Duroc, Caulaincourt, and Lobau. My presence there is indispensable; only from there can I restrain the Austrians and the Prussians. Without doubt they will hesitate to declare war against me when they know that I am at the head of the French nation and of a new army of twelve hundred thousand men. . . . I make over the command to the King of Naples. I hope that the most perfect harmony will prevail among you."

After these words Napoleon arose, shook hands affectionately with his lieutenants, embraced them all, and got into his carriage with Caulaincourt. On the seat were the Mameluke Rustan and a captain of the Guard, Wonsovitch, a Pole, who was to act as interpreter on the way. Duroc and Lobau followed in a sleigh. It was ten in the evening. The thermometer marked 18° F.

The next day the army learned that the Emperor had left. It was in such a state of misery and discouragement that it paid scarcely any attention to the departure which, a few days before, would have caused a feeling of keen surprise and of profound disappointment. Every one felt that Napoleon was no longer the protector of his army; that his genius, once capable of wonders, had suddenly become powerless, both against the winter and against fate.

V.

DECEMBER 5, 1812, the day Napoleon left his army like a fugitive, Paris was perfectly tranquil. Salvos of artillery were fired as a signal for rejoicing, and to announce for the next day the anniversary of the coronation and of the battle of Austerlitz. This holiday had been postponed from the 2d of December to the 6th, because the 6th was a Sunday. That day the Empress Marie Louise was to leave the Palace of Saint Cloud and establish herself for the winter at the Tuileries. At midday she received the Diplomatic Body, surrounded by the Princes, Ministers, Grand Eagles of the Legion of Honor, High Officers of the Crown, and the members of her household and of that of the Emperor. After the audience, she went to the chapel, where she heard mass and the *Te Deum*. In the evening, in the palace theatre, she heard Cimarosa's opera, the *Horaces*. Madame Grassini and Madame Sessi sang the principal women's parts. The Tuileries and the city were illuminated; and yet, what cause was there for joy? The real illumination was that of burning Moscow.

68

It was not the playhouses, but the churches that should have been crowded, to pray for the dead, to try to avert God's wrath which had fallen so heavily on France.

The bad news had not yet arrived, but a vague presentiment made every one uneasy. People said that the wonders of Austerlitz could not be repeated, and no one counted on the thunderbolts to which Napoleon had accustomed the world. No change was visible: officials and courtiers seemed to believe the Emperor's fortune eternal: the Empress's face was always calm ; but, in spite of her inexperience, the young sovereign was intelligent to detect the gradual modification of public opinion even before messengers came with the evil tidings.

Meanwhile, Napoleon in his latest bulletins had made use of every euphemism to calm men's minds. His 25th bulletin, dated October 25, and published in the *Moniteur* of November 9, announced the evacuation of the City of the Czars in these terms : "The Emperor left Moscow October 10. . . . Moscow is not a military position. Moscow has no longer any political importance, inasmuch as this city is burned and ruined for a hundred years. The Marshal of Treviso remains there with a garrison. The weather is very fine, like that in France in October, perhaps a little warmer. But early in November cold weather may be expected. Everything makes it necessary to prepare for winter quarters. This is necessary for the cavalry especially ; the infantry

has rested at Moscow and is in excellent condition."
The 26th bulletin, dated October 23, and published
in the *Moniteur* of November 16, betrayed no anxiety.
" The Duke of Treviso," it said, " blew up the Kremlin October 23, at two o'clock in the morning. The
arsenal, the barracks, the magazines, were all destroyed. This ancient citadel, which dates from the
foundation of the monarchy, — this first Palace of the
Czars, — has ceased to be. The Emperor intends to
start the 24th, to reach the Dwina, and to take a
position within eighty leagues of Saint Petersburg and
of Wilna, — a twofold advantage, being thus twenty
marches nearer both the means and the end. . . .
The Russians are amazed at the weather of the last
three weeks, in which we have had the bright sun
and the pleasant days of our visits to Fontainebleau.
The army is in a very fertile region, which compares
favorably with those of France and Germany."

The 27th bulletin, which was dated October 27,
and appeared in the *Moniteur* of November 17, was
equally optimistic: " The weather is superb, the
roads are good; it is the end of the autumn; this
weather will last for a week, and by that time we
shall have got into our new positions. The Italian
guard distinguished itself at the battle of Maro-
Jaroslawitz. The old Russian infantry is destroyed.
The Russian army now exists only by means of the
numerous reinforcements of Cossacks recently arrived
from the Don." The 28th bulletin, dated at Smolensk, November 11, and published in the *Moniteur*

of November 29, was not perfectly reassuring, but it did not tell a hundredth part of the disasters: "The weather was very fine until November 6, but on the 7th the winter began. The earth is covered with snow. The roads have become very slippery, and very hard for the draught horses. We have lost many of them by the cold and fatigues. Since the storm of the 6th we have lost more than fifty thousand draught horses, and nearly a hundred caissons have been destroyed. The Emperor's health has never been better."

Do not these bulletins read like cruel jests? Could the truth be better hidden? This terrible retreat, the most disastrous known to history, was represented as a strategic march, somewhat impeded by unfavorable weather. But public opinion was not reassured, and in spite of the official optimism, men began to think of nothing but ruin and destruction.

For his part, Napoleon had skilfully prepared for his own return. Three days before leaving his army he had sent on as a forerunner, one of the aides of the Prince of Neufchâtel, Major de Montesquiou, who was to inform Europe of some of the recent events, while setting them in a favorable light. The instructions he carried ran thus: "Selitche, December 2, 1812. M. de Montesquiou will leave at once for Paris. He will give the Empress the enclosed letter. On his way he will see the Duke of Bassano at Wilna, to inform him of the necessity of stopping individual soldiers, and of feeding them, and especially of pro-

viding a great quantity of supplies, bread, meat, and
brandy, in order to give the army abundance after its
present distress. Everywhere he is to announce the
arrival of ten thousand Russian prisoners, and the
victory gained on the Beresina, in which were captured six thousand Russian prisoners, eight flags, and
twelve cannon. He will also announce it at Kowno,
Königsberg, Berlin, and to M. de Saint Marson, and
publish everywhere in the gazettes: 'M. de Montesquiou, aide-de-camp of the Prince of Neufchâtel,
has passed through, bringing news of the victory of
the Beresina gained by the Emperor over the united
armies of Admiral Tchitchakoff and General Wittgenstein. He is carrying to Paris eight flags, taken
from the Russians in this battle, in which six thousand prisoners and twelve cannon were captured.
When this officer left, the Emperor Napoleon was at
Wilna, in excellent health.' M. de Montesquiou
will travel as rapidly as possible, in order to contra-
dict everywhere false rumors. He will say that
they tried to divide the French, who, however, scattered them to the four winds; that they have reached
Wilna, where they have found numerous stores, and
that they will soon have recovered from their sufferings. On reaching Paris he will give the Empress
details of the Emperor's good health, and the state
of the army. Then he will await new orders."

Napoleon continued his speedy flight. He did not
even enter Wilna, but passed through Wilkowiski,
where he changed his carriage for a sleigh, and in

the same clandestine way reached Warsaw December
10. He did not even dare to go to his Ambassador's,
M. de Pradt, Archbishop of Malines, but sought re-
tirement in a wretched inn, where he had great difficulty in getting a fire lit. Caulaincourt called on
the Ambassador, greatly surprising him by his unexpected appearance. The archbishop at once went
to the inn where the sovereign of so many nations
resembled the obscurest traveller. The conqueror
himself was struck by the contrast, and said to the
Ambassador, with a forced laugh, "It's but a step
from the sublime to the ridiculous." Then he added
in a calm voice : " Who has escaped reverses? It is
true that no one has ever had any like these, but
they had to be proportionate to my fortune, and
besides they will be soon repaired." Then he summoned the principal Polish 'ministers, urged upon
them absolute silence concerning his presence in
Warsaw, promised to return speedily with three hundred thousand fresh troops, and continued his journey under an assumed name, still accompanied by
Duroc, Caulaincourt, Lobau, Captain Wonsowitch,
and the Mameluke Rustan.

Meanwhile M. de Montesquiou, in accordance with
his instructions, had inserted in all the papers of
Lithuania and Germany the statement that the
Emperor was at Wilna in good health, but at Wilna
no one had seen Napoleon. Every one was wondering
what had happened. Had he disappeared like Romu-
lus in a storm? Had he fallen into the hands of the

Cossacks? Was he buried in the snowdrifts? Had some German fanatic stabbed him? Was he a prisoner? or dead? Nothing was known about this man who a moment before had stood forth before a dazed world as an Agamemnon, king of kings, as a second Charlemagne! From Lithuania to the heart of Austria the rumor suddenly spread that he was no longer alive, and the breath of whole nations paused in solemn expectation. The sleigh was gliding on, and no one who saw it passing like a flash over the plains of Poland and Saxony imagined that the fragile sleigh was carrying Cæsar and his fortunes.

December 14, the illustrious fugitive reached Dresden by night and took quarters, still incognito, at the Ambassador's, M. de Serra. At Dresden, where a few months before he had held a magnificent court of kings and princes, and where his face was distinctly remembered, he had to take the greatest precautions to escape recognition. He received secretly the King of Saxony, the best and most faithful of his allies, and tried to reassure him by grand promises. Then he wrote this letter to the Emperor of Austria: —

"December 14, 1812. MY BROTHER AND MY DEAR FATHER-IN-LAW: I stop for a moment at Dresden to write to Your Majesty and to give you news of myself. In spite of rather severe fatigues, my health has never been better. I started from Lithuania the 5th of this month, after the battle of the Beresina, leaving the Grand Army under the orders of the King

of Naples, the Prince of Neufchâtel still holding his
post of major-general. In four days I shall be in
Paris, where I shall spend the winter to look after
my most important affairs. Possibly Your Majesty
will decide to send there some one in the absence of
your Ambassador, whose presence is of such service
to the army. The different bulletins which the Duke
of Bassano cannot have failed to send Count Otto
will have informed Your Majesty of everything that
has happened since our departure from Moscow. It
is important, in the present circumstances, that Your
Majesty should mobilize his corps in Galicia and Tran-
sylvania, thus raising his forces to sixty thousand men.
I have perfect confidence in Your Majesty's feelings.
The alliance we have contracted forms a permanent
system to assure the triumph of the common cause,
and to bring us speedily to a suitable peace. You
may be sure that I for my part shall always be found
ready to do everything in my power to please you and
to convince you of the importance I attach to our
existing relations, as well as to give proofs of the
perfect esteem and high consideration with which
I am Your Majesty's affectionate brother and son-in-
law, NAPOLEON."

The Emperor left Dresden as stealthily as he entered
it; and always buried in thick furs, concealed under a
false name, he continued his swift journey in a sleigh
with the same companions. This strange journey
was not unpleasant to him. Curious and romantic
experiences suited his adventurous nature, which was

greedy of emotions. Then, too, it was a real consolation no longer to have before his eyes the lamentable
spectacle of his army, whose terrible sufferings would
have awakened, if not remorse, at least pity, in the
coldest heart. Possibly Napoleon fleeing in his sleigh
over the snowy plains was not so unhappy as one might
at first suppose. His reverses, though as vast, as
portentous as his triumphs, had not at all discouraged
him. What he had seen on the bridge of the Beresina,
as on that of Arcole, was his unexpected good fortune,
— what he always called his star. He comforted
himself with the thought that any one else in such
circumstances would have perished, and he prepared
himself for new adventures. The thoughts that flashed
through his mind as he hurried along through Germany, exposed to any fanatic who might recognize
and assassinate him, were not those of moderation,
prudence, or repentance, but those of pride, victory,
and dominion. He was like a bold rider who, on
being once thrown, thinks only of vaulting into his
saddle, and of whipping, spurring, and mastering his
wayward steed. His steed was fortune. What did
he think of what the Abbé Perreyve called "that
army invisible to the bodily eye, but too visible to
the mind's eye, which begins its bloody march, that
grand army of the dead, the slain, the abandoned,
the forgotten, the army of those atrocious sufferings
and those prolonged infirmities, which proceeds in
mournful procession behind what we call glory"?
Away with phantoms and odious memories! That is

past; now for revenge! The loss of the highest stake never broke the spirit of an untiring gambler. Like Don Juan before his guest of stone, he hardened himself against Fate. Fate summoned him to repentance; he did not repent.

Feverishly he seized again the dice, again to shake them once more in the box, proud and confident before the final throw. He made no recriminations, uttered no laments. He had to reign again, remount his horse, hold reviews, summon a huge army of conscripts to arms, and once more to make Europe tremble. When Francis I., returning from captivity in Madrid, crossed the Bidassoa, and found himself free again on the soil of his kingdom, he exclaimed: "Here I am, king once more! I am king! I am king again!" When Napoleon had crossed the Rhine, he was able to say, "I am always Emperor!"

Yes, he was always Emperor; yet what gloom his advent in the capital was to call forth! This was the second time he had abandoned his army; but what a difference between the return from Egypt and the return from Russia! From Egypt he had returned alone, but victorious, and his soldiers were at Cairo; from Russia he returned alone, but his army was annihilated and no longer at Moscow. Any one else so returning would have feared the criticisms or the blame of the populace; he was returning to Paris as proud as if he had just signed a glorious peace, and the Grand Army were following his triumphal chariot. The nearer he drew to the

frontier, the more his confidence and satisfaction
increased. The thought of seeing once more his
wife, his son, his Palace of the Tuileries, his Imperial
throne, filled him with rapture. After being washed
overboard by a terrible tempest, he was about to pace
the deck once more and to take the helm again.

All his prestige was needed to diminish the disastrous impression which was produced by the bad
news that had just arrived. He was not to reach
Paris until the morning of December 18, and no one
expected him, when, on the morning of the 17th,
there was published in the *Moniteur* the 29th bulletin, which announced many of the catastrophes. It
came like a thunderbolt. For nearly three weeks no
word had been received from the army. The 28th
bulletin, the last that had been received, had been
published in the official sheet, November 29, and
as we have seen, it was full of exaggerated optimism. Since then nothing had been heard. Judge,
then, of the universal stupefaction when the 29th
bulletin burst upon them like a funeral knell! He
owned to the loss of more than thirty thousand
horses in a few days, the melancholy condition of
the dismounted cavalry, of the artillery, and of the
train. He said: "Men whom nature had not made
sturdy enough to rise superior to all the chances of
fate and fortune, seemed overwhelmed; they lost
their gaiety and good-humor, and thought of nothing
but woe and disaster; those whom it made of sterner
stuff preserved their cheerfulness and habitual com-

posure, seeing new glory to be won in almost insurmountable difficulties." The bulletin confessed that the Cossacks, "that contemptible cavalry which simply makes a noise, and is incapable of breaking through a company of light infantry, was made by circumstances most formidable." While omitting much, he announced the crossing of the Beresina, and closed thus: "That the army needs to reform its discipline, to form anew, to get new horses for the cavalry, the artillery, and its baggage train, is evident from what has been said. Its first need is rest. In all its movements the Emperor has continually marched amid his guard; the cavalry being commanded by the Marshal, the Duke of Istria, the infantry by the Duke of Dantzic. Our cavalry was so short of horses that all the officers who had a single horse had to be collected, in order to make four companies of one hundred and fifty men each. Generals served as captains; colonels as uncommissioned officers. This sacred squadron, commanded by General Grouchy, and under the orders of the King of Naples, never lost sight of the Emperor in all his movements. His Majesty's health was never better."

In this famous bulletin there certainly prevailed a tone of frankness which was not without grandeur, and it lent the figure of the Emperor, in better health than ever amid so many trials, an epic and majestic air; yet Napoleon's adversaries, especially the Royalists, reproached him with it most bitterly. Chateaubriand thus speaks of it in his *Mémoires d'outre tombe :* " Bonaparte was always guarded by a sacred battalion which never lost sight of him in all his movements, in compensation for the three hundred thousand men slain; but why had not nature tempered them finely enough? Then they would have preserved their usual appearance. Did this vile meat for cannon deserve to have its movements watched as preciously as those of His Majesty? This bulletin, like many others, ends thus : ' His Majesty's health was never better.' Families, dry your tears! Napoleon is well! After this report there appeared in the papers this official remark : ' This is an historic utterance of the highest rank. Xenophon and Cæsar thus wrote, one his Retreat of the Ten Thousand, the other his Commentaries.' What madness of pedantic allusion! We had sunk to the contemptuous scorn of a flattery which exhumed memories of Xenophon and Cæsar in order to insult the eternal grief of France."

M. de Montesquiou reached Paris the night of December 17. He had left the Emperor on the 2d, the date of the despatches he was carrying to the Empress, and since then had heard nothing from him. Hence he could give Marie Louise only very meagre information, and no one knew where Napoleon was, or when he would return to the capital. This absolute uncertainty, added to the gloom produced by the 29th bulletin, arroused widespread uneasiness. Meanwhile the Emperor continued his journey without an obstacle. On his way through Weimar he borrowed the carriage of his Minister, M. de Saint-Aignan, and pushed on through Hanau and Mayence without being recognized. At a short distance from Paris, his carriage having met with a slight accident, he took a post-chaise, which brought him swiftly the rest of the way.

December 18, at half-past eleven at night, Marie Louise, sad and ailing, had just gone to bed in the Tuileries. The lady-in-waiting, who was to sleep in the next room, was making ready to lock all the doors, when suddenly she heard the footsteps of two men. Who could it be at that hour? The drawing-room door opened, and two men, wrapped in thick furs, made the lady utter a cry of surprise: one was the First Equerry, Caulaincourt, and the other the Emperor himself. At first they had been refused admission to the palace, and both had found some difficulty in getting the porter to recognize them. Marie Louise, who was suddenly awakened, sprang out of bed, and when she saw Napoleon, embraced him with delight.

VI.

ADULATION.

ANY one but Napoleon would have been disturbed at the thought of meeting his Ministers for the first time after a war which he had been the only one to desire, and which had ended so lamentably. But he, so far from feeling the slightest embarrassment, determined to assume their position and to appear as an accuser. Malet's conspiracy gave him exactly the pretext that he desired. The feeling that his presence inspired was mainly fear. His attitude, he decided, should be what it would have been if the Russian campaign had been one long triumph. Instead of rendering an account, he meant to demand one.

On his arrival at the Tuileries, December 18, at half-past eleven in the evening, the Emperor summoned the Princes holding high positions, the Ministers, and the high officers of the Crown for the next morning. First he received the Archchancellor Cambacérès, then the Ministers in succession, according to the length of the tenure of their offices, so that the Chief Justice and all the Ministers, with the sole exception of the Minister of Commerce, came before Savary, Duke of Rovigo, the Minister of Police.

" Of all who were there," says the Duke of Rovigo in his Memoirs, "there was not one who would have wished to stand in my shoes. They all seemed unwilling to speak to me, lest they should pain me. The Emperor detained every Minister, except the Minister of War, only a short time, so that I was ushered into him very soon. When I passed through the crowd which had gathered about the door of the drawing-room where the Emperor was, they made way for me as if they were letting a funeral procession pass on its way to bid farewell to the court. What especially helped to confirm this opinion was the return to Paris of the Duke of Otranto, whom the Emperor had recalled from Aix in Provence, where he was living: every one looked upon him as my successor. Some who had been my friends in the days of my first success took pains to let me know everything that was said while I was with the Emperor."

The Duke of Rovigo remained nearly two hours with his sovereign. " I can imagine," said Napoleon, " that you might have been arrested by fifty men, but it is very much to be regretted that you should not have been able to defend yourself. As for me, I am at the mercy of the first officer who is on guard at my door." The Minister entered into long explanations, which the Emperor received very kindly, and he soon saw with surprise and pleasure that he still retained his master's confidence. "When I left the Emperor," he says, "it was interesting to see the curiosity of the courtiers, who tried to read in my face whether they should do well to approach me. However, they regarded the length of our conversation as a favorable sign, and it was that evening (for it was four or five o'clock in the afternoon) that those ridiculous rumors which had been current about me for a month, came to an end. Afterwards I had many excellent opportunities to make their authors repent their rashness, but I did nothing about it. My friends returned when they saw I was in favor; I received them all without bearing malice."

Although Napoleon reached the Tuileries in the evening of December 18, the *Moniteur* of the 19th made no mention of his return. It contained, however, the following paragraph: "December 5 the Emperor called together, at headquarters at Smorgoni, the King of Naples, the Viceroy, the Prince of Neufchâtel, and the Marshals, the Dukes of Elchingen, of Dantzic, of Treviso, the Prince of Eckmühl, the Duke of Istria, and told them he had appointed the King of Naples his lieutenant-general, to command the army during the winter. His Majesty, in passing through Wilna, accorded an interview of several hours to the Duke of Bassano. His Majesty travelled incognito in a single sleigh, under the name of the Duke of Vicenza. He visited the fortification of Praga, passed through Warsaw, and spent several hours there without being recognized. Two hours before his departure he sent for Count Potocki and the Minister of Finance of the Grand Duchy, with whom he conversed for a long time. His Majesty reached Dresden the 14th, one hour after midnight, and stayed with Count Serra, his Minister. He had a long conversation with the King of Saxony, and left immediately, by Leipsic and Mayence."

Napoleon's return was thus announced in the *Moniteur* of December 20: " Paris, December 19. His Majesty the Emperor arrived in Paris yesterday evening at half-past eleven o'clock. He has received the Princes holding high positions, the Minister, and high officers. The Duke of Cadore has been sworn in as Minister and Secretary of State *ad interim* in the place of Count Daru, who remains until further orders with the army, as Commissary General. His Majesty has commissioned the Bishop of Nantes, one of his almoners, with the administration of his chapel, in the absence of the Grand Almoner."

Etiquette moved on with perfect regularity; Napoleon had never seemed more calm and more confident. At the Palace of the Tuileries one would have thought that the Russian campaign was nothing but a bad dream, a nightmare that the day had dispelled, but in the city the distress and uneasiness were very great. The Duke of Rovigo says: " The Emperor's arrival in Paris completed the change of public opinion. When once black thoughts began, imagination knew no bounds, and the army was regarded as a horde of exhausted and half-frozen men, rather than as a band of cohorts, who for so many years had been the admiration of their contemporaries and had enriched history with so many glorious feats."

The time had come for Napoleon to display all his audacity and to seat himself, in proud majesty, upon his throne like the Jupiter of the Imperial Olympus. Sunday, December 20, at noon, he assembled in his palace the great bodies of the State, and it was on his throne that he received them, surrounded by Princes, Cardinals, Ministers, the High Officers of the Crown, and the Grand Eagles of the Legion of Honor. The Senate advanced first, introduced by the Grand Master of Ceremonies, and presented by His Most Serene Highness, the Prince Vice-Grand Elector Talleyrand, former Bishop of Autun, and afterwards Minister of Louis XVIII.

Advance, Senators, who in less than sixteen months will proclaim your master's fall, who in speaking of him will pass all bounds in your invectives and anathemas, you who will be for him perfect examples of ingratitude and insolence! Burn all the incense you have left! Bind together the flowers of your servile rhetoric! You still draw your pay. The gilded embroideries of your uniforms are still bright. So long as the lilies have not taken the place of the bees, be more ardent Imperialists than the Emperor; you will soon be more ardent Royalists than the King! You will return to this same palace, you will bow before the same throne. Another monarch will be seated there, another flag will be flying above the dome. But what does that matter? You will not have altered your character, and you will succeed under the white flag through the same qualities as under the tricolor. The birth of the Duke of Bordeaux will be for you the same thing as the birth of the King of Rome. The same language will seem to celebrate the two Princes; the same cradle will do for both, like the same throne.

The President of the Senate began his speech after congratulating the Emperor on his "happy arrival amid his people"; he went on: "Sire, while Your Majesty was eight hundred leagues from his capital, at the head of his victorious army, men, escaping from the prisons where your Imperial clemency had saved them from death, which they merited for their past crimes, tried to disturb the order of this great city. They have suffered the penalty of their misdeeds. Happy is France, Sire, in being secured by its monarchic constitution from civil discords, from the sanguinary hatreds begotten of partisanship, and from the horrid disorders that follow in the train of revolutions!"

There was no need for the Senators to wax indignant with General Malet's forged decree of the Senate; the one they voted April 2, 1814, certainly expressed no greater fidelity to the Emperor. They themselves it was who were to accuse Napoleon of having " broken the compact which united him to the French people, by levying taxes otherwise than through the law, by unnecessarily adjourning the Legislative

Body, by illegally issuing several decrees of condemnation to death, by annihilating the responsibility of the Ministers, the independence of the bench, and the liberty of the press." They were to accuse him with completing the misfortunes of their country "by the abuse of all the means entrusted to him, both men and money, for war, and his refusal to treat on conditions which the national interest required him to accept." They themselves, the accomplices of his faults, were to proclaim his fall. Malet only forestalled their feelings, their language; only they did not wait to be told that the Emperor was dead. Malet's conspiracy was not merely a prophecy; it was the exact programme of the different revolutions still hidden in the future. October 23, 1812, no one gave a thought to the King of Rome; who, July 29, 1830, was to think of the Duke of Bordeaux? of the Count of Paris, February 24, 1848? September 4, 1870, of the Prince Imperial?

The President of the Senate continued his address. "The Senate," he said, "is the Emperor's first Council; its authority exists only when the Monarch calls for it, and sets it in motion; it is established for the preservation of this monarchy and the inheritance of your throne in our fourth dynasty. France and posterity will find it always faithful to this sacred duty; and all its members will ever be ready to die in defence of this palladium of the national security and prosperity." Chateaubriand, commenting on this passage, says: "The Senate, in presuming to con-

gratulate Napoleon on the public welfare, is nevertheless appalled at its own courage : it fears even
to exist, and takes care to say that the authority of
the Senate *exists* only when the sovereign calls for
it and *sets it in motion.* There was so great danger
that the Senate would be independent!"

/ Then followed lyrical outbursts of enthusiasm.
"Sire, Your Majesty has hoisted the French eagles
on the towers of Moscow. The enemy was able to
oppose your success and to thwart your plans only
by having recourse to the ghastly measures of des-
potism, by turning its boundaries into deserts, and
by giving to the flames his capital, the centre of his
wealth, and the product of many centuries. They
little know, Sire, Your Majesty's heart when they
thus revive the barbarous tactics of their savage
ancestors. You would gladly have renounced trophies which were to cost so much human blood and
suffering. .... May Your Imperial and Royal Majesty deign to accept this tribute of the gratitude,
love, and unalterable fidelity of the Senate and of
the French people! . . . The affection which the
whole nation bears for the King of Rome proves,
Sire, both the attachment of the French for Your
Majesty's family, and that inward conviction which
reassures every citizen, and shows him in this august
child the security of his own, the safeguard of his
fortunes, and an invincible obstacle to all civil agitations and political upheavals, the greatest misfortunes
that can distress a people."

The Emperor replied to the Senators: "What you say is very agreeable to me. . . . Our fathers had adopted this rallying cry: 'The King is dead; long live the King!' These few words express the main advantages of a monarchy. I think that I have carefully studied the feelings that my people have shown in different ages: I have reflected on what has been done at different epochs of our history; I shall still ponder them. The war I am waging against Russia is a political war. I have carried it on without animosity: I should gladly have spared that country the evils it has inflicted upon itself. I might have armed the greater part of the population against the others, by proclaiming the emancipation of the serfs: many villages urged this upon me; but when I saw the degraded condition of this large class of the Russian people, I refused to take this step which would have consigned many families to death and to the most awful torments. My army has suffered losses, but these are due to the premature severity of the winter. I accept the expression of your feelings."

One would have said, to hear the Emperor, that the retreat from Russia was merely an unimportant episode in the vast romance of his career. To the terrible catastrophes which had practically wiped out his army, he referred only with these few words, "My army has suffered losses." Of his own blunders, his own imprudence, his refusal of the advice of all who knew the geography, the character, the climate of Russia, he said not a word. The Council of State, with even more fulsome flattery than the Senate, went into raptures over "the prodigious development of an august character which was greater than ever." What was his reply? He talked — strange as it may seem — about ideology. "It is to ideology, the science of ideas, to that obscure metaphysical speculation, that study of the obscure first causes, which busies itself with establishing the foundations of legislation rather than with adopting laws in accordance with our knowledge of the human heart and with the lessons of history, that we must attribute the misfortunes that have befallen France. These errors necessarily introduced the reign of the men of blood. In fact, who announced the principle of insurrection as a duty? Who flattered the people by announcing a sovereignty which it was incapable of exercising? Who destroyed the sanctity and the respect of laws by making them dependent, not on the sacred principles of justice, on the nature of things, and on civil justice, but merely on the will of an assembly composed of men ignorant of civil, criminal, administrative, political, and military laws? When one is called upon to regenerate a state, it is the opposite principles that should be followed." Why did not Napoleon impeach, instead of innocent ideology, the guilty winter, the author of most of the disasters of the Russian war, and charge it with high treason?

The time was set; the official flattery was to grow

in obsequiousness, and Napoleon was never to tire of
the incense burned before him. Instead of thinking
of mournful subjects, some great solemnity, some
magnificent splendor, was called for, such as the coronation of the Empress and of the King of Rome.
That, said the courtiers, will be a fine opportunity for
France to express its devotion and loyalty to the
Imperial dynasty: the Emperor had but to go to the
capital; there he would hear nothing but applause.
December 27, in the Throne Room of the Tuileries,
he received a deputation of the electoral college of
the Department of the Tiber, and the President spoke
in these high-flown terms: " The Romans will not
belie the name of their ancestors; and while some
shall fight beneath victorious banners, others shall
cultivate the arts in order to make eternal, by majestic
monuments, your glorious exploits, and to transmit
their memory to the remotest posterity. Sire, to
crown the happiness of the city of Rome, you have
only to honor it with your presence and to permit it
to behold you seated on a throne reared in the Palace
of the Cæsars. In that shrine you will hear unending applause; there you will see the famous monuments, rescued from the ravages of time, which your
munificence has restored to the fine arts. The
Romans will bind your brow with undying laurel,
and your entrance into the capital will be the most
solemn, the best applauded, and the most deserved of
your triumphs. It will efface the vaunted ovations
of ancient warriors, of the most illustrious emperors.

Deign, Sire, to accept and to appreciate the unanimous wishes of the city of Rome and of its department which we have been commissioned to lay on the steps of your throne."

Paris and the Eternal City tried to outdo each other in adulation. After the Roman delegate, the Prefect of the Seine made his address: "What joy, Sire, the presence of your sacred person imparts to every heart! What hope and security it inspires! Your glances everywhere give life; and then what glory during your absence! Our wishes, our homage, our admiration, followed Your Majesty's footsteps as he flew from victory to victory, planting his eagles on the turrets of Moscow, and in those even more glorious moments when he manifested how even against the fury of the elements could prevail that constancy, that firmness of soul, which have won for him the proudest triumph that it could be granted to mortals to attain!"

The evening of December 27, 1812, the day when he had listened to these two addresses in the Throne Room, the Emperor went to the opera with the Empress and saw a performance of *Jerusalem Delivered.* The audience was very large, and, according to the *Moniteur*, the two sovereigns were greeted with most enthusiastic applause.

Constant, his valet de chambre, says in his Memoirs: " I took my old place in the Emperor's service, and found him exactly as he was before he left for the campaign; his face was precisely as serene; one

would have said that the past was of no importance
in his eyes, and that living already in the future he
saw victory again perched upon his banners, and his
enemies humiliated and defeated . . . A few days
after I arrived in Paris, Their Majesties went to the
opera, where the *Jerusalem Delivered* was given. I
was an eye-witness of the way the Emperor and
Empress were received. I never saw greater enthusiasm, and I must say that it seemed to me a very
sudden transition from the recent crossing of the
Beresina to such a magical performance."

The illusion was complete. Just as in the last
days of royalty, a few months before the murder of
Louis XVI., the King and Queen were received with
an outburst of enthusiasm in the brilliant Opera
House, so, after the Russian campaign, a few months
before the invasion, before the deposition, Napoleon
and Marie Louise received in public, at the theatre,
a welcome as warm as those of the most brilliant
evenings of 1810 and 1811. There was the same
brilliant spectacle, the same glory; but, alas! the
power and splendor of the Empire were about to
vanish like a scene of the opera itself. Other persons were soon to come upon the stage. Everything
was changed in a moment, as if at the machinist's
whistle.

Nevertheless Napoleon was able to deceive himself.
He had found all again, — his wife, his son, the throne,
his palace, the courtiers. But the artificial world in
which he lived, surrounded with flattery as in the

most brilliant periods of his career, was not the real, suffering, weeping France. And outside of France there was Europe, which was impatiently gnawing its bit, awaiting the terrible hour of a general uprising. Every wise observer was sure that terrible convulsions were approaching. To prevent them there was demanded infinite wisdom, and wisdom was just what this exceptional man most lacked; for his superabundant genius did not possess the good sense which was required as a balance. Napoleon needed counsellors: he listened only to flatterers.

VII.

WHILE Napoleon had found once more his courtiers at the Tuileries, and had been greeted by them as if he were triumphant, what had become of the Grand Army? The day after his departure the weather had become even worse; snowflakes filled the air; birds fell to the ground frozen stiff: it seemed as if nature, paralyzed and motionless, had ceased to live. "Then," says General de Ségur, "no one spoke, no one murmured; the absolute silence of despair prevailed, broken only by sounds of weeping. Unhappy shades seemed alone to glide about in this realm of death. The dull monotony of our footfalls, the creaking of the snow, and the faint moans of the dying, alone disturbed this vast and lamentable silence. There was no anger, no cursing, nothing which supposes that any warmth was left; there scarcely survived sufficient strength to pray: most fell without complaining, whether from weakness and resignation, or because complaints imply the hope of relief or sympathy." And the brave general who wrote this account, which is as epical

as the song of Roland, exclaims in patriotic anguish:
"This was the army that had sallied forth from the
most civilized nation in Europe, the army once so
brilliant and victorious over the enemy until its last
moment, and whose name still ruled over many conquered capitals. Its bravest warriors, who had just
crossed the field of many of its victories, had lost
their noble bearing. The men, clad only in rags,
with feet bare and bleeding, dragged themselves
along on branches of pine, and all the strength and
perseverance they had shown in conquering, they
now employed in flight."

Their confusion was complete; the regiments had
lost their formation; the men retained neither the
arms nor the uniforms of soldiers; they were unable
to face any other enemy than hunger and cold; no
one thought of anything but his own safety: bands
of eight or ten combined to plunder together. These
little bands being themselves broken up by their
sufferings, a crowd of starving men would rush upon
a dying horse to eat it. Such continual scenes of
horror and desolation met the survivors of the retreat
at every step. When, December 13, they reached
the Niemen, which they had crossed six months before under a bright sky, numbering four hundred thousand men, with sixty thousand cavalry, and twelve
hundred cannon, in all the pride of power and glory,
the comparison of that brilliant scene with their
present misery made even these veterans weep. Instead of three French bridges, brought five hundred

leagues and thrown across the river with the boldest promptness, there was now but one bridge — a Russian one. This was used by the remains of the Grand Army. Musket in hand, Marshal Ney, at the head of a hundred brave men, defended it to the last moment, and was the last to leave the fatal land. In spite of their terrible sufferings, Napoleon's soldiers still had so great a reputation that the enemy, as if astonished at their success, which was due to the winter, advanced no further than to the banks of the Niemen.

There were some men whose prodigious courage was not shaken for a moment by their fearful sufferings. Marshal Davout wrote, December 12, to his wife: "I take advantage, my dear Aimée, of the departure of a courier, to reassure you regarding your Louis's health, which is excellent in spite of the inclemency of the season. You will notice that my hand trembles as I write; I swear to you that the cold is the only reason, and that I feel it all the more because I am writing in the open air, so as not to lose the courier." He wrote again, December 17: "Everywhere the Russians have been beaten, and when the army has rested a little, they will meet their conqueror again. The conduct of the troops is excellent; not a murmur is to be heard. It seems as if the humblest soldier felt that no force, no genius, could overcome the harm the weather has inflicted." And December 24: "We must soon hear of the Emperor's safe arrival in Paris. This news will be agreeable to every Frenchman, and especially to his soldiers; with him in France, the harm that the unexpected and unprecedented cold has done, will be soon repaired." Yet there was a limit to human strength; the retreat could not have lasted many days more. Even those whose spirit was not broken for a moment, were physically exhausted; and Marshal Davout himself, prodigy of heroism as he was, wrote to his wife from Thorn, December 23: "It was high time, my dear wife, for me to arrive. I hope a few days' rest will set me on my legs again, especially as my weakness is due to nothing but fatigue. I never could have believed that I was so strong: I have certainly come four-fifths of the way from Moscow on foot."

Towards the end of December, the letters from the officers and men of the Grand Army began to arrive in France after a long interruption. There is this justice to be rendered to the Imperial government, that it did not intercept one of them, and that the survivors of the retreat were free to describe with perfect frankness the disasters they had just experienced. I ask for no other proof of this than this letter from my father, who died a general, and, during the Russian campaign, was serving as captain in Marshal Davout's corps: —

"Königsberg, December 21, 1812. MY DEAR AUNT: I am willing to bet that since I learned to write, not one of my letters has ever given you so much pleasure as you will get from this one. For a

long time you must have been in most painful uncertainty about me, and I need not tell you that it has
been impossible to send you a line from a country
where there were no mails, houses, or inhabitants.
Doubtless you know that I have come from a vast
desert which contains nothing but snow, ashes, and
corpses. From the Niemen to Moscow, every village
was burned without a single exception. We had to
cross this region again to get from Moscow here.
When we began the war, we had a hundred regiments
of cavalry. All the horses are dead and have been
devoured by the remains of a famished army. I
should have to write a hundred pages to tell you all
we have suffered. Since the world began there has
never been such a war. We have had to fight against
cannon, fire, famine, and water. Among the few
survivors it would be hard to find one whose nose,
feet, or ears have not been frozen; but, thanks to my
good luck, I got here *whole*, and in excellent health,
except a heavy cold from which every one is suffering: this is not strange, considering that for seven
months we have had to sleep in the open air, in good
and bad weather, in a country where in November
the thermometer fell to 24° F.

" I encountered unheard-of dangers at the battle of
Moskowa, September 7: for ten hours I was in continual peril. All my friends were shot down by my
side. November 28, at the crossing of the Beresina,
I was also terribly exposed; my only way of escape
was to leap with my horse into the river; the cakes

of ice carried him away, and I saved myself by swim-
ming, all dressed and armed as I was. The bridge
was blocked and the river was full of bodies.

"December 13, at midnight, I was taken prisoner
with four officers of my regiment. I am the only one
of the five who succeeded in escaping. After running for an hour through the snow, which was up to
my knees, across ditches and palisades, and falling
seven or eight times, I was out of breath, like a stag
pursued by hounds. Then a dozen Cossacks, who
had been pursuing me, caught up to me, and took
my cloak, cartridge-box, epaulettes, cross, money,
watch, in short, everything I had on, except my
trousers. They were so greedy over the spoils, that
of all those things not one was left whole. I suffered
from their excessive haste in stripping me, but otherwise I have no cause to complain of their treatment.
When that operation was finished, they carried me
away with a considerable band of prisoners, and they
doubtless would have sent me to Siberia, to end my
days there, if I could have got so far; but Providence,
who has always aided me in peril, favored me once
more. I took advantage of a moment when my
guards were more occupied with their booty than
with their prisoners, and by running like a madman,
managed to get to the Niemen, which was only a
quarter of a league away. When I got there, since
it was frozen, I hid in the reeds. I nearly froze
myself. I was half naked, and I needed all my
courage, which never left me for a moment. At

daybreak when I was able to see where I was, and to look about me, I started through some woods, and by dint of scurrying on managed to rejoin the rear-guard; there I found some friends who lent me some money and covered me with a ragged cloak with which I reached Königsberg. Of all the horses, uniforms, and luggage of all kinds, of which I had more than four thousand francs' worth at the beginning of the campaign, I have nothing left but one pocket-handkerchief. So I have had to supply myself with headdress, boots, epaulettes, cartridge-box, arms, uniform, linen, horses, etc., and I have not a penny. So you see I am in a more embarrassing position than when I received my commission, because then I had at least a coat on my back, while now I find myself in the condition I was in, November 30, 1788, when my mother's monthly nurse carried me to the fire.

"I am now going to tell you a most interesting piece of news. Since October 11, I have had the cross, so that now I am an old knight of the Legion of Honor; you may judge how gratifying that is. The delight it gave me has all passed away; I have suffered so much since then that the charm of novelty is gone; I am indeed terribly melancholy. I have lost all my best friends; their death has been so tragic that my whole life will be saddened. I have seen too many horrors ever to forget them."

The families that were in receipt of letters like that were sad; but how much sadder those that could receive none! How many were absent! for that is what the dead were called in official language. The lists were long of the innumerable absences published every day in the official announcements of the *Moniteur*. France, so long accustomed to triumph, was overwhelmed by its defeats. The winter had been exceptionally severe even in Paris. If there was suffering in comfortable, well-warmed apartments, with abundance of nutritious food, and thick clothes, what must have been the tortures of the unhappy soldiers amid blood-stained snowdrifts? Every one was moved by immense compassion.

There was another feeling, which was quite as general, — the desire for peace. The Senate had not dared to say the word, but it was in every one's heart. Every one yearned for peace, except one man, and that man was the Emperor. While the suffering and exhausted people cared for nothing but rest, he was thinking of nothing but conscription, armies, plans of campaign, strategic marches, battles, revenge. The Emperor of Austria, on the other hand, who was still sincere in his paternal interest for the Napoleonic dynasty, was above all things desirous of peace and reconciliation; and if Napoleon had accepted his father-in-law's views and had frankly consented to a few concessions of territory, which had become indispensable, he would certainly have preserved the Austrian and possibly the Prussian alliance.

It would not be fair to say that at this moment the Emperor Francis was deceiving his son-in-law. Since the beginning of December the Cabinet of

Vienna had made known its programme which could
be named in one word, — pacification.   M. de Floret,
First Secretary of the Austrian Embassy at Paris,
was sent to the Duke of Bassano, Minister of Foreign
Affairs, who was still at Wilna, where Napoleon had
made him stay during the war.   M. de Floret was
bearer of this despatch from the Count Metternich : —

"Vienna, December 9, 1812.   There are moments
and events which decide the fate of empires as
that of individuals.   At such times, illusions are
fatal; one must face the truth, however painful it
may be.   The attempt to bring Russia to terms, from
the centre of its wilds, has failed.   I will say nothing
of what ought to have been done ; we think too highly
of the first general of our century to presume to criti-
cise his military operations. . . .   The effect produced
by the first unsuccessful undertaking of Napoleon
upon all the nations of Europe is none the less incal-
culable.   It is in view of this circumstance that I
must beg you to ask the Duke of Bassano to pay the
greatest attention to the calculations and opinions of
the Minister of the power most capable of judging
this important question.   He addressed him with
perfect frankness; we are more directly called upon
because the proofs of the most loyal and political are
wholly in our favor.   I do not make a hasty statement when I aver that Austria alone, by the calm
and imperturbable firmness of her attitude, restrains
fifty millions of men who are ready to rise.

"However difficult a general peace may appear, it is doubtless easier — granted that the Emperor of the French desires it — than a separate arrangement. The only European power that is called on to speak first of this eminently desirable peace is Austria. We hold this conviction as a strong and central power. We should acquire it, if we did not already hold it, from the attempts of every sort which are made by the powers at war with France, to persuade us to abandon our present alliance. The Emperor Francis alone can use to France, England, and Russia a language, compromising neither the self-respect of rival and hostile governments, nor the national feelings of the people.

" The ties of blood which unite the two Imperial houses of France and Austria give an especial character to every step taken by our august master. Undertaken by any other power, such steps would fail to appear as disinterested, and as favorable to the French sovereign as are those of Austria. The Emperor Francis is interested, not merely in the maintenance, but also in the well-being of the new dynasty reigning in France, — a consideration without weight with the other powers. The Emperor of the French seems to have foreseen what has happened at this moment, when he said to me so often, that his marriage had altered the face of things in Europe. The time is approaching, it has perhaps come, when the Emperor Napoleon may derive real profit from this alliance."

Metternich's despatch ends thus: " Our august master, when he heard of the evacuation of Moscow, expressed in a few words the basis of his sentiments and of his policy. ' The time has come,' he said, ' when I can prove to the Emperor of the French who I am.' I simply give you these words of His Imperial Majesty, and authorize you to quote them to the Duke of Bassano: they would only be injured by any commentary."

The Emperor of Austria tried to gain additional weight to his proposition by a personal letter to his son-in-law, which ran as follows: —

" Vienna, December 20, 1812. MY BROTHER AND VERY DEAR SON-IN-LAW: I was on the point of sending the Count of Bubna to Dresden when I received the letter which your Imperial Majesty kindly sent hither. Consequently I have modified this officer's instructions, and he will have the honor of handing you this letter. The course of · events has occupied me painfully for many weeks. I flatter myself that Your Majesty will have gathered from the communications that I had presented to him through my *chargé d'affaires* at Wilna, the conviction of the continual interest I feel in him. They will also show my way of judging the state of affairs, and what are my wishes. These have no other aim than Your Majesty's well-being — to which I am personally attached by the most sacred bond — and no other motive than the greatest good of our peoples. It is to me a matter of the greatest interest to know thoroughly Your Majesty's plans, which have so direct an influence upon the future, that I cannot hesitate to beg you to explain them with all the frankness of friendship. You can readily understand how much I am interested in the fate of the brave army which I have added to your own, and what must be my anxiety for the safety of my most exposed provinces. General Bubna has orders to rejoin me at the earliest possible moment. I am engaged in selecting the man whom I shall commission to represent me with Your Majesty until the return of the Prince of Schwarzenberg. Accept the assurances of the sincere attachment, and of the high regard with which I am, my brother, Your Imperial Majesty's affectionate brother and father-in-law,

"FRANCIS."

General Bubna, who reached Paris towards the end of December, carried, besides the letter of the Emperor of Austria to Napoleon, another letter from him to his daughter; a letter in which he expressed his wishes for an early peace. Marie Louise answered, sending her father good wishes for the new year, and a present of a porcelain breakfast service adorned with views of all the Imperial palaces of France. "May Heaven grant," she said in her letter, "the fulfilment of your wishes, and that we may soon have peace!" A few days later she wrote to her father: "May Heaven grant that the Emperor shall not leave me! The thought of his departure terrifies me after all the anguish I endured last year. . . . I share your

desire to see soon a long peace, for I don't dare to
think of the moment when my husband shall return
to the battle-field."

Marie Louise was very anxious for peace. She
desired it for herself, for her husband, for her son,
for her father, for her two countries, France and Austria. The Countess of Montesquiou, the governess
of the King of Rome, added these words to the prayer
which the Prince Imperial repeated every evening before going to sleep: " O God! fill papa with a desire
to make peace for the happiness of France and of us
all!" One evening when Napoleon was in his son's
room, he heard the little Prince stammering out this
prayer, and he began to smile. Alas! when the
Emperor tenderly gazed on the boy sleeping in his
cradle, why did he not think of all the mothers whom
his headstrong ambition was to deprive of their sons?
How could fatherly love, that deep and gentle feeling,
be reconciled with such disdain of human lives sacrificed for a doubtful glory and for such short-lived
plans?

VIII.

THE CONCORDAT OF FONTAINEBLEAU.

AT the beginning of 1813 Napoleon might still have saved his Empire and himself; he had not broken with his father-in-law, or with the Princes of the Confederation of the Rhine, or even with the King of Prussia, and he had command of immense resources in men and money. His great mistake lay in supposing that an unprecedented disaster, like that of the Russian campaign, was an unimportant episode. He ought to have consented with a good grace to throw something overboard, in order that all should not be lost. Instead of that, the Emperor, staking his whole fortune on a single card, took for his motto: All or nothing. Resolved to accept no diminution of territory or influence, he thought that at his New Year's reception of the great bodies of the State and of the High Officials, he could be, January 1, 1813, what he had been January 1, 1812. He hardened himself the more because his enemies wished to humble him; and he had been so long accustomed to the favors of Fortune that he imagined that she had been guilty of only a temporary infidelity.

Nevertheless, Paris was despondent. The year 1813 began on a Friday: this number 13 and the Friday impressed the superstitious. People said that since Josephine was no longer with Napoleon to give him good luck, fate had condemned him to misfortune. A number of officers and soldiers returned, some having lost an arm or a leg, others with hands or feet frozen. They described the terrible disasters they had witnessed, and their stories dismayed their hearers. The French, who were recently so warlike, had became most peaceable. As for the Emperor, he tried by every means in his power to react against this general depression. He had this paragraph inserted in the *Moniteur:* " Paris, January 10. His Majesty the Emperor was yesterday at the Théâtre Français, where the tragedy of *Hector* was given. This modern piece is an especial favorite of His Majesty. This morning, Sunday, after mass, there was a parade, and His Majesty spent three hours on foot, in spite of the mud and the bad weather, in inspecting, organizing, and reviewing his troops. He saw a great number of newly arrived conscripts. The men are excellent, full of enthusiasm, and very eager."

Napoleon commanded the High Officials and Queen Hortense to give the usual festivities. " Every one was compelled," says Chateaubriand, " to go to the balls with death in his heart, silently weeping for relatives and friends. . . . In the drawing-rooms was seen what is met in the streets: namely, unhappy

creatures seeking distraction by singing their un-
happiness to divert passers-by." The Emperor would
have liked cheerfulness even in the retreat from
Russia. He had said in his 29th bulletin, " Those
whom nature had made of sterner stuff preserved
their gaiety and usual manners." Among the exceptional men whom nothing could daunt, the
General de Narbonne was mentioned with great
admiration ; for every morning, in his bivouac, he
used to have his hair done and powdered in the
midst of the snow, while he chatted freely with the
officers of his staff. When he had returned to Paris,
his friends congratulated him, and applied to him the
famous passage in the 29th bulletin ; but he exclaimed
sadly, " Ah ! the Emperor may say what he pleases ;
but 'gaiety' is a rather strong word ! " And he turned
aside to hide the tears which sprang to his eyes.

Napoleon knew no such attacks of melancholy.
Never had he displayed more eagerness or greater
confidence in his good luck. He was never tired of
saying that his next campaign would open with twice
as large forces as had fought in the previous campaign.
While waiting for the hour of battle, he devoted
himself most warmly to the pleasures of the chase,
that mimic war. " At the end of 1812, and the
beginning of 1813," says his valet de chambre Constant, " I noticed that the Emperor had never hunted
so frequently. One day, when Marshal Duroc was in
his room, and he was putting on his green coat with
gold facings, I heard the Emperor say, ' I must be

active, that the newspapers may speak of it; for the English papers are saying every day that I am ill, cannot move, am good for nothing. Have patience; I shall soon show them that I am well in body and mind.'"

January 19, 1813, a hunt had been commanded near Melun, at Grosbois, the estate of Berthier, Prince of Neufchâtel, who was that day to entertain the Emperor and Empress. After a breakfast at the castle of Grosbois, the hunt was about to begin when, to every one's surprise, Napoleon had a post-chaise brought, and after entering it, he drove, not to Paris, but to Fontainebleau. Constant says that the Empress and the ladies in her suite had actually nothing with them but their hunting-dresses, and that the Emperor was much amused at their sufferings when they found themselves on the way to Fontainebleau without proper dresses.

The palace towards which Napoleon thus suddenly started had contained, since June 19, 1812, an illustrious and venerable guest. This guest, or, more exactly, this prisoner, was the Pope Pius VII., the most famous of the victims of the Imperial policy. The Emperor, fearing that the English might make a descent on Savona, where the Holy Father was first confined, had ordered him to be carried to Fontainebleau; but remembering how the Vicar of Christ had been greeted at Grenoble, Avignon, and Nice, on his way to Savona, he had given orders that this time the journey should be made secretly. Pius VII. was obliged to take off his white slippers to have them stained with ink and the embroidered cross removed. The string was cut which held the gold cross that the Popes always wear around their necks ; he had to put on a simple priest's hat, and thus disguised, to leave Savona secretly the night of June 9; not until a week later did the inhabitants know that he had left. He was very ill at the time, and on his painful journey was several times at the point of death.

Still he uttered no complaint, and after passing through Chambéry and Lyons by night, without any one's suspecting his presence, he reached the gate of the Palace of Fontainebleau about noonday, June 19, 1812. The porter, who had received no instructions, refused him admission ; but taking pity upon him, found him temporary lodging in a little house near the palace. That evening the Duke of Cadore arrived, and gave orders that rooms should be at once made ready for the Pope. These rooms, which looked out on the Courtyard of the Fountain, were the same that he had occupied in 1804, at the time of the coronation. A detachment of foot-grenadiers and of the chasseurs of the Imperial Guard were in attendance upon him ; and, as if to disguise what was really his captivity, the officer who was charged with guarding him was dressed as a chamberlain. The presence of this austere and venerable man in this gilded prison was a touching spectacle. When, sad and solitary, he passed through the brilliant gallery of the Festivities and those of the Bourbons, his air

of an anchorite made an imposing contrast with the
pagan memories of which this spot was full. As he
gazed at the mythological frescos of Primaticcio, the
Vicar of Christ thought of the emptiness of all
human glory and splendor, and he said to himself
that palaces pass away, but the cross remains. He
cast a glance of utter indifference upon the useless
luxury with which they pretended to surround him.
The carriages and horses offered to him might have
come from the Imperial stables ; he was firmly
decided never to use them. He refused to officiate
publicly in the chapel of the palace. He asked for
and secured the transformation into an oratory of
the drawing-room nearest his bedroom, and it was
there that he said mass every morning. He never
consented to leave his rooms on any pretext, not
even to take the air in his garden. His sole prome-
nade was to walk a few steps in the gallery. The
inhabitants of Fontainebleau never set eyes on him.
He lived like a monk, devoting his days to fasting
and prayer, patching his worn-out clothes. The
palace of Henri II. and Diane de Poitiers, of Henri
IV. and Gabrielle d'Estrées, had become a monastery.

For seven months to a day Pius VII. had led the
life of an anchorite at Fontainebleau, when, January
19, 1813, at nightfall, just after his frugal meal,
while he was talking with the cardinals and bishops
who lived with him, he saw Napoleon suddenly enter
in hunting-dress ! His surprise and emotion were
great at seeing face to face the conqueror whose

image, even when at a distance, was ever present in his thoughts.

The emotion of Pius VII. was all the greater, because the Emperor, to whom two years before he had written many letters with his own hand, had refused to answer him, and had treated him in the severest, most insulting manner, even going so far as to send him a message through the Prefect of Savona, that he would have to resign his position as Sovereign Pontiff for incapacity. And now, as if nothing had happened; as if they were still in the happy days of 1804; as if the Palace of Fontainebleau was not a prison, Napoleon, with a happy face, a kind expression, a smile on his lips, ran up to the holy old man, took him in his arms, and overwhelmed him with signs of friendship.

How much had happened since the Pope and the Emperor had parted nearly nine years before! Pius VII. no longer found with Napoleon the amiable Josephine, to whom he had been so kind, so fatherly; whose marriage he had legitimized before the Church, and whose divorce he had not, at any price, consented to pronounce. Where was the time when the new Charlemagne had inspired the successor of Saint Peter with such great hopes? How often in his captivity the Pope, recovered from his illusions, thought of Notre Dame of Paris, and of the brilliant ceremony of December 2, 1804! How often, too, Napoleon, Catholic by his Italian origin, must have felt a secret remorse when he thought of the Sovereign Pontiff who had come to crown him! He still exercised over his victim a sort of fascination, an irresistible charm; so the old man became embarrassed and troubled at the thought of being alone with this terrible charmer. He feared to be drawn into concessions which he should later repent, and which would wring his conscience.

For his part, the Emperor was determined to employ all the means of action, intimidation, and seduction of which he possessed the secret. The conference was put off till the next day, January 20. It took place between Napoleon and Pius VII., who shut themselves up alone, and lasted not less than five days. "It is evident," said the Abbé de Pradt, "that the Emperor wished to put an end to the business by a sudden and unexpected step, and that he trusted to the effect that his presence, a direct discussion, and his personal skill, would produce on the Pope. He was then at the height of his fame, and no one had any suspicion of the Island of Elba, still less of Saint Helena." Napoleon finally subjugated his antagonist and brought him to the point he wanted. The Concordat of Fontainebleau contained eleven articles, and might be regarded as an implicit renunciation by the papacy of the temporal power of the Popes. The first article stated that His Holiness would fulfil the duties of the pontificate in France, and in the kingdom of Italy, in the same way and with the same forms as his predecessors. Residence in Paris was not imposed upon the Holy Father, but

he was obliged to reside in the States, whether French
or Italian, of Napoleon. Avignon is said to have been
the city which Pius VII. preferred, but it is not mentioned in the new Concordat. Article II. stipulated
that the ambassadors, ministers, *chargés d'affaires* of
the powers to the Holy Father, and the ambassadors,
ministers, and *chargés d'affaires* whom the Pope might
send to foreign powers, should enjoy all the immuni-
ties and privileges of the members of the Diplomatic
Body. By Article I. the Emperor promised to pardon
the cardinals, bishops, priests, and laymen who had
fallen into disgrace on account of recent events.
Article II. ran thus: "The Holy Father adheres to
the above arrangements in consideration of the present state of the Church, and in the confidence inspired
by His Majesty that he will accord his valuable protection to the numerous needs of religion in the times
in which we are living."

Napoleon no longer insisted that the black cardinals — those who had refused to be present at his
marriage with Marie Louise and had been deprived
by him of the cardinal's robes — should be blamed,
and he did not compel the Pope to banish forever
from his presence Cardinals di Pietro and Pacca.
Napoleon also made various concessions in regard to
the nomination of bishops. In the evening of January 25, 1813, when all was finished and there was
nothing to do but to sign the Concordat, Pius VII.
endured a moment of indescribable anguish. The
cardinals who were living with him at Fontainebleau

were present at this last conference. He looked at
them earnestly, betraying his mental anguish and his
stings of conscience; his look seemed to say: Am I
right or wrong? What ought I to do? A word, a
sign, from the four cardinals, and all would perhaps
have had to be done over again. Not one stirred.
Respecting the venerable Pontiff's painful perplexity,
and unwilling to influence him in any way, they kept
a profound silence, lowering their heads. Then the
Pope took the pen in his trembling hand and signed.

When the Emperor thus overcame the resistance
of the Vicar of Christ, did he suspect that he too, in
this same Palace of Fontainebleau, would soon endure
distress, anguish, doubts, and scruples no less terrible
than those of the Holy Father It was at Fontainebleau that he compelled the Pope to abdicate his
temporal power, and it was at Fontainebleau that,
one year later, he was to abdicate the Empire. Possibly he then, when he had to trace the letters of the
fatal word, recalled what the Pope had suffered at his
hands. Deeds of violence almost always, even here
below, bring their punishment, and Providence appears as the great distributor of justice to peoples and
rulers.

As soon as the Concordat had been signed, Marie
Louise went, at her own suggestion, to congratulate
the Pope. It was especially in view of Austria and
of Southern Germany, essentially Catholic countries,
with which alliance was necessary, that Napoleon had
set so much store on some arrangement with the

Pope. It is sometimes when the papacy appears feeblest that it is really strongest. The captivity of Pius VII. had been worse for the jailer than for the prisoner. One was to die at Saint Helena; the other was to return in triumph to Rome. Napoleon had a vague instinct of the great importance of the religious question, and when he imagined that he had settled it by the Concordat of Fontainebleau, he felt a joy which was to be shared by his wife and father-in-law. Marie Louise, who remembered that the black cardinals had refused to be present at her wedding, and knew that Pius VII. had opposed the divorce, was both flattered and touched by the warmth of the Holy Father's greeting. As soon as the Concordat was signed, she wrote to the Emperor Francis: " We have been at Fontainebleau for six days. The Emperor and the Pope have settled the affairs of Christianity in the best way. The Pope seems very happy. Since yesterday morning he has been most easy and gracious; he signed the treaty in less than a quarter of an hour. I have just seen him ; I found him very well. He has a very handsome and interesting face. This reconciliation will, I am sure, please you as much as it does me."   .

Napoleon, too, hastened to send in confidence to his father-in-law the text of the new Concordat, with a letter to which the Emperor Francis replied February 17, 1813, as follows : —

"My Brother and very Dear Son-in-law: It is with great pleasure that I have received Your Imperial Majesty's last letter. You know how much interest I take in the real welfare of your government. The condition of the Church has a great interest for France, and a definite arrangement of its affairs has no less for my Empire. I am very anxious that Your Imperial Majesty should be equally successful in settling with the Holy Father the temporal question with which is closely connected that of the perfect independence of the head of the universal Church. It is this independence which especially interests the Catholic powers; it is not without points of great utility to Your Majesty himself. I shall keep the secret you desire concerning the text of the transaction which you have been kind enough to communicate to me."

February 18, 1813, Count Otto, French Ambassador at Vienna, had already written this despatch on the same subject: "Yesterday morning I was admitted to a private audience, in which I handed His Majesty's letter to the Emperor. He did not open it in my presence, but I hastened to tell him that it contained a copy of the Concordat concluded by the Emperor with the Pope. The Emperor expressed the liveliest satisfaction. He told me he had always desired this arrangement as one of the essential bases of public peace in France and in the rest of Europe. 'I often spoke on this subject,' he said, 'to your master during his stay at Dresden. The influence of religious opinions is far too powerful not to become with you, as elsewhere, one of the leading principles

of internal policy. I draw from it the happiest augu-
ries for a general peace.'"

In appearance everything was settled; in fact,
nothing was. The Concordat did not contain a
formal renunciation, on the part of the Holy Father,
of the possession of the Roman States; it spoke only
of the Pope's promise to exercise his pontificate in
the Emperor's states, and Pius VII. made only an
implicit abdication. More than this, the very evening
of the signature Napoleon had dictated to the Bishop
of Nantes so strange a letter that, according to the
Count d'Haussonviile, it is hard to make out whether
it was inspired by amiability or whether it contained
bitter sarcasm. This is the letter: " Your Holiness
having appeared to fear at the moment of signing the
articles of the Concordat which put an end to the
divisions that afflict the Church, that this implied a
renunciation of the sovereignty of Rome, I take pleasure in assuring you by this letter, that never having
felt justified in demanding it, I cannot conceive that
there has been any renunciation, direct or indirect,
of the sovereignty of the Roman States, and I have
intended to treat with you only in your capacity as
Head of the Church in spiritual matters." Had
Napoleon forgotten, when he wrote this letter, that
he had styled his son the King of Rome, and that the
Eternal City was the capital of a French department,
the Department of the Tiber? No; doubtless he had
not forgotten it. He knew well that in the eyes of
Pius VII. the true King of Rome was not the little

Prince Imperial, but himself, the Pope. The restoration to favor of the black cardinals cost the Emperor a bitter pang. He especially feared Cardinal Pacca. " He is my enemy," he often said. He signed with reluctance the decree setting free the prelate and the Cardinal di Pietro. He felt sure that these two cardinals would fill with scruples and anxiety the troubled conscience of Pius VII. " When the Cardinal di Pietro arrives," he said to the Pope, half ironically, " you will confess to him."

Napoleon and Marie Louise, before leaving Fontainebleau, January 27, 1813, took affectionate leave of the Holy Father. But no sooner had the Pope seen the mighty conqueror depart than he fell into deep dejection and bitterly repented the concessions he had made. His timidity plunged him into deep anguish; he fancied himself false to his duties and to the cause of Heaven. When he looked at the pine-trees which Louis XVI. had planted opposite the gloomy rooms where Monescalchi was assassinated, he suffered moral tortures like those that had wrung the heart of the martyred king when the Pope had written to him, " If you were disposed to renounce even the rights inherent in the royal prerogative, you have no right to alienate or to abandon what is due to God and to the Church, whose eldest son you are."

When Cardinal Pacca presented himself at Fontainebleau, he found, he said, " His Holiness in a pitiable and alarming state. When he spoke of what had happened he was overwhelmed with the deepest remorse. This distracting thought robbed him of sleep and let him eat only enough to avoid starvation." In his despair the unhappy man exclaimed, "All this will make me die mad, like Clement XIV." The only alleviation to his grief was the thought that he had yielded only to force ; yet he bitterly reproached himself for not preferring martyrdom to concessions which he regarded as dishonorable and criminal. From that moment, but one idea possessed him, — to recant, whatever might be the consequences of such temerity. May 24, 1813, he gave to the officers in charge of his person a letter, in which he declared to Napoleon that he regarded the Concordat of January 25 as null and void; then he read to the cardinals who were with him an allocution in which he said to them in a transport of mystic joy, "Blessed be the Lord, who has not removed his mercy from us. He wished to humiliate us by a salutary confusion. May this humiliation be for the good of our soul ! To him for all time be praise, and honor, and glory ! " From that day, calm took possession of the successor of Saint Peter, and, freed from remorse, he recovered his health and moral peace ; his sleep and a heart at peace.

IX.

IT is curious to notice how formidable Napoleon continued to be, even after the retreat from Russia, and how much he was dreaded. The blood-stained snows had wrought no injury to the pedestal on which stood that colossal figure. Even Germany, though cowed and impatient, did not dare to express her hatred openly. It was in secret councils and mysterious meetings that the general insurrection was prepared. Judging from the diplomatic conditions, Napoleon seemed to enjoy the same power. His representatives at Berlin and at Vienna, the Count of Saint Marsan and Count Otto, were treated with the utmost respect. Austria and Prussia appeared, officially at least, desirous of maintaining and even of strengthening the French alliance. The two ambassadors received the most cordial assurances and the most lavish promises. We have inspected the correspondence of these two diplomatists and that of General the Count of Narbonne, who, in 1813, succeeded Count Otto as French Ambassador at Vienna. The greater number of the despatches we quote have

124

never been printed. They set before us, one might almost say from day to day, the growth of the evil by which two countries that, during the war of 1812, had been the vassals rather than the allies of France, passed from obedience to discussion, from discussion to disagreement, and ended with declaring war on their ally. These despatches are mainly interesting to diplomatists; but others, we hope, will find them not unworthy of attention.

The situation of the Prussian court was especially difficult at the end of 1812. Napoleon had done too much or too little for it. From the moment he had forborne to destroy it, he should have treated it more kindly. By imposing French garrisons upon it, and weighing it down with burdens of every sort, he had produced a feeling of exasperation which for many years was latent and was sooner or later to break forth. A country like that of Frederick the Great, accustomed to glory, could not resign itself to such a humiliated condition.

King Frederick William, guarded by the French troops who occupied Berlin and the fortified towns, bore more likeness to a hostage than to an independent sovereign. The misery of his ruined and humiliated people had grown till it filled castles as well as hovels; no one's fortune had been spared; private sufferings rivalled those of the state. Napoleon took account of all this, and his position with relation to Prussia was as false as Prussia's position with relation to him. On one hand, he owed the Prussian govern-

ment money for food and supplies, and on the other
he had every reason to believe that the money he
should pay this government would be spent against
France. The Count of Saint Marsan, the Emperor's
Minister at Berlin, was highly thought of then; but
circumstances are stronger than men, and in spite of
all his zeal, intelligence, and loyalty, this skilful and
honest diplomatist was unable to stem the torrent.

Still, at the end of 1812, Prussia was still trembling before Napoleon, and the King had not shown
by a word, a gesture, or a movement of his face, the
slightest indication of resistance.   Perhaps even at
this moment he was sincere in his desire of maintaining an alliance against which the national feeling
protested, but which was to be broken by the government only after long hesitations and a real terror.

On passing through Dresden on his way from
Russia, the Emperor, December 14, 1812, had written to Frederick William, the King of Prussia, that
it was very important that the Prussian contingent
should alone constitute an army corps, and should be
raised to thirty thousand men.   "In asking Your
Majesty to augment his troops," it was said in Napoleon's letter, "I show how much confidence I have
in the system you have adopted."   The letter ended
with congratulations on the courage and discipline
displayed by the Prussian troops during the campaign.
It was handed to the King at Berlin by the Count
of Saint Marsan, who addressed the following report
to the Emperor, December 17, 1812: "The King

received me with his usual kindness. I handed him Your Majesty's letter. I had a long audience, and I have the satisfaction of announcing to Your Majesty that I found the King in the most compliant mood, without a cloud on the loyalty and frankness of his character. The King added that he did not fear factious spirits, that I ought to have seen that he had taken some measures, and that orders had been given to keep a rigid oversight and to punish everything of the sort that showed itself, no matter how trivial, even if a mere jest. In general, Sire, I was able to see that the King was gratified by two things: one by the satisfaction Your Majesty expressed with the conduct of his troops, and the other, the mark of confidence and consideration you gave in asking him to unite his contingent in a single army corps consisting of his troops alone, thus treating him like Austria."

The Count of Saint Marsan did not conceal from the Emperor the extreme agitation which was beginning to show itself in Prussia, and in this report he said: "I ought not to keep it from Your Majesty, the foes of this system of union with France are working most eagerly to excite every one. The King, who is of frank, loyal, and scrupulously upright character, is not, I think, open to the attacks of those who would like to lead him into another system, especially since he is endowed with a certain firmness which some may call obstinacy, that is no less useful at this moment. The Baron von Hardenberg, who is of an upright and loyal character, and who is especially anxious not to pass for a frivolous politician, is too clear-sighted not to see that if Prussia changes her system she would begin by being overwhelmed by France, and that if she escaped ruin, she would become the prey of Russia. On the other hand, this Minister thinks that at the moment when Your Majesty shall be able to give a firm and solid peace to Europe, Prussia, having faithfully followed your system, will seem, too, destined to form a constant ally of France and her northern frontier, and that Your Majesty will assign to this country, not the military place which it has occupied and which was exaggerated, but the rank that it held in the political system for the equilibrium of Europe. I know that he goes so far as to think that if Poland is not so strongly constituted as to assure its existence, it might occur to Your Majesty not to unite Poland with Prussia, but to make the King of Prussia the King of Poland, in order to strengthen the frontier, by combining the interior lines and countries. . . . The greater part of the nation have always regarded the system of union with France as the safeguard of Prussia, but at this moment they are disturbed by all the intrigues of the opposite party, which is smaller but more active; and the sufferings, which are really excessive, and the burdens that weigh upon proprietors, do not act in our favor."

The first news of the French disasters were not believed in Prussia, where it could not be imagined that the unrivalled army which had been seen in its splendor a few months before was nothing but a phantom. But the arrival of the wounded made the truth known, and from that time thoughts of revenge fired every Prussian heart. Nevertheless, M. de Saint Marsan had no suspicions of Frederick William's feelings about Napoleon, and he wrote to the Emperor at the end of December: "All sorts of talk are still prevailing at Berlin. Part of it is due to the French wounded who are passing through. Malcontents are agitating, but it amounts to nothing more serious than drawing-room talk, especially on the part of a few women. The King and the Ministry are faithfully following a line of conduct such as I am able to approve. The King thinks that Your Majesty intends to devote the great resources of your genius and the strength of your Empire to collect an army still more formidable than the first; that then you will negotiate a peace, even a general peace. . . . When the King heard that the Duke of Bassano meant to pass through Berlin, he expressed to me his satisfaction. He gave orders to have a house prepared for him, and when he was told that I meant to have him stay with me, sent me word that he hoped that the Duke would at least make use of his horses and carriages; that besides his desire to testify his esteem and regard for the Duke of Bassano, it was well that the public should know what he felt for Your Majesty's Minister."

There was a strange contrast between the language of the Prussian court, which was always gracious,

courteous, and respectful towards Napoleon, and the
deep-seated anger which the country no longer sought
to conceal; but M. de Saint Marsan no less persisted
in building great hopes upon the King and his
Ministry.   December 22, 1812, he wrote a despatch
to the Duke of Bassano : " Clamor and malice are
under full headway.   The Chancellor continually
urges the police to keep close watch.   It has been
suggested to him to issue a special order on the subject: he thinks this useless, and possibly dangerous
at this moment.   I agree with him.   We have agreed
that every overt act or attempt shall be severely
punished, and that the greatest publicity should be
given to the measures adopted by the government
for the promotion of the common cause, which will
be of the happiest effect, and produce an excellent
impression upon the nation. . . .   With respect to
its main policy, without regard to special circumstances, I believe that if Prussia is sure of the confidence of France, she will always prefer the French
alliance to any other."

The illusions of the French diplomatist were
doomed to have a terrible awakening.   December
30, 1812, a thunderbolt fell.   On that day, General
York, who commanded the twenty thousand Prussians of the rear guard, and almost the whole of
General Macdonald's army corps, concluded, at
Tauroggen, a capitulation by which he and his
troops entered into the Russian army corps that
was pursuing him.   The Prussian soldiers shouted

with joy when they heard the order of the day that announced this defection, which was the first outbreak of the feelings that were to manifest themselves in the whole nation. At the same time, General York wrote to his King: "If I have made a mistake, I am willing to be shot, and will meet my fate with calmness and serenity, being conscious that I have always remained a faithful subject and a good Prussian. The time has come for Your Majesty to escape from the disastrous demands of an ally whose views concerning Prussia, if fortune had remained faithful to him, are still wrapt in impenetrable obscurity. These are the considerations that have decided him. Heaven grant that they may further the well-being of my country!"

For his part, General Macdonald wrote, January 1, 1813, to Major-General Berthier: "General York has fully justified my estimate of him: I had clearly seen that he was our deadliest foe, but I should never have deemed him capable of such black treachery. I have always had the greatest consideration for his troops, and thoroughly confided in their honor."

King Frederick William had no part in General York's defection. As soon as he heard of it, he summoned the Count of Saint Marsan, and earnestly disavowed the general's conduct. The French Minister was convinced by the King's loyal utterances, and told him that he would disbelieve the whole world before he would doubt the King. January 5, 1813, he wrote to the Duke of Bassano: "Last evening, at eleven o'clock, the King sent to me the Baron von Hardenberg to announce his decision. His Majesty was amazed and indignant at General York's defection. His first words were, ' It's enough to give one an attack of apoplexy.' What is to be done? The King has decided that His Majesty the King of Naples shall be asked to announce, in an order of the day of the French army, the King's disavowal and indignation; that if General York cannot be arrested, he shall be judged in default; that Prince von Hatzfeld shall go at once to Paris to convey to His Majesty the Emperor the expression of the King's feelings, and to manifest the same feelings to all Europe, by means of this exceptional mission." The Count of Saint Marsan wrote again to the Duke of Bassano, January 7: "It is impossible, my lord, to exhibit more loyalty and exactitude in discharging one's obligations, than is shown here." And Count von Goltz, Prussian Minister of Foreign Affairs, sent to all the King's legations a circular letter, in which he said: "The King has done and will do all that lies in his power to prove that he remains faithful to his system and to his promises. (January 9, 1813.)"

In reality, Frederick William had not yet made up his mind; he was hesitating. Never, perhaps, was a sovereign in a more perplexing position. Whichever way he looked he saw nothing but trouble, uncertainty, and misery. He asked himself what he ought to do, and his conscience gave only a confused and undecided reply. Being forced either to break his

word to France, which was able to crush him, or else
to fight for her against friends who represented themselves as liberators, this naturally loyal ruler strug-
gled with doubts and hesitations which were really
torturing. Is it credible? Even after General York's
defection, even after the extraordinary hatred of
everything French that broke out in the whole
Prussian kingdom, Frederick William was far from
decided to break loose from Napoleon.

It is a very significant detail that at this very
moment, early in 1813, the Prussian court seriously
contemplated a matrimonial alliance between the
Crown Prince and a Princess of the Emperor's family. The despatch of the Count of Saint Marsan
referring to this proposed marriage is dated January 12, 1813, and it is very curious. It has never
been published, and shows better than anything the
ascendancy which Napoleon still exercised. In this
despatch the Count began by reporting the remarks
the King had made to Prince Hatzfeld, who was
about to leave for Paris to visit the Emperor.

"The King," said the Minister of France, "has in
the first place overwhelmed Prince von Hatzfeld with
attentions. He has shown him how highly he appre-
ciates his services, the purity of his feelings, the
justice of his opinions. . . . He then said to him,
'Assure the Emperor that nothing can move me from
my plan of alliance with him. Take every means of
ridding him of every trace of suspicion or mistrust
which he may feel toward Prussia. It is true that

most of my friends are ill-disposed towards the
French, and very naturally; but unless they are
forced by the necessity of unendurable sacrifices,
they will take no active steps; it thus is no occasion
for surprise at what happens in places whither the
enemy penetrates; but in those very places the inhabitants have greeted the French army in the warmest
way, when it was exhausted by all it had endured;
and this proves the purity of our intentions and their
obedience to my orders. I think that I have seen
proof that Austria will remain firm in its alliance
with France. If that were otherwise, my position is
very different from that of that power; I am the
natural ally of France. If I were to change my system, I should always be sacrificed by the Russians,
and then again by the French, who would treat me
as an enemy, and with justice. I know there are
madmen who look upon France as exhausted, but
you will soon see it presenting an army of three hundred thousand men, as fine as the first one. I suppose that I shall have dark moments and sacrifices
to endure; I shall endure what I must to assure the
peace and future prosperity of my family. Tell the
Emperor I can make no more pecuniary sacrifices;
but if he will give me the money, I can still raise
fifty or sixty thousand men for his service. Moreover, in the present circumstances it is fortunate that
Prussia is tranquil; for if there were to be an insurrection in this country, it would be the spark that
would set Germany ablaze."

In this despatch the Count of Saint Marsan spoke thus of the matrimonial project: " The idea has been started here that it might be possible to conclude a family alliance between France and Prussia by the marriage of a Princess of the Imperial family of France with the Crown Prince of Prussia. This idea, which suggests the union of all their interests between the two powers, — a union already natural in view of the political condition, — has necessarily made an impression on the mind of so enlightened a minister as the Baron von Hardenberg, and has inspired him with the hope of seeing his work thus consolidated; and after having assured the existence of Prussia, by a political alliance with France, of obtaining its restoration by a family alliance, which would remove all suspicion and mistrust, and engage France to restore Prussia to its place and make it her northern frontier."

M. de Saint Marsan, further on in the despatch, thus reported Frederick William's conversation with Prince Hatzfeld concerning the proposed marriage: " Coming thus to the plan of the marriage, this is what the King said to Prince Hatzfeld: ' If you have an opportunity, listen to what is said; express your own opinions, but make no promises unless you have received orders.' Then the Prince asked if he could know what he really thought of it, and if in any case he would follow this plan. ' I cannot conceal from you,' said the King, ' that as father of a family, I am averse to contracting an alliance from merely political motives. Nevertheless, if I see that there will result considerable advantages that will place my kingdom in a higher position than it now holds, I shall not hesitate.' "

The French Minister thus closed his despatch: " Your Excellency may assure the Emperor that this report of the King's conversation with Prince Hatzfeld is absolutely accurate. Besides, it is in harmony with the King's upright and loyal character, and with the feelings he has always had for France, even when he was led into the war of 1806, to which it is notorious that he was opposed. Hence if Your Excellency gives Prince Hatzfeld any encouragement, you will find him eager to discuss the matter, although unofficially. As for me, I have spoken about this affair freely, because it is well known that I received personal confidences, and consequently I have been free to utter my own personal opinions. I have endeavored to convey the impression that I regard an event of this sort as certain to assure not merely the prosperity of Prussia, but also the peace of Europe, since it would dig the ground from beneath the feet of those evil citizens of Germany who are always hoping to lead their sovereigns into some course of action that would bring about general disorder."

January 15, the Count of Saint Marsan was still convinced that the Franco-Prussian alliance could be maintained. "If His Majesty the Emperor," he wrote to the Duke of Bassano, "judges it well to show confidence in this government, I am convinced that this alone would suffice to defeat the propositions which might be made by England and Russia. Also that some consideration in the sacrifices to be demanded, a little money for securing stores, and the maintenance of discipline among the soldiers, would prevent any explosion on the part of the inhabitants."

While the French diplomatist was in full enjoyment of this optimism, Baron von Stein and General York were convoking the provincial states at Königsberg, and securing a decree to arm the entire population and to employ every resource against France. As for the King, he had not yet decided to speak out against Napoleon; but he wished already to hold an intermediate position, to obtain the neutrality of Silesia, and by a general peace to secure the complete freedom of Prussia. Nearly thirty thousand French still occupied its capital, and, moreover, the Russians were approaching. He then made up his mind to take refuge at Breslau, whither he betook himself with the Ministers of France and Austria, and to await events. His Ministers continued to give the Emperor's representative the most friendly assurances. The Count of Saint Marsan wrote to the Duke of Bassano: —

"Breslau, February 15, 1813. Baron von Hardenberg has sworn to me twenty times to-day that the system has not changed; that there have been no overtures, direct or indirect, with regard to approaching Russia. He has told me that he awaits with the greatest uneasiness and impatience an answer from Paris, because if, in view of the circumstances, His Majesty the Emperor approves the steps made towards establishing the neutrality of Silesia, and will himself give some aid to Prussia, the system will be more firmly consolidated than ever, and nothing but despair can throw Prussia into the arms of Russia. He has repeated to me how much the King's conduct since the retreat of the Grand Army proved his loyalty; that if he had lacked this and had wished to change his system, he would not have waited for this moment, but would have availed himself of his earlier opportunities; and that, moreover, they are not so foolish as to forget that nothing is easier than for France to make Prussia repent a breach of faith. . . . A little repression is being put on the utterances of the young men. A severe reprimand has been given to a professor accused of exciting his pupils, indicating that the next enemy they would have to fight would be the French. The police have received instructions on this subject, and they needed them, for they are very incompetent."

The Count of Saint Marsan, when he followed the King to Breslau, had left at Berlin the First Secretary of Legation, M. Edouard Lefebvre, who wrote to the Duke of Bassano, February 17, 1813: "The greater the discrepancy between events and what appears to be promised by the King's loyalty and the Minister's good disposition, the readier we must be to

THE COUNT OF SAINT MARSAN. 139

believe that matters are unsettled at Breslau, and
that possibly no definite decision has been made.
The King's timorous and hesitating character would
justify this opinion. . . . I sent to Your Excellency,
by yesterday's courier, the *Gazette* containing an
edict which declares that all young men more than
twenty-four years old may enlist, if they choose, and
that the King and the country will be grateful for
this proof of devotion. The upshot is that enlistment
is compulsory from seventeen up to twenty-four, and
voluntary from twenty-four up to an undetermined
age."

Only one thing could have prevented the explosion ;
that was the success of Prince Hatzfeld's mission in
Paris ; but this fell to the ground. The Prince was
unable to obtain from the Emperor either reimburse-
ment for the supplies furnished or the evacuation of
the strongholds. These two refusals discouraged the
last French inclinations of the King, and drove him
still more towards Napoleon's enemies.

Meanwhile Frederick William still continued impenetrable, and gave the Count no chance to suspect
his speedy decision; and the Minister thus wrote in a
despatch dated Breslau, February 21, 1813: " There
has been no change in the way I am treated. The King
sees no one here, as at Berlin, except at his dinner,
from which the Diplomatic Body is excluded; but he
goes into private company, even when he has to pay.
I met him the other evening at a ball of this kind
where I knew that he was going ; he came up to me

at once; talked with me a long time; asked me often what news I had from the Emperor, talking at great length about his indefatigable activity, and the immense advantages his strength gave him; he said nothing about the condition of the country; besides, the place was too public. The Crown Prince and the other young Princes who were with the King also sought me out for particular attentions; and all this caused great surprise in the assembled company."

February 27, the Count of Saint Marsan gave up every illusion. In a despatch dated that day he wrote: "There is no longer, in my opinion, any doubt that Prussia is about to abandon the alliance with France. Baron von Hardenberg said to me: 'If Prussia should ever change its system, it could not be denied that it had been forced so to do by the harshness with which it has been treated, and by its receiving no answer on so important a subject as that of its advances at a time when, left to itself, it would be desired that it should neither make use of its own means, nor seek to lessen its misfortunes.' He assured me, moreover, that the condition of neutrality was always in such a state that it could be revoked on forty-eight hours' notice; but he did not conceal from me the fact that Russia is making all sorts of advances to Prussia."

The next day, February 28, 1813, the courts of Saint Petersburg and Berlin concluded at Kalisz a treaty of alliance which was at first kept secret. Russia engaged to provide one hundred and fifty thousand men for the war against France ; and Prussia, eighty thousand men. The two powers agreed to use all their efforts to secure the adhesion of Austria. The Emperor Alexander promised not to lay down his arms until Prussia should be restored to the condition she was in before 1806.

The existence of this treaty was kept hidden from the Count of Saint Marsan, and he was treated as courteously as ever. He wrote to the Duke of Bassano : —

" Breslau, March 1, 1813. Although the agreement with Russia, and the perfect harmony existing between the two courts is as evident as was the alliance with France scarcely a month ago, there has been no change in the formality and respect with which I am treated, not only by the court, but also by the public and the leading members of society. As to business, nothing is ever said about it ; and I, for my part, remain entirely passive ; I should only compromise myself, and consequently the dignity of His Majesty the Emperor, if, after all I have said, I should demand new explanations." M. de Saint Marsan already guessed the secret which was kept from him. He had written to the Duke of Bassano, March 2 : " I have said that Prussia could not long play a doubtful part. I have just heard some news which leads me to think that it has decided, and that the threats and promises of the Russians have produced their effect. I understand that General Blücher has been set free." And yet the French diplomatist still thought that the Prussian alliance might be saved. In the same despatch he said: "If His Majesty the Emperor does not judge it well to do anything for Prussia, it will declare against us, and will be forced to do this willy nilly. If anything is done for it, I am far from despairing of its retention in the system. Inasmuch as I am entirely without orders and instructions, and have no knowledge of what are the intentions of His Majesty the Emperor, and am, in consequence, unable to utter one word in the way of promises and positive encouragement, I confine myself to general discussion, to axioms and hypotheses, which I turn over and over in every way. . . . Prince Hatzfeld has sent a report dated February 14, in which he indicates a hope of obtaining something. The original was immediately read to me in confidence. In our last interview Baron von Hardenberg said to me: 'I cannot understand why His Majesty the Emperor does not consent to do anything for the King, and to give some sort of a positive promise; he would never have a more faithful ally than he. He has proved this by the enormous sacrifices he has already made; but no one seems to take any account of these.' "

We are inclined to think that Napoleon could not have easily conciliated the Prussian nation, although he might have kept the government in his system of alliance if he had made it in time the indispensable concessions. King Frederick William and Baron von Hardenberg were distinctly frightened by the demagogic tendencies which manifested themselves. Towards the end of 1812 they were, we think, still well disposed; and if the Emperor had restored its strongholds to Prussia; if he had paid for the supplies it had furnished; if he had conceded some territory, it is our impression that the Cabinet of Berlin would have declared itself satisfied, and would have done its best to stem the torrent which threatened to carry away everything. Possibly it would not have succeeded, but it would at least have tried. If the nation in its enthusiasm especially yearned for revenge, what the calmer and more cautious government preferred was peace; but an honorable peace, that should assign to Prussia an important position in Europe, instead of the enfeebled condition in which it was left.

The die was cast; Napoleon, who, with wisdom, might have found a way to disarm the hatred of the Prussian people, was confronted by a bitter, implacable adversary. The passions which republican France unchained against Europe were turned against imperial France. Sovereigns, ministers, generals, were about to become demagogues, to borrow the French phraseology of 1792, to promise constitutions as a means of arousing the different peoples against the ruler of the continent. Secret societies uttered cries of vengeance. Religion and science fostered the warlike spirit. Church pulpits and teachers' chairs were turned into public tribunes. The Prussian people seized their arms and rose like one man; women, rich and poor, sent to the Treasury all their gold and silver and jewels, even their wedding-rings. These

offerings were received with a gratitude that only added
to the patriotic enthusiasm; in exchange there were
given objects in iron, of the same form, bearing this
inscription : " I have given my gold for iron. 1813."
The revolutionary weapons, which Napoleon had
refused to employ against the King, were about to be
used against him; and to oppose them he had only
the regular resources of monarchies by divine right.

March 15, 1813, the Emperor Alexander had
entered Breslau. King Frederick William had gone
to meet him, and the two sovereigns on horseback
had been greeted by the applause of the troops.
Two days later, March 17, M. de Saint Marsan
received official notice of the treaty concluded, February 28, between the two monarchs. " Your Excellency," he wrote to the Duke of Bassano, " will have
concluded from the reports which I have had the
honor of sending to you that the alliance between
Prussia and Russia is definitely settled; that the
King and the government are carried away, one may
say, by the German revolutionary party, and that all
possible means will be tried, and all the most turbu-
lent individuals employed to arouse the whole German nation." The Count lingered a few days at
Breslau, and did not receive his passports till March
27. In a despatch dated that day he wrote: " I
have had to exercise much patience and self-control
to stay here as a spectator of all that has taken place;
nevertheless, I must say that both the government
and private citizens have treated me most consider-

ately.   I venture to flatter myself that I have com-
plied with His Majesty's wishes, and have closely followed the line of duty by leaving Breslau, without
orders from His Majesty the Emperor, only when the
government demanded it."   War was declared between France and Prussia.

X.

COUNT OTTO.

IN 1812 the French Ambassador at Vienna was a diplomatist of great merit, Count Otto, who had for many years represented the Emperor Napoleon at the court of the Emperor Francis, and had been one of the principal negotiators of the marriage of the Empress Marie Louise. By his tact, his experience, and his conciliating character, he had won general sympathy at the Austrian court, where he was what in diplomatic language is called a *persona grata*. His despatches do him great honor. He knew how to tell the truth to Napoleon in the most respectful forms, and it was certainly not his fault if his sovereign indulged in illusions, which were destined to be fatal, on the character and extent of the Austrian alliance.

The main cause of Napoleon's errors was that politically he set too much importance on his marriage with an archduchess. He should have known that before becoming the father-in-law of the Emperor of the French, the father of Marie Louise was the Emperor of Austria, and that if, after his defeat at

146

Austerlitz and Wagram he had to choose between his paternal affection and his interests as a ruler, his choice was not doubtful. From the moment when Russia, Prussia, and England promised him to restore Illyria, the Tyrol, and the Lombardo-Venetian Kingdom, while France could only promise Illyria, — and even that was doubtful, — family considerations could have but little weight. Still, even after the Russian war, Napoleon might have made use of Austria. She would have been of great service in helping him to make an honorable peace with all the powers; but to secure this peace he would have had to make considerable concessions, and that is what Napoleon did not wish to do. This is at least what we conclude from Count Otto's correspondence, many of whose despatches, almost all unpublished, we are about to quote.

October 31, 1812, the Ambassador informed the Duke of Bassano, Minister of Foreign Affairs, of the excitement which was beginning to pervade Austria.

" I was told this morning," he wrote, " that the Archduke John had said at dinner at Duke Albert's, that at last the time had come for sharpening their daggers and falling on the French. It was added that I had sent a note to complain of this violent utterance. This specimen will give you, my Lord, an idea of the lies in circulation here, which, it is hoped, will disturb the good understanding between the two governments. Often these lies are accompanied by so many plausible details that it is hard for

me to defend myself. Some agitator, who saw me a
few days ago leaving the Palace, had the insolence to
spread abroad the rumor that I had been to Laxen-
burg to inform the Emperor of the sad condition of
our army and to ask for a re-enforcement of fifty
thousand men."

November 10, 1812, Count Otto informed the Minister that Austria intended not to continue the war
as a French ally, but to endeavor by diplomacy to
secure a general peace : " In my frequent interviews
with Count Metternich I have been able to see that
he was inclined towards a plan, which he could hardly
hope would succeed, and which he feared to communicate to me. Being unused to this reserve, I tried
to find out his secret, and it was only after many
conversations that I was able to convince myself that
the Austrian Cabinet desired to be charged by us with
the honorable duty of carrying messages of peace not
merely to Russia, but even to England. If I had any
doubts about these intentions, they would have been
removed by the interview that I had yesterday with
His Majesty the Emperor of Austria, on the occasion
of the Festival of the Order of Saint Stephen. After
expressing to me his hopes for the success of Count
Lauriston's mission, he said : ' In the winter you will
have time to negotiate ; all Europe craves peace ; in
case you cannot come to an understanding with the
court of Saint Petersburg, I will speak to it in your
name, if your master gives me authority, for you
understand, of course, that I shall do nothing without

your consent. I think, moreover, that my interven-tion will not be without result. But peace to last, must be general, and England should share in it: I have no relations with that power; nevertheless, if your master desires, I will gladly take steps to learn its intentions.' "

In the same despatch Count Otto expressed the wonder whether Austria was sincere or was playing a double game. " I confess," he went on, " that so far nothing justifies such a supposition. Austria has an evident interest in the humiliation of Russia. The Viennese court has rejected with scorn the propositions that have been made to it since the beginning of the war; it has acted at Constantinople in perfect [conformity with our views; it has done everything to prevent the ratification of the treaty of Bucharest; and appears to have at least delayed it. Its ruler's tastes, its financial condition, make it more and more desirous of peace : it asks for nothing better than a chance to repair its losses in the late wars, and the public itself is so convinced of this, that, in spite of the outcries of the enemies of France, it is mainly to the French alliance that it should ascribe the prosperous state of its new issue of notes, — a real barometer of public opinion."

Nevertheless, the Ambassador noted the progress which Napoleon's enemies were making in Vienna. " The Russians," he wrote, November 25, " have on their side almost all the aristocracy of the Continent, and the English are the allies of all the bankers and

merchants of every country. Hence there is no
need of surprise at the inconceivable speed with
which false rumors spread through Europe. Here
the Greek merchants, who control two-thirds of the
commerce of Vienna, are entirely in the interest of
Russia. A few days ago they started the rumor
that Napoleon had been taken prisoner. This absurd
statement brought about a fall on 'Change of ten
per cent; so great is the contradiction between
public confidence and the passions of the moment."

When the disasters in Russia became fully known,
these passions spread alarmingly. Count Otto wrote
a letter to Napoleon himself, December 18, 1812, in
which he said: "Your Majesty knows the elements
that compose the Viennese public too well not to
conjecture the impressions caused by recent events.
The most alarming rumors, the most painful conjectures and hopes have followed one another rapidly.
Nothing was talked about but the destruction of the
Grand Army, and the impossibility of beginning
another campaign. The Emperor and his Ministry,
who have a better knowledge of the resources of
France, took a fairer view of the condition of things.
They are confident of the success of a second campaign; but they none the less desire to be commissioned by Your Majesty with the honorable task of
trying to negotiate during the winter." In the same
letter Count Otto confessed with noble frankness the
dangers of the situation. "Such," he added, "is the
force of the passion of the moment, and such the

blindness of the multitude, that they persist in seeing and dreading nothing but France, although she
alone is capable of some day saving Austria. At
the present time, Sire, Russia is full of attentions to
Austria; all the intrigues of the Cabinet and of its
numerous agents have but one aim, — that of bringing
the court of Vienna into a new alliance, which would
be for her a new source of misfortune."

Ten days later, December 28, 1812, the Ambassador wrote to the Duke of Bassano: "However
painful may be the picture of what is going on here,
it is my duty, my Lord, to draw it for you without
concealment. It is perhaps without a precedent that
the government of a great power should have formed
the idea of deserting an ally, after its first reverses,
to join the flags of its enemy. Nevertheless, this is
what the majority of the influential men of this
country have dared to urge immediately after the
news of the disastrous retreat of our army. The
endeavor has been made to circumvent the Emperor
by all the means which intrigue and corruption
could employ against his good faith. It has been
represented to him that since France no longer had
an army, it would be absurd to try to continue the
war alone against the Russian giant; that the court
of Berlin was unable to continue its armaments; that
Bavaria, the Duchy of Warsaw, and Saxony had
neither men nor money left; that the North of Germany was ready to hoist the standard of revolt and
to drive out the sovereigns who had been merely

French prefects; that consequently it was necessary to recall the auxiliary corps, to change his policy, and to profit by this favorable moment to retake the province he had lost; that more than sixty millions of Germans and Italians were ready to declare for Austria, and to make common cause with her; that France herself was on the eve of a great revolution; that the last conspiracy in Paris had had many far-spreading roots in England, in Spain, and even in the Grand Army, where the Emperor Napoleon had narrowly escaped assassination by some partisans of Malet and Lahorie; finally, that the time had come to deliver Europe from a yoke that had become insupportable, and to restore to its people their old laws and their independence."

The Empress of Austria, the step-mother of Marie Louise, was desirous of playing the part which the beautiful Queen Louisa had taken at Berlin before the battle of Jena. Count Otto knew very well that the wife of Emperor Francis was secretly at the head of the party which desired war against Napoleon, and in this same despatch of December 28, 1812, he said, speaking of this Princess's views: "Although the Empress is not free to make her opinion known, it is notorious that she favors exclusively all the enemies of the present policy, and that she associates only with the boldest and most zealous coalitionists. One recent anecdote may serve as an example of her opinions. Before the last Austrian war, the Archduke Charles had shown some opposition to a new appeal to arms; she went to him, fell at his feet, and besought him not to oppose a measure which might restore to the monarchy its former glory and avenge all the insults it had endured. It is said that the Archduke Charles could not resist her tears, and that he voted, against his judgment, for a war of which he foresaw the disastrous issue. I have to-day been informed that, like her brother Maximilian, she has joined the Society of the Friends of Virtue."

Count Metternich, who was accused of sympathizing with France, was violently attacked by all the intimates of the Empress. The Emperor's Ambassador thus expressed himself on this subject in the same despatch: "While thus breaking out against France, the faction has not forgotten to attack the main defender of the French alliance, Count Metternich. Not a day passes that they do not invent some new way of discrediting him, and announce authoritatively that he is about to be replaced by M. von Stadion. Count Metternich has so little support at court and in society, that he is obliged to associate with his most active enemies, in order to persuade them to pardon him for the decision he has made. Nine-tenths of the public have been in succession misled by the false rumors, the lampoons, and even the caricatures which are allowed to circulate."

What was the attitude of Emperor Francis amid this general excitement? He acted with the greatest prudence, coming out neither for nor against

Napoleon. At heart he yearned for continued harmony with his son-in-law, and in no way desired a restoration of the Bourbons to the throne of France. The memory of many centuries of rivalry between the Bourbons and the House of Austria was always fresh. The Emperor Francis, we are convinced, sincerely desired the consolidation of the new French dynasty; but this desire did not go so far as to sacrifice to its sovereign the essential interests of his monarchy. At any rate, at the end of 1812, he was perhaps, of all the Austrians, the one least hostile to Napoleon. When at this decisive hour he wished to inspire his son-in-law with ideas of moderation and wisdom, he was not false to him: he loyally sought the best means of saving him.

Count Otto thus spoke of this monarch in his despatch of December 28, 1812: "The Count of Sickingen said to me, 'After the interests of his own country, the Emperor has nothing nearer his heart than to see the French government and the new dynasty establish itself. He fears that the distractions and the ever-renewing wars may not leave the Emperor Napoleon time enough to finish his work. He is afraid for his daughter and for his grandson, whom he loves much. His uneasiness has affected his health. The intrigues of malcontents torment him without moving him. It is desirable that the Emperor Napoleon write to him often, to strengthen the confidence with which he inspired him at Dresden. You cannot think how great an influence a

letter from your sovereign has on the Emperor's state
of mind. Whenever he receives one, he talks about
it for several days, weighing every word and encour-
aging himself with the hopes it contains.' . . . I
concluded by thoroughly reassuring the Count of
Sickingen on the turn our affairs must take within
two months. He left me to go to the Emperor, with
whom he passes every evening in absolute solitude.
Minister Metternich spoke to me to the same effect.
He is anxious that the two sovereigns should have
very close relations, and that they should write to
each other their impressions with perfect freedom.
'Arrange matters,' he said to me yesterday, 'so that
they shall speak to us unreservedly, and that we shall
know exactly what the Emperor Napoleon means.
We think that we can be useful to him; we who are
outside of the vortex which surrounds you, can get
another view of things from yours, and in this case
we will give you our opinions frankly.'"

A few days later, when the defection of the Prussian contingent was known in Vienna, Count Metternich, while still protesting affectionate sentiments
towards France, noticeably modified his attitude. He
began by clearing away the vagueness which had
hitherto shrouded his thoughts. Taking courage
from what had happened in North Germany, he
announced certain ideas which seemed at the time
to be only wishes, but were almost ready to become
demands. Count Otto perfectly understood the im-
port of this altered policy. "In uttering the word

peace," he wrote to the Duke of Bassano, January 10, 1813, "the Austrian Cabinet modifies its position, and puts the nation and the army on its side. Hence public opinion gives it a power which it cannot expect from either its troops or its finances. But this word will not be uttered, until authority has been received from its august ally. That, my Lord, is the point of view from which the present condition of things should be regarded. This Cabinet will have great power as an armed mediator, and very little as an ally; and when we consider the internal passions that agitate the monarchy, we cannot withhold our gratitude from the Sovereign and his Prime Minister for so firmly resisting the shock of recent events. Austria's feelings are unalterable, in spite of the solicitations of every sort by which she is beset. I have new proof of this in the interview with which the Emperor honored me this morning, on the occasion of the festival of the Order of Leopold. His Majesty renders perfect justice to our ability to carry on the war, but asks what will be the result of it. He thinks that France and Russia can do each other no real harm; that these two giants will grind to powder whatever happens to be between them; and that at the end of the bloodiest conflict the world will ever have seen, peace will be made at last on nothing but heaps of ashes."

Anxiety had so wrought on the health of the Emperor Francis that the great reception announced for New Year's Day had been given up. Metternich told Count Otto that he had seen this monarch in very difficult circumstances, when his own life and the preservation of the Empire were at stake; but that he had never seen him more troubled than he was at that moment.

The Emperor Francis was still hesitating; but Metternich had drawn up a programme which he thus sums up in his Memoirs:

"Napoleon's failure against Russia has altered the situation of the Emperor of the French, as well as that of the other powers.

"The result for Europe will be peace.

"To bring about a peace is the true task of Austria.

"What course is to be followed to secure peace; a real peace, not a disguised armistice, like all the treaties concluded with the French Republic and with Napoleon?

"The only course is to compel France to withdraw into limits which warrant the hope of a durable peace, and of the re-establishment of a political equilibrium between the powers."

The Austrian statesman added to the statement of this programme: "The attitude of Austria as an armed mediating power is in accordance with both the geographic situation of the Empire and with its strength, and will permit the Emperor Francis to have the last word in war, as in peace. We should work unremittingly to arm ourselves to make war. The Emperor's pact will be made sure by the time which we shall thus gain."

Napoleon, on the other hand, imagined that Austria, instead of mediating, would be his ally, offensive and defensive; and without asking anything for herself, would aid in preserving all the French Empire, even Rome, even Holland, even the Hanseatic towns. The lack of harmony was not proclaimed, but it existed in a latent condition; and early in 1813 it was easy to foresee that the son-in-law and the father-in-law would soon quarrel in spite of the protestations of friendship which they lavishly uttered, and in spite of the announcement of an early formal coronation of Marie Louise and of the King of Rome — a ceremony which Napoleon thought would touch the paternal heart of the Emperor of Austria and strengthen the bonds of alliance.

Nevertheless the French Ambassador at Vienna wrote to the Duke of Bassano, January 18, 1813: " In the most critical moments I have endeavored, my Lord, to betray no distrust. I think that nothing would so injure our relations with the Emperor of Austria as the idea that he was misunderstood by his august ally. Long study of this monarch's character has convinced me that with a very just mind he combines principles of uprightness and delicacy, of which I have received most touching proofs. It is not he who has been able to conceive the idea of profiting by the impression made in different parts of Europe by the disasters of the Grand Army; the faintest show of such a suspicion would pain him greatly. . . . The news of the approaching corona-

tion of Her Majesty the Empress and of the King of
Rome has produced the most favorable impression
here. I know that the Emperor has been touched
by it, as a new proof of the confidence of his august
son-in-law. . . . The Minister told me that the
French court must have seen from all the communications made to it, how devoted is this government
to the principles of the alliance, and how interested
it is in the happiness and prosperity of the Imperial
household of France. The well-known feelings of
the Emperor for his beloved daughter leave no doubt
on this subject."

The coronation of the Empress Marie Louise and
of the King of Rome, which in fact never took place,
had been set for March 7, 1813. Count Otto thus
spoke of it in his despatch of January 19 : "Every
one knows, my Lord, that France is invulnerable ; she
can be weakened only by her own dissensions. The
solemn ceremony of March 7 will be a new benefit
from our regenerator, and a new bond between the
French Empire and Austria. After long and terrible
disturbances, this bond, which the wise policy of His
Majesty has formed for the happiness of Europe will
be the warrant of a long repose which His Majesty
can enjoy by busying himself solely with efforts
to raise his people to that high degree of strength,
wealth, and greatness to which his genius has never
ceased to aspire since the memorable day of Brumaire."

After this, unfortunately inexact, prophecy, the
Ambassador went on : "Being thus for a long time

sent out as a scout far from my country, I am accustomed to sound an alarm at the first sight of danger. But Your Excellency would judge me ill if he should imagine that here I use the language which is to be found in my letters. Firm confidence in the principles and in the strength of my government, a calm attitude in difficult situations, a habit of yielding trifles in order to have the right to insist upon important matters, great consideration for the self-respect of the Emperor and his Minister, and an unremitting effort to place everything in the light of their interest rather than of ours — that, my Lord, is the method I have adopted; I have found it successful in other equally difficult missions, and it has received His Majesty's approbation and your own."

This line of conduct was wise, and the Ambassador's position was certainly as good as circumstances permitted. Yet Napoleon, whose suspicions were justly aroused by the strange retreat of Prince Schwarzenberg's auxiliary corps on Cracovia, and by Austria's vast armaments, imagined that some one else than Count Otto would more easily detect the real designs of the Viennese court, and early in February he sent as his successor General the Count of Narbonne. So far from uttering the least complaint, Count Otto wrote, February 6, 1813: "After a continuous residence of eleven years in a foreign country, Your Excellency will readily believe that the announcement of my recall has given me great pleasure. I shall lay on the steps of His Majesty's throne the expression of the sentiments which have always animated me in his service, and the profound conviction that my efforts have not been without their use. Whatever may be the task with which His Majesty may in future deign to entrust me, he will always find me zealous in carrying out his orders, and in giving proofs of my unbounded devotion to his person and to the glory of his reign."

Count Otto remained for some weeks in charge of the Embassy, and did not make over the post to his successor until the middle of March. Up to the end of his service he was in receipt of protestations of friendship from the Emperor Francis and from his Minister. In a despatch of February 13, 1813, he wrote: " Count Metternich said to me, ' Our alliance with Russia was monstrous; it had but one ground, and that was a very precarious one: the exclusion of English commerce. It was a military alliance, extorted by the conqueror. It was doomed to be broken. Our alliance, on the other hand, rests on the most natural and most permanent interests. It must be as lasting as the needs that have produced it. It is we who have sought it, and we concluded it only on ripe reflection. If we had it to make over again, we should not draw it up differently. We desire it just as it is. It will secure peace, and tend afterwards to strengthen it. When the Emperor of Austria decided to send to Paris an Ambassador Extraordinary to be present at the coronation of the King of Rome, he chose Prince Esterhazy, the mem-

ber of his court who was most conspicuous for his
wealth and the vast extent of his estates. The
Prince seemed much flattered by his selection, and
he intends to perform his duties in the most brilliant
way. He will leave in a few days. Prince Schwarzenberg arrived yesterday. He intends to start at
once for Paris, with the twofold object of explain-
ing to His Majesty the present condition of affairs,
and of giving Europe an unmistakable proof of the
intentions of Austria, by showing at the French
court the commander of the auxiliary forces reporting to his commander for orders.' Those are the
Minister's own words. He takes the greatest pains
to use the language best fitted to convince the courts
of London and Saint Petersburg of the close harmony
existing between France and Austria."

Judging from the remarks which Metternich still
made to Count Otto, the Emperor Francis's sympa-
thies appeared to be for Napoleon, and all his mistrust to be of the Czar. "Our alliance with France,"
said the Minister, "is so necessary that if you were
to break it to-day, we should propose to you to
re-establish it on the same terms and with the same
conditions. France has done us much harm, but it
is for our interest to forget the past. We wish to be
of use to her at this moment, because at some other
time she will be able to render the same service to
us. This alliance is not the result of war, or a condition of peace, like that of Tilsitt. It is the product
of ripe reflection, and has been prepared by succes-

sive, spontaneous advances, as well as by the close
union of the two Imperial families. Receive it,
then, as a fact, and regard it as an incontestable truth
that we seek only your good; that we no longer
fear France, but the Russians, whose power you
have augmented by your successive concessions."
(Despatch of February 17, 1813.)

In the same report Count Otto spoke at length of
the alarm felt by the government about revolutionary
tendencies, which were growing every day: "There
is another enemy whom the Cabinet of Vienna fear
much more than the Russians; that is the populace,
or rather the spirit of resistance which is beginning
to show itself all over Europe. The Hungarians
have proposed to the government to organize what
they call an insurrection; but the Cabinet will take
good care not to accept this offer, which seems to
hide a secret intention of arming in accordance with
the Russian designs. The conviction prevails here
that the Russians, in concert with the English, are
making every effort to persuade the populace of
different nations to declare themselves independent
of their rulers; that the greater part of Europe is
threatened by a terrible conflagration; that all the
sovereigns allied with France have become so unpop-
ular that the slightest breath would overthrow them;
finally, that nearly all Germany is on the eve of the
most terrible disturbances. Silesia especially arouses
distrust, and it is thought certain that the centre of
the Russian army is marching directly on this prov-

ince to foment an outbreak. From a mass of letters
which the Minister is receiving from all quarters, it
seems that the Emperor Alexander is acquiring a
moral force which is very dangerous in the existing
circumstances. His most pretentious promises are
justified by his gentleness, which extends to the
Poles. Austria's attitude will be able to stem this
torrent until our armies can act. She is convinced
that in concert with France she can put an end to this
revolutionary invasion, and she wishes to make use
of her central position to pacify Europe. Although
she does not count much on the success of her first
steps towards England, she will thus be able to
make Russia uneasy and force her to peace. But
she judges a congress indispensable for this happy
result, and she intends by means of the continental
peace to induce England to make one. The Minister
said that France once at peace would put an end
to the temporary importance of the Russians, and
that she would regain all the ascendancy which her
strength, her wealth, and her moderation ought to
guarantee to her forever; finally, that peace alone
will be for France and for Austria, her ally, a much
more solid conquest than any successful campaign
could win."

Count Otto always thought that Marie Louise's
marriage would establish a useful friendship between
the two Empires, but he did not hide the perils of
the situation, and especially the excitement of all
Germany. In his despatch of February 19, 1813, he

said: "The solemn ceremony preparing in France cannot fail to produce the happiest results, by showing His Majesty's just confidence in an Austrian Archduchess. Never has a princess deserved better of the nation, or been placed on the French throne under happier auspices. She has become the precious pledge of a political alliance, which but for her would never have existed, or, at least, would have been extremely precarious."

After this homage to the Empress, the diplomatist added with praiseworthy frankness: "Europe has need of calm; evils of all sorts have too long weighed on its populace not to irritate them to the furthest point. I beg Your Excellency not to form any illusion on the feelings that have been seething in Germany for six years, which the governments are no longer able to restrain. Probably most of the allied sovereigns are loyal; but the people are against us, with scarcely an exception, and only a long peace can efface the memory of their sufferings. Foreign agents, who may express other views in Paris, do not deserve your confidence, and would give the lie to everything generally known of the tone reigning in the capitals of the Confederation, and often in their rulers' cabinets. Never has a government more urgently needed to conciliate the nation than Austria. It is hard to give you a just idea of the agitation that prevails as the Russians approach the frontier. . . . Count Metternich said to me: 'I spend four or five hours every day with the Minister of Police. Our prisons are full of people whom we have had arrested to prevent the harm they might do. Every day there is danger that the Emperor will be insulted, or that I shall be assassinated. Soon the Prussian insurrection will spread to the Rhine. In Westphalia the discontent is extreme. The explosion will come when it is least expected. Nothing can equal Russia's crafty policy. Those people are of every country; they speak all languages; they flatter every passion. They demand of the people no sacrifices, and appear in the guise of liberators. The Confederation formed under your auspices at Warsaw has made no sensation in Galicia; but as soon as the Russians had mentioned the restoration of the kingdom, the leading men of that province noticed a great excitement, and told us every day of their anxiety.' While speaking, the Minister's eyes filled with tears; he confessed that in every branch of the administration he encountered an opposition which rendered his position very painful. With the exception of the Emperor and Prince Schwarzenberg, he did not mention a single man of mark who belonged to his party."

Count Otto thus concluded his energetic despatch: "In this state of things, my Lord, France can count only on herself and her immense force. The people, misled by Russian machinations, are ready to break every bond which unites them to the reigning dynasties. The next campaign cannot fail to drive the Russians back to their icy deserts. But Germany,

Poland, Prussia, and perhaps Austria itself, will present nothing but centres of insurrection, hate, and vengeance."

In a despatch of February 28, Count Otto once more insisted on the extreme seriousness of the situation, and on the cries of alarm uttered by Count Metternich: "The position of this government," he said, "becomes more delicate every day. The Minister has shown me documents proving the existence of a plot to assassinate him. Two officers were charged with this deed. They have been arrested as well as a secret committee of which they were members. He showed me other papers disclosing other conspiracies of the sort fostered by Russia. 'It is supposed,' he added, 'that the French alliance depends on my life. I am ready to lose it for a principle which I deem useful for my country, but we are so beset that we have to keep these plots secret in order not to add to the excitement. . . . Our position would be less painful if you would be franker with us. We keep you informed of all our views and actions. You make no reply; we are left in absolute ignorance of your political plans. Do treat us like friends, anxious to serve you, and give us strength by having confidence in us.' "

This confidence did not exist on either side. Napoleon desired war, and his father-in-law desired peace. Napoleon was anxious to retain everything, and the Emperor Francis thought he should give up some of his territory. The Cabinet of the Tuileries refused any clear explanation with the Cabinet of Vienna, because it felt that only by equivocation could be kept up, if not the reality, at least the appearance of harmony. It must be acknowledged in justice to Count Otto, that he neglected nothing to free his sovereign's mind from dangerous illusions, and to set before him in true colors the condition of Germany in general, and of Austria in particular. Napoleon would have done well if he had listened to the wise and respectful advice of this diplomatist, a man of honor, who, at the risk of displeasing his master, had the courage to tell him the whole truth.

XI.

VILLEMAIN says at the beginning of his *Contemporary Memories, Historical and Literary:* "I do not believe that at the end of the last century, and in the first years of this, two epochs crowded with extraordinary events and with men famous in politics and war, there was a rarer and more cultivated mind, a more generous heart, a man more agreeable in the commerce of life, or one bolder, more sensible, or more capable of great things, than Count Louis de Narbonne, a Minister of King Louis XVI. under the Legislative Assembly, and an aide-de-camp of Napoleon, in 1812. Fortune alone was wanting to this man, whose merit, in the judgment of the best and wisest heads of the Empire, such as Daru and Mollien, seemed sufficient for anything. Although her favorite on a few rare, memorable occasions, even then she offered him only situations that were too far gone, too fatal and desperate, in which one thought of winning honor and then dying, but not of repairing too great errors, or of putting a stop to their inevitable consequences."

169

Napoleon had a special fondness for the Count of Narbonne, appreciating to the fullest extent his education, courage, and agreeable character. He drew back from his exile this émigré who had lived out of France for seventeen years, and in 1809 restored him to the French army with the grade of Division General. The Emperor whose instincts were at bottom very aristocratic, delighted to see in the former knight of honor of one of the daughters of Louis XV. a finished type of courtesy, which recalled at the court of the Tuileries the best traditions of the court of Versailles. After he had selected this former Minister of War of Louis XVI. for his aide-de-camp, he congratulated himself on the discovery that no officer of his guards was more at his ease in a drawing-room, or more light-hearted in a bivouac. In the disastrous retreat from Russia no one displayed more coolness and courage. Hence, Napoleon, in the beginning of 1813, thought at a critical and decisive moment no one would so well represent him at the court of Vienna as this man of the old régime, whose solid and brilliant qualities could not fail to be recognized by the high Austrian nobility.

In the Emperor's eyes, the Count of Narbonne, who had entered the diplomatic service only a few months before, was a model diplomatist. We read in the *Memorial of Saint Helena:* "Speaking of his Ambassadors, the Emperor remarked that M. de Narbonne was the only one who really deserved this title, and had really discharged its duties. And this,

he said, he did by his personal advantages, not merely
those of his intelligence, but much more those of his
old-fashioned morals and manners, and of his name;
for as long as one has simply to give orders, the first
comer will do; nothing more is required; possibly an
aide-de-camp is the best person to employ. But when
one is compelled to negotiate, it's a different thing;
then one ought to send to the old aristocracy of ·
Europe representatives of that aristocracy, for it is
after all a sort of Freemasonry. If an Otto, an
Andréossi enter the drawing-rooms of Vienna, all
expression of opinions is hushed, all easy intercourse
ceases; they are intruders, outsiders; the mysteries
are interrupted. It's just the other way with a Narbonne, because with him they have affinity, sympathy,
identity; and a woman of the old nobility may grant
every favor to a plebeian without betraying to him
the secrets of the aristocracy."

We incline to think that Napoleon exaggerates
a little the importance of the aristocratic element in
diplomatic affairs, and we must say that in spite of
charming manners and fascinating intelligence, this
model Ambassador did not prevent Austria from
declaring war with France. But to quote again
from the *Memorial:* "The Emperor," says the Count
of Las Cases, "was very fond of M. de Narbonne;
he was much attached to him and mourned his loss
deeply. He made him his aide-de-camp only because
Marie Louise, he said, through some intrigue of
her household, refused to receive him as her knight

of honor; a post for which, Napoleon added, he was exactly suited. Until he was appointed, he added, we were dupes of Austria. In less than a fortnight M. de Narbonne had seen through everything, and Metternich was greatly annoyed by this appointment. Yet, said the Emperor, how complicated fate is! It was, perhaps, the very success of M. de Narbonne that wrought my ruin. His abilities were at any rate rather injurious to me than useful; for Austria, seeing that she was found out, threw aside her mask and hastened her action. Had we been blinder, she would have been more reserved, and slower. She would have prolonged for some time her natural indecision, and meanwhile other chances might have arisen."

Let us now hastily run over the most important despatches of the Count of Narbonne which we have examined in the archives of the Ministry of Foreign Affairs ; they are mainly unpublished.

The new Ambassador wrote to the Duke of Bassano, March 22, 1813 : "Your Excellency will, I hope, forgive me, if in these first moments after my arrival, which are necessarily taken up by duties and cares of every sort, my correspondence is far less useful than that of my predecessor. I can only speak of my presentation to their Majesties and to the members of the Imperial family. Externally everything went off in the most decorous way, and my first audience with the Emperor, who treated me with the utmost kindness, had, outside of his genuine interest in the health and happiness of his august son-in-law, no other result than a number of tolerably vague speeches on the universal necessity of peace; on the strength of the army which France was about to send forth; on the decision already taken by the King of Prussia who had been forced to it, the Emperor said, by unanimous opinions of all classes of his subjects. It was easy for me to lay weight on the terrible danger there was for princes who preferred obeying to commanding, and who let themselves be driven to what had already reduced Prussia from the rank of a great power, and was possibly to complete its ruin. The Emperor agreed that this state of things was already one of revolution which was more disastrous than any defeat; this naturally gave me an opportunity to say that no Prince who had received so many proofs of the devotion of his people could fear to be abandoned by them when he ordered what alone could assure their present and future tranquillity. A promise to assent to whatever the Emperor shall do or desire to bring about peace; the necessity of a great development of the forces of France to bring this about, a thorough knowledge of the vastness of its resources and their great power were then mentioned. The sincerity with which all this was uttered tempted me to speak at once of an active co-operation which should abridge and put a speedy end to all difficulties; but I discerned his fear of any discussion which for me too would have presented many difficulties that were not settled before I left Paris; moreover I wished to avoid the appearance of seeking an immediate and direct answer."

So for both Emperor and Ambassador the only way
of seeming to have an understanding was by avoiding
an explanation. "The Emperor," M. de Narbonne
continued, "appeared grateful for my reserve, and
spoke with pleasure of the happiness which his
daughter, Her Majesty the Empress, enjoyed."

Then the Ambassador spoke of his reception by the
Empress of Austria, who was compelled to conceal
her hatred of Napoleon and of France beneath the
forms of politeness. "My audience with the Empress gave me no light. She was very glad that the
Emperor had returned in good health, and sympathized
with our Empress's pleasure who is always writing
about her numberless grounds for content. There
were many affectionate questions about the King of
Rome, many inquiries about the state of the arts in
Paris; very little was said about the last campaign,
and there were numerous most civil commonplaces.
The Empress's faintness put an end to the audience."

As for Metternich, he greeted the new Ambassador
with extreme courtesy, but he did not hesitate to say
that Napoleon ought to give up some of his territory.
M. de Narbonne wrote, March 24: "M. de Metternich
said that if the Emperor of France was willing to be
a monarch thrice as strong as Louis XIV., and master
of Europe solely by the weight of his strength, his
position, and his genius, all difficulties would soon
arrange themselves; but that it was necessary that
England should acquire a conviction of this truth;
that this power alone had the indisputable power of

treating directly with France, and that he believed, for example, that she would never consent to leave us Holland, unless new and repeated triumphs on the part of the Emperor should accustom her to the necessity of giving way. . . . I should be unjust to M. de Metternich if I seemed to infer from what I have said that he is not perfectly loyal to us in every respect. A thousand reasons incline me to think thus."

The Count of Narbonne was at first over optimistic; but a few days sufficed to give him an exacter appreciation of the state of things. " It seems impossible, my Lord," he said in his despatch of April 1, 1813, " to refuse to believe that the excitement now prevailing threatens Germany with a most violent, wide-spread, and possibly, sudden explosion. Every country into which any Russians have been able to make their way seems to have earnestly set about to turning every German into an implacable foe of France; I say every German, because they pretend to recognize no national differences; and now, more than ever, publications on the present state of affairs urge the disregard of whatever might weaken the common hatred of us, which should inspire every one who lives between the Rhine and the Niemen. These publications infest the whole Austrian Empire. In a word, the whole condition of things here repeats that of Prussia before the battle of Jena. It is plainer to me than ever that on our side we have, as you truly said to me, only the Emperor, M. de Metternich, and

M. de Schwarzenberg. Doubtless, the Emperor holds to France by interest, loyalty, and sentiment; but surrounded as he is by our enemies, fed with all the poisons presented to him in every form, terrified by the consequences that may follow every decision, it is almost impossible that he should not often hesitate and grant concessions which will only strengthen our foes."

Austria was to change gradually, but quickly, from an active alliance to a passive one; then to neutrality; then to armed mediation; finally, to a declaration of war against her former ally. M. de Narbonne foresaw and predicted this threefold phase of the Austrian policy. "As for M. de Metternich," he added in the despatch of April 1, 1813, " I am always glad to repeat it, I believe in his complete good faith toward the French policy; but only so far as this shall lead us to peace; and since every day inclines me more to respect his acuteness and ability, I wonder if it would be strange that in case he saw this peace impossible, he might not think it well to say: 'I have above all things wished to try to secure peace, the sole, real happiness of my country, and for that purpose I have braved everything; but I have not neglected to prepare for war. France has refused to agree to reasonable propositions which had been accepted by all the other powers; now I propose to place Austria at the head of your enemies, and to resume in Europe our proper attitude and rank.' Cannot this language and this conduct insure Austria the preservation of its position, which a change of policy, without apparent cause, would compel it to abandon?" Alas! why did not Napoleon pay attention to this really prophetic despatch?

One of the causes for the protracted hesitation of the Cabinet of Vienna to pronounce against France, was the dread of the revolutionary ideas promulgated by Napoleon's enemies. M. de Narbonne wrote to the Duke of Bassano, April 6, 1813: "I had the honor of informing you that M. de Metternich appeared quite as alarmed as I at the terrible consequences that would follow the appeal to the people, which now, all the enemies of France are making,—an appeal which seems to transform the counsellors of Russia, Prussia, and Sweden into a committee of public safety. General Wittgenstein's proclamations naturally brought up this matter. M. de Metternich thinks that the absurdity of these proclamations has diminished their danger. But that of Kutusoff, also addressed to the Germans, whom it treats as one people, without speaking of Austria, especially attracts his attention. In fact, it speaks in the name of Russia and Prussia, which affirm that the shameful yoke of the Confederation of the Rhine is broken, of restoring liberty to Germany by means of a constitution for which both kings and people shall be consulted. 'Is it a National Assembly, or a Cortes, that their constitution promises us?' asks M. de Metternich. 'What a fire-brand is thrown on what is already ablaze!'"

The Austrian Minister added, "But let the Emperor

Napoleon help us to resist this movement which is as violent as it is general. Now that you are here, you can see the strength and the skill with which the Austrian government has to contend. We may despise and triumph over the clamors of society which urges war with the wildest passion; but the reasonable and reasoning majority of the nation, which desires nothing but peace, and has hitherto been held back only by the hope of obtaining it, how is that to be satisfied, if, as Count Bubna writes, the Emperor of France should consider himself driven to a war to the death with Prussia and Russia, in which we cannot feel sure that we shall not be implicated? Be sure that if Prince Schwarzenberg's army corps, which the Emperor Napoleon has blamed for not going to Minsk, could have been there, which would have made it experience the fate of the rest of the allied army on its return, nothing could have prevented the Austrian army from marching against the French, whatever the government might have tried to do."

Metternich no longer tried to conceal his thoughts. "The Austrian government," he said, at the end of his interview with M. de Narbonne, "is like a swimmer struggling with strength and courage against the current, and hoping to succeed; it would be certain, if the Emperor Napoleon were willing to aid it a little; that is to say, if he were to consent to conditions of peace equally compatible with his glory and his honor."

M. de Narbonne did not confine himself to questioning the court and the ministry whose real intentions he soon divined; he examined with an intelligent eye all classes of Austrian society. He wrote to the Duke of Bassano, April 17, 1813: "Turning to the petty details of the spectacle offered at this moment by the city and court of Vienna, I find every café and place of meeting full of nothing but hatred of the French; they are charged with the desperate financial condition, the ruin of commerce, and the horrible dearness of everything not of the strictest necessity. If I observe the army, I find no officers who do not tremble at the idea of making war for us, and none who, thinking they will no longer have to face the Frenchmen who have so often humiliated them, do not believe and say that the time is come when they can easily recover with interest their honor and the territory of Austria. I need not repeat what has so often been told Your Excellency about the spirit which animates society."

Encouraged by events, Metternich, while maintaining an air of perfect courtesy, went so far as to give it to be understood that Austria would be glad to see Napoleon lay aside his title of Protector of the Confederation of the Rhine. "If Prussia and Russia," he said to M. de Narbonne, "regard the suppression of the title of Protector of the Confederation of the Rhine as an indispensable condition of peace, we cannot in conscience fight to defend it and to assume its preservation." The Ambassador in reporting the Austrian Minister's remarks, in his despatch of April

10, adds, "I replied that in such a proposition I could see nothing but a somewhat extraordinary desire to humiliate the Emperor, who did not like conditions of that sort. At this, M. de Metternich seemed frightened at the mere idea that I could credit him with a desire of that sort, and I must confess that I have never heard him utter a word which was not an expression of his respect and admiration for the Emperor's person and genius, and, above all, never one which had the slightest air of a threat."

The Count of Narbonne clearly discerned beneath the formulas of official politeness the real plan of the Cabinet of Vienna, and his only hope, though it was but a vague one, was not the co-operation, but the neutrality of Austria. He wrote, April 14, 1813: "The government, even if it were as well disposed in our favor as my predecessor liked to hope, would not put upon its shoulders the burthen of universal blame by hoisting the French colors. But a complete, absolute neutrality would, I think, prove an attraction; at the present moment it would allay the general agitation and satisfy the dignity of the government by giving it an air of resoluteness as well as the spirit of expectation and fickleness which reappears at every epoch. . . . There remains to examine what should be the guaranty of such neutrality. That is a question which I am not called upon to solve. Doubtless the surest would be the success which awaits His Majesty's arms. I will only add that if by force of circumstances which it is impossible to foresee, these successes should be lessened or deferred, co-operation, supposing it possible, would at once change neutrality into absolute defection. The Austrian government is not in a position to withstand the force of public opinion. The feelings of alliance and affection for France, which the Emperor preserves with more constancy than firmness, if I may so say, are insufficient to raise him above the exasperated passions of the multitude."

At the moment Napoleon was about to open the campaign, M. de Narbonne, who was more a man of honor than a courtier, deemed it a patriotic duty to inform him of the truth. "Everything convinces me," he wrote to the Duke of Bassano, April 23, 1813, "of the understanding which exists between the Emperor of Austria and our enemies, and I confess that I think him almost ready to support all the propositions which Austria will finally announce, and which will be, I think, very different from what our Sovereign has the right to expect. I could not help being extremely struck by hearing the Emperor of Austria say in a very peremptory way that his forces shall never be employed for our master unless he shall accept reasonable propositions, by his keeping silence when I asked him who shall be the judge of these conditions, and what he will do if he is not satisfied with them. It is impossible not to perceive in this silence exactly what has been repeated to me by M. de Metternich, that, in this last case, taking part against us would be the natural result of his position as armed mediator." At the risk of offence, the Count of Narbonne had the noble courage to tell his sovereign what he thought. By this loyal frankness, he followed the dictates of his conscience, and impartial history has no fault to find with him.

XII.

WHILE Europe was preparing to enter upon a struggle for life or death with Napoleon, he, as confident, as eager, as in the glow of his youth, was arming for the colossal war with untiring activity. It seemed that he had but to stamp on the ground to call forth numberless legions. In three months an army of three hundred thousand men was raised, equipped, and brought together. As General de Ségur says: " At any hour of the day or night the Emperor, whatever he was doing, could have told the numbers, the composition, the strength of every one of the thousands of detachments of every branch of the service which he had set in movement from every part of the Empire, the way they were uniformed and equipped, the number of marches each one had to make, the day, the place, even the hour at which each one was to arrive."

His language had never been haughtier. He went in pomp at the head of a grand procession to open the sittings of the Legislative Body, January 14, 1813, and said with an air of great dignity: "The

disasters produced by the severity of the climate
have thoroughly demonstrated the strength and
greatness of this Empire which is founded on the
co-operation and the affection of fifty millions of citizens and on the geographical wealth of the finest
countries in the world.   It is with keen satisfaction
that we have seen our people of the Kingdom of
Italy, those of Holland and of the united departments rivalling with the French, and feeling that they
have no other hope, future, or happiness than in the
consolidation and triumph of the great Empire. . . .
The French dynasty reigns and will continue to reign
in Spain. . . . I am satisfied with the conduct of all
my allies. I shall not abandon one of them; I shall
maintain the integrity of their states. The Russians
shall return to their terrible climate."   Alas! every
sentence was a new illusion. The new Frenchmen
were about to turn against France; the French
dynasty in Spain was to be driven out. It was not
Napoleon who was to abandon his allies, but his allies
who were to abandon Napoleon. The Russians were
not to return to their terrible climate; it was our
magnificent climate to which they were to advance.
The great man was no longer a prophet.

Forgetting the insignificance of family alliances
where politics were concerned, and the many wars
waged in the Middle Ages and in modern times
between closely related sovereigns, Napoleon imagined that the Emperor Francis would never be able
to abandon the cause of his daughter and his grand-

son, and with a simplicity unworthy of so mighty a genius, he fancied that a few friendly letters and a few affectionate words would outweigh the interests and ambitions of the Austrian policy. Marie Louise readily lent herself to her husband's illusions, and wrote to her father letters full of serene confidence, as if the thought had never entered her head that clouds could arise between Austria and France. The young Empress's courtiers were never tired of speaking to her of her husband's certain triumph. She imagined that he was invincible. All who went near her, the members of the Austrian Embassy as well as the French themselves, spoke in the most confident terms. No disagreeable truth ever came to her ears. Happy as a wife and as a mother, she looked forward to the future with calmness, and golden visions floated above the palaces in which she lived.

Marie Louise's letters to her father, even after the campaign had begun, were sprightly. " The Emperor," she wrote to him, " sends many kind messages; he displays much affection for you, and not a day passes that he does not tell me how much he loves you, especially since he saw you at Dresden. . . . The Emperor begs me to assure you of his friendship and to write to you often. You may judge whether he has to tell me twice. . . . You will have seen in the newspapers all the patriotic gifts the French have made to their Sovereign. The people show the warmest devotion ; this love moves me to tears. . . . The Emperor is very well ; very cheerful, in spite of his hard work. It is said that he already has a large number of troops. More are going to start in a few days. It is really touching to see the activity, the patriotism, and the military ardor of the nation. . . . The armies are said to be magnificent. The Emperor is perfectly satisfied, and hopes soon to force his enemies to make a lasting peace."

Before opening the campaign Napoleon wished to visit the Invalides with the Empress. This visit took place March 7, 1813. The old soldiers were drawn up in line of battle in the large courtyard. The Emperor talked with them for some time and decorated a good many. Then he went into the church with Marie Louise and heard a *Te Deum.* After that he visited with the Empress the bakery, the refectories, and the infirmary where four centenarians, who had been present at the battle of Fontenoy, were presented to him.

Napoleon, who was in perfect health, robust, full of hope, and more eager than ever for war, impatiently awaited the opening of the conflict. Yet wishing to provide for the chance that he might be slain, and recalling Malet's conspiracy, he decided, before leaving, to make the Empress Regent. Hitherto, during the Sovereign's absence from the Empire, the government had been confided to a Council of Ministers, presided over by Cambacérès. But it might happen that a Minister should die or fall ill, and in that case no one was authorized to assume his signature unless by an Imperial decree. Napoleon wished to obviate this inconvenience by establishing a regency. He had an investigation made of what had been done in France at different periods of its history when Regents had governed the country. Then when all was ready he summoned a Privy Council at the Elysée, March 30, 1813, to which were admitted the Empress, the Queen of Spain, and Queen Hortense. After the reading of the decree establishing the regency, Marie Louise swore to discharge her duty as a good wife, a good mother, and a good Frenchwoman, according to the laws and constitutions of the Empire, and to surrender her powers whenever the Emperor should desire. She sent a messenger to Vienna to inform her father of her new dignity. "You can readily understand," she wrote, "how much I am flattered by this new proof of the Emperor's confidence." March 31 Marie Louise was present at the Council of the Ministers. She was intelligent, attentive, and seemed to take a serious interest in the business. When the reports of the police were about to be read, Napoleon listened to a few, and said to Archchancellor Cambacérès: "It is not necessary to sully a young woman's mind with certain details."

To lighten the task which the regency imposed upon the Empress, the Emperor appointed the Baron of Méneval her private secretary. He was, according to the Duke of Rovigo, "the man in whose honesty he had the completest confidence, his own private secretary. He submitted to his loss, and

begged M. de Méneval to write to him every day."
Cambacérès was made First Counsellor of the Regency. Marshal Moncey was given the part of General commanding the Empress's Guard, and the Duke
of Cadore that of Secretary of State during the
absence of Daru, who accompanied the Emperor to
the war.

The functions of the Regent were carefully defined
in an order signed by Napoleon at Saint Cloud, just
before his departure, April 18, 1813. This said:
" The Empress-Regent will preside over the Senate,
the Council of State, the Council of Ministers, the
Privy Council, and the extraordinary councils to be
holden whenever the Empress-Regent shall think
proper — when urgent circumstances shall demand
prompt measures that cannot await our decision.
She shall have the right to grant pardon, to commute
punishment, and to grant reprieves to the execution
of sentences and condemnations. . . . She may sign
decrees containing nominations of minor importance,
or when urgent circumstances shall require it. By
minor importance is understood, for the War Department, second lieutenants, lieutenants, captains; in the
Navy Department, officers up to and including the
rank of lieutenant; and in the Law and Administrative Departments, the officials whom we do not
appoint by our own choice. . . . If the Empress-
Regent does not choose to preside over the Senate,
her place shall be taken by our cousin, the Prince
Archchancellor, by virtue of the general commission

granted by this order, which commission also confers upon him the right of presiding, when the Empress-Regent does not herself preside, over the Council of State, the Council of Ministers, and the Privy Council."

It was arranged that Marie Louise should hold every month, and oftener if necessary, diplomatic receptions, without taking any part in the discussion of foreign affairs, and that she should receive every day a report from the Duke of Lodi, the Chancellor of the Kingdom of Italy. The Archchancellor Cambacérès, First Counsellor of the Regency, and General Savary, Duke of Rovigo, Minister of the General Police, were to send a daily report to the Emperor, who at a distance, as well as at home, held in his hand the reigns of government.

Wishing to make her duties as Regent easy for a young woman of twenty-one, Napoleon had decided to trace for her in his letters the line of conduct she was to follow, and to send to her minutes of the letters she was to write, or of the speeches she would have to make ; she herself desired this. These letters were separate from the private correspondence ; they had an official character and a special form.

The Emperor, aware that he might lose his life in the terrible conflict he was about to begin, desired, by assuring the position of the Empress, to give her a proof of his affection, and he caused the Senate to arrange the dower she should receive if she should become a widow. This was fixed at an annual income of four million francs, part to be paid by the nation, and part from the Crown estates. The estates set aside for the dower were the castle and forest of Compiègne and the forest of Laigle, valued together at eight hundred thousand francs; the forest of Villers-Cotterets, the forest of Eu and of Aumale, with the Castle of Eu, the forest of Soignes, valued together at one million two hundred thousand francs; and in addition two million francs in funds of the Treasury. The Empress, too, was to have a life use of the Palace of the Elysée and of the Great and Little Trianon.

Prince Schwarzenberg, who had just arrived in Paris, and in the presence of Napoleon seemed like a subordinate before his chief, took very good care not to disturb the Empress by any indication of the possibility of a rupture of the alliance between Austria and France. To all appearance the relations of the two empires had never been more cordial. So great was still the ascendancy of the hero of Wagram that Prince Schwarzenberg, who had been sent to insinuate to him that Austria would not draw the sword unless in view of peace, and of a German peace, did not dare to make the statement. Napoleon overwhelmed him with attentions, and with his lists in his hand, tried to convince him that in France, Italy, Spain, and Germany, he had eleven hundred thousand men under arms, and that these men outnumbered the Prussians and Russians. He showed himself disposed to give to Austria Silesia, a million Poles

and Illyria, and he pretended to believe that his
father-in-law meant to remain faithful to the treaty
of alliance of March 14, 1812. According to this
treaty, an Austrian auxiliary force was placed under
the direct orders of the Emperor of the French.
Consequently Napoleon told Prince Schwarzenberg
that he was going to command this Austrian army
corps to march to upper Silesia to fight against the
enemies of France. Prince Schwarzenberg bowed
without making any objection, and Napoleon thought
himself justified in looking upon General Frimont,
then at the head of the Austrian contingent, as his
subordinate. Hence, he wrote to the Emperor
Francis : —

"Saint Cloud, April 13, 1813. MY BROTHER AND
VERY DEAR FATHER-IN-LAW : Prince Schwarzenberg
has handed me Your Majesty's letter. I read it with
great pleasure, and I have talked with him for a long
time with perfect frankness. I can only refer to
what he will report to Your Majesty. I have been
much pleased with General Bubna's conduct during
his stay here. I should be glad if Your Majesty
would give him some mark of your satisfaction. I
am on the point of starting for Mayence; I had not
meant to be there before the 20th, but the news I
have received of the enemy's movements on the left
bank of the Elbe have decided me to hasten my
departure by a few days. So I intend to enter
Mayence the 15th or 16th. As soon as the campaign
is opened, I shall send from Prague orders to General

Frimont to denounce the armistice and to assume command of the army corps of Prince Poniatowski. I shall keep Your Majesty informed of what goes on. I beg you not to doubt of my sincere attachment; it is unalterable."

The Emperor knew very well from the Count of Narbonne's reports that he ought to distrust Austria; but he hid from others, and perhaps from himself, his suspicions; and fancying that a single victory would suffice to preserve the alliance of his father-in-law and of all the princes of the Confederation of the Rhine, he tried to inspire his wife, as well as his generals and Ministers, with his own confidence in a speedy and brilliant triumph. He imagined himself still in the days of Austerlitz and Jena.

As for Marie Louise, she saw with sadness her husband's departure. The thought of being Regent of the vast Empire and of the Kingdom of Italy, flattered her but little. She had never been ambitious, and fear of the responsibility outweighed the delights of power. She was, moreover, determined blindly to follow the orders of her husband, who should rule the Empire from afar.

After an affectionate leave-taking from his wife and his son, Napoleon started to assume command of his armies, and the *Moniteur* announced his departure from Saint Cloud by this simple sentence: "April 15, His Majesty the Emperor left for Mayence to-day at one in the morning."

A few hours after her husband's departure, the

Empress-Regent wrote to the Baron of Méneval, her secretary : —

" You know, of course, that the Emperor is gone. I like to think that you, too, miss him. I beg of you, if M. Fain is still there, to tell him that I should like to have him give me news of the Emperor; I have had no chance to say this myself. I beg of you also to send me a copy of the list of guests which the Emperor desired sent in the course of the day. I beg of you to believe me your attached

" LOUISE."

The Regent appeared in her new dignity, April 18, at a reception of the Diplomatic Body at Saint Cloud. Surrounded by Princes in high positions, Ministers, high officers of the Crown, Grand Eagles, a lady of honor, officers and ladies in waiting, she wore her new rank with dignity and affability. " General satisfaction was felt," says the Duke of Rovigo in his Memoirs, "at seeing the Empress Marie Louise clad with this authority; she was known to be kind and tender; she was much loved and esteemed; those who had to do with her in private life had nothing but good to say of her, and it is true that she had won the esteem of the nation, which had much affection for her. This was due to the fact that on every occasion when she had to appear, she was always surrounded with the splendor which etiquette demanded."

Marie Louise still believed in the friendship of her father and her husband; and if she had been able to

foresee how imminent was war between Austria and
France, she would have felt even keener regret at
Napoleon's departure.   As for him, he knew full
well that the part he was about to play was full of
peril.   But for men of his sort, danger is a pleasure.
With their pride and audacity they find joy in tempt-
ing, braving, and defying fortune.   The need of
strong emotions is the keynote of their character.
They like neither repose nor safety.   To rulers of
that kind a prosperous but uneventful reign seems
like a degradation, and desiring for their subjects as
well as for themselves excitement and adventures,
they think themselves sent into the world to provide
material for history.   Such was Napoleon, a high
player and a great actor, who lived for posterity.

XIII.

THE day after Napoleon's departure, Prince
Schwarzenberg found the Empress-Regent sad
and anxious. He was more open with her than he
had been with her redoubtable husband, and he let her
see the possibility of a break between her father and
her husband. Marie Louise's eyes filled with tears.
Prince Schwarzenberg spoke in a still more alarming way to the Duke of Bassano. He considered
the possibility of Napoleon's not accepting Austria's
mediation, and went so far as to say: "Politics made
the marriage; politics may unmake it."

For his part, the Count of Narbonne, the French
Ambassador at Vienna, wrote to the Duke of Bassano,
May 2, 1813: "People who have not been outside of
this city for twenty years, say that never has society
been so scandalously frank in its opposition to what
appears to be the professions of the Emperor and
his Minister. Is it the fault of the government, or
its intention? Or, being unable to prevent it, is it
this spirit which causes so much uncertainty and
condemns the government to a course, which, in

any other circumstances would prove the blackest treachery! That is a question which one cannot help asking one's self."

Marie Louise, who read the despatches, was much disturbed by the state of affairs. She had an interview with the First Secretary of the Austrian Embassy, M. de Floret, who after Prince Schwarzenberg's departure, was in charge of the Embassy. "I am assured," she said to him, "that Austria means to side against France."

M. de Floret seemed sincere when he besought the young sovereign to cast out such fears from her mind. "But I hear it said every day," the Empress went on. "The Emperor is very uneasy about it, not merely on my account, but also because of his friendship for my father since he saw him at Dresden. Judge for yourself how this condition of things distresses me. I think that at Vienna my husband's real strength is not understood. Soon his armies will be very much larger even than they now are. I know this, now that I see the lists. The French have never shown such ardor. If my father should declare war against France, the most terrible consequences for himself and for Austria might follow. Write to Vienna. My father will believe you more than he will believe me."

M. de Floret did his best to reassure the Empress. He told her that the Emperor Francis's character and his affections for a beloved daughter were a guaranty for the future; that he had had enough of war, and

now desired nothing but peace, which was necessary
for both Austria and France; and that he wanted
quietly to devote the rest of his life to his people and
his family. This comforted Marie Louise, who began
to talk about Napoleon, of his kindness as a family
man, of his domestic excellence which made him a
model husband, and she persuaded M. de Floret to
promise to write this to Vienna. She herself sent her
father a letter, in which, after expressing her fears,
she invoked the ties of blood. "The Emperor said
to me," she wrote, "the Sovereign to whom I am
most strongly bound is your father. I am sure that
if he should let himself be led by his wife he would
regret the loss of my friendship." At this time
Marie Louise had a sincere affection for her husband,
and the idea that she might one day desert him never
occurred to her. She discharged her duties as Regent
like a good Frenchwoman, a good wife, and a good
mother.

Meanwhile, Napoleon delighted to be once more at
the head of his troops, plunged into his duties as
commander-in-chief. Never had he more ardently
loved war. The terrible lessons of the Russian campaign had been completely thrown away upon him.
He was confident that his revenge would be most
brilliant, and fancied that though he might have had
to yield to the elements, men would never conquer
him. The victory he won at Lützen, May 2, 1813,
made him imagine that he would always be the master of Europe. His soldiers, who were scarcely more

than boys, did wonders. Marshal Ney had said to
him: "Sire, give me those young and brave conscripts, I will lead them wherever you please. Our
old fellows know as much as we do; they judge the
difficulties and the field, but these brave boys are
afraid of nothing; they don't look to the right or
the left, but always straight ahead; it's glory that
they want." In the battle the French conscripts and
the Prussian students rivalled one another in bravery
and daring. Almost every general was wounded.
While the King of Prussia and the Emperor of
Russia looked down upon the carnage from the top of
a hill, Napoleon was in the middle of the fire, spurring on his recruits by words and gestures. "To-day
belongs to France," he shouted. "Forward! The
country is watching you. Learn how to die for it."
And after the battle he said: "In the twenty years
that I have commanded French armies I have never
seen more bravery and devotion. My young soldiers'
honor and courage streamed from every pore." Yet
this victory, which was hotly disputed, was incom-
plete. After all his obstinate efforts and a loss of
twelve thousand men, Napoleon had captured only
two thousand prisoners, and having no cavalry, he
could not pursue the enemy.

From Pegau he wrote, May 4, 1813, the following
letter: —

"MY BROTHER AND VERY DEAR FATHER-IN-LAW:
Knowing the interest which Your Majesty takes in
my success, I hasten to inform you of the victory

which it has pleased Providence to grant to my forces in the field of Lützen. Although I was anxious to direct myself all the movements of my army, and was thus exposed at times to the musketry fire, I was untouched, and, Heaven be praised, am in the enjoyment of the best of health. I have heard from the Empress, with whom I continue to be very well pleased. She is now my Prime Minister, and discharges her duties to my great satisfaction. I must tell Your Majesty this, for I know how it will gratify your paternal heart. Your Majesty must believe in the esteem and thorough respect I feel towards him, and especially in my sincere interest in his happiness."

The same day Napoleon wrote to the Archchancellor Cambacérès : —

" MY COUSIN : You will see by the despatches sent to the Empress what is the present state of affairs. It could not be better. The bravery, zeal, and devotion the young soldiers show is unexcelled. They are full of enthusiasm."

May 6 the Emperor sent to the Minister of Public Worship the text of a circular which the Empress-Regent was to forward to the bishops of the Empire. It ran thus : —

" BISHOP : The victory won at Lützen by His Majesty the Emperor and King, our very dear husband and Sovereign, can only be regarded as a special act of divine Providence. We desire that on receipt of these presents you should make arrangements for the singing of a *Te Deum*, and for returning thanks

to the God of battles; and that you should add such
prayers as you may think proper to secure the divine
protection for our armies, and especially for the preservation of the sacred person of His Majesty the Emperor and King, our very dear husband and Sovereign.
May God guard him from every peril! His safety
is necessary for the happiness of Europe, and for
religion, which he has aided and is called upon to
strengthen.   He is its sincerest and truest protector.
This letter having no other aim, we pray God to have
you in his holy keeping.   Given at our Palace of
Saint Cloud."

No pains were spared to kindle the enthusiasm of the
Parisians.   Lützen was celebrated with more pomp
than Austerlitz.   Sunday, May 23, 1813, the Empress-
Regent went in state to Notre Dame, to be present at
the *Te Deum* sung in honor of the new victory.   The
church was sumptuously decorated with lights, hang-
ings, and carpets.   In the choir, to the right of the
altar, stood the Empress's throne.   At one o'clock
she started for the Tuileries in a state coach, and
followed by a brilliant company, drove to the cathedral.   The Archbishop of Paris at that time was the
great orator of the Constituent Assembly, Mirabeau's
rival, the former Abbé Maury, who had been made
a cardinal.   When Marie Louise reached the thresh-
old of the cathedral he addressed her as follows:
"Madame: The presence of Your Imperial and Royal
Majesty in this sanctuary makes known to your people the new and conspicuous blessings with which the

Most High has crowned the ever victorious arms of
your august spouse. If all the French people are overwhelmed with joy at having to-day in their love to
thank God for so much glory, what must be the happiness of a heart called upon to share it upon the throne?
Religion is about to enrich itself, in its prayers, with
all the credit which is assured by your virtues at the
moment when your piety has selected it for the expression of your gratitude to the King of kings."

After this ingenious bit of flattery, the eloquent
cardinal went on, alluding to the coronation of the
Empress and of the King of Rome, which, it was
supposed, would take place when the war was over,
as an epilogue to the victories. "The same temple,"
he said, "in which the whole Empire meets to raise
to Heaven the pious transports of its gratitude, will
soon be opened, Madame, to celebrate in your honor
another historic rite as dear to our Sovereign as to
his subjects. Then we shall see again, amid universal
applause, the august heroine of this national festivity,
deservedly placed before our altars, by the side of the
restorer and the heir of the throne of Charlemagne.
Religion, happy to consecrate such a blessed day,
will congratulate itself on then proclaiming all the
resplendent glory of your happiness and the public
joy. But, Madame, we cannot too soon tell Your
Majesty, in the name of this religion, as holy as it is
necessary, that it will always regard as the greatest
of your benefactions the publicity of religious principles and the protection of your example."

When he had finished his speech, the Archbishop walked in front of the Empress-Regent, as she was led to the choir in a procession, beneath a canopy supported by canons. The procession advanced in the following order: the Ushers, the Heralds at Arms, Pages, Aides, and Masters of Ceremonies, the Officers in Waiting, the Grand Eagles, the High Officers of the Empire, the Grand Master of Ceremonies, the High Chamberlain, the Princes holding high positions, the Regent beneath the canopy, the Lady of Honor, the Knight of Honor, the First Equerry, the First Almoners, the Marshal, the Duke of Conegliano. The Empress on reaching the choir knelt on a cushion before the altar, and then took her seat on the throne; and after the *Te Deum* was sung, she went back to the Tuileries as she had come.

The next day the *Moniteur* took up its lyric trumpet, and thus described the ceremony: "It is hard to paint the emotion inspired by this solemn rite. It was a spectacle at once magnificent and touching: the estates of the Realm, guardians of the Empire; the worthy magistrates, charged with the maintenance of order and justice; the warriors, the honor of their country; the young students, the hope of France; the flower of the vast population of Paris, gazed with tenderness at the gentle majesty of virtue mounting on the most glorious throne in the world, and they with rapture united their prayers with hers, to thank the God of battles for the success with which he has crowned the noble conceptions and swift efforts of our immortal Emperor. Gratitude for his feats, regrets for his absence, prayers for his safety, enthusiasm for what had been done in six months in the way of repairing losses, the many conspiracies brought to naught in one day, the visionary schemes destroyed by one victory, the miracles wrought by his genius, evoked in every heart a multitude of intense, noble, and tender impressions, which sought expression in every way. In the sanctuary, outside of it, and all along the path followed by the Empress-Regent, with her noble suite, there was assembled a vast throng, and their applause attested the love and veneration with which she has inspired the whole French people."

In order to make a favorable impression on the nation, in the number of the *Moniteur* containing the description of the *Te Deum*, it was announced that the Emperor had just proposed a congress at Prague to discuss a general peace, and it was added : " His Majesty offers to agree to an armistice between the different armies, in order to put a stop to the shedding of blood. These principles are in harmony with the views of Austria."

Marie Louise was happy because everything seemed to betoken a speedy and glorious peace. After her return from Notre Dame, she wrote to her father: " I come back deeply moved by seeing the love with which the Emperor inspires the people. Never have the French more warmly cheered his name. He is victor and peacemaker."

At Vienna the impression made by the battle of Lützen was immense. The Count of Narbonne wrote, May 10, 1813, to the Duke of Bassano: "However accustomed one may be to the wonders accomplished by His Majesty, it is impossible not to be struck by a new admiration or new terror on seeing how his genius dispenses with everything, fills every void, takes the place of cavalry, renders the army experienced, and finds a way to turn everything into an instrument of victory. I hastened to inform Prince Schwarzenberg, who seemed delighted and not at all surprised."

Napoleon made a victorious entry into Dresden where he was rejoined by the King of Saxony, once more his faithful ally. The Emperor of Austria sent thither General Bubna with this letter: —

"May 11, 1813. MY BROTHER AND VERY DEAR SON-IN-LAW: I despatch Count Bubna to Your Imperial Majesty at this moment of the greatest importance for our Empires. This is the moment when I demand your frankest confidence. If Your Majesty aids my efforts by a moderation which will establish his reign among the most glorious, which will assure the happiest future to Your Imperial Majesty, by establishing on the firmest basis the dynasty which you have founded, the existence of which is closely bound up with my own, I shall congratulate myself on having contributed to this good end."

In another letter written the next day, Emperor Francis thanked his son-in-law for sending him word of the victory of Lützen: —

"My Brother and very Dear Son-in-law:
I warmly thank Your Imperial Majesty for the attention paid me in sending me news of your health after
the bloody day of Lützen. You only do justice to
my eager interest in yourself, by thinking me anxious
about the dangers to which you expose yourself only
too much. What you say about the Empress gives
me great pleasure. When I gave you my daughter,
I was sure that I gave you an excellent wife who
was endowed with all the qualities necessary for
domestic happiness. The development of these
which renders her worthy to govern the Empire is
doubtless due to the wise lessons and the example of
Your Imperial Majesty. It is my heartiest wish that
my daughter may always contribute to your happiness, on which, my brother, my own in a great measure depends."

Napoleon thus answered this affectionate letter: —

"Dresden, May 17, 1813. My Brother and
very Dear Father-in-law: What Your Majesty
tells me in your letter about the interest you feel,
touches me deeply. I deserve it by the genuineness
of my feeling for you. If Your Majesty is concerned
about my happiness, may you guard my honor. I
have decided to die, if need be, at the head of the
brave French army, rather than to become the laughing stock of the English and to allow my enemies to
triumph. May Your Majesty think of the future!
Do not destroy the fruit of these years of friendship,
and do not renew the old plots which will drive

Europe into unending convulsions and wars. Do
not for petty considerations sacrifice the happiness of
our generation, of your life, and your subjects' real
interests, — why should I not say those of a part of
your family which is sincerely attached to you! May
Your Majesty never doubt my attachment!"

The same day that Napoleon sent this letter to the
Emperor of Austria, he received warmly General
Bubna and appeared to enter sincerely into the views
of the Viennese cabinet. The same day he wrote
again to Emperor Francis : —

" My Brother and very Dear Father-in-law :
I have had an interview of several hours with Count
Bubna. I told him frankly and sincerely what I
thought. I desire peace more than any one. I consent to open negotiations for a general peace and to
the assembling of a congress in some city placed
between the different belligerent courts. As soon as
I shall have heard that England, Russia, Prussia, and
the allies have accepted this proposition, I shall hasten
to send a Minister Plenipotentiary to this congress,
and I shall urge my allies to do the same. I shall
make no objection to the admission to the congress
of the Spanish insurgents to present their claims. If
Russia, Prussia, and the other belligerent powers
wish to treat without England, I also consent to that.
I shall be ready to send my Minister Plenipotentiary
as soon as I shall have heard that this proposition is
accepted, and I shall urge my allies to do the same
thing as soon as I shall know the date of meeting.

If, after the opening of the congress, the belligerent powers desire to conclude an armistice as was the case in Paris with Prince Schwarzenberg, I am ready to agree to it. Your Majesty will see from what I say, which is what I said six months ago, that I desire to avoid the effusion of human blood and to put an end to the troubles which afflict so many nations."

The Emperor Francis trusted in his son-in-law's sincerity, and at first thought that the congress would be of importance. Metternich, who really desired peace, was confident and happy. The Count of Narbonne wrote to the Duke of Bassano, May 21, 1813 : "Since my arrival here I have not seen M. de Metternich so satisfied as he appears at this moment. ' Well,' he said to me, 'I hope that the time is come when the Emperor Napoleon will be convinced that we are neither fools nor traitors. Confess that I was right in guessing that he would at last do us justice, and see that the simplicity of the plans required no explanation or development. His letter to his father-in-law, which I have not yet read, though I have heard most of its contents, is exactly what I should have desired, and at any rate, what we hear exceeds all my hopes. Though I have not been to Laxenberg, but am going to-morrow with Bubna, I can tell you now that His Majesty is delighted, and will send him off with instructions which ought to please Napoleon.' I repeat it. I have never seen him more thoroughly pleased. . . . Day before yesterday at Laxenberg, a man whom I know was speak-

ing of the embarrassment Napoleon must be in, in
spite of his victories, and was dwelling with great
satisfaction on his dangerous situation.   Emperor
Francis answered with a proverbial phrase of an
Austrian dialect, ' I am not troubled about him ; he
will be playing one of his old tricks.'   Do you care
to know the opinion of Russian and Prussian society?
The same persons who a fortnight ago were offering
to bet a hundred to fifteen on a war against us, yesterday refused even the odds reversed.   An intimate
friend of Prince Schwarzenberg tells me that he left
with the greatest possible satisfaction, and accounted
for this change on the ground of the pleasure he
must feel at holding the brilliant position of commander of the Austrian forces with the certainty
that he would not have to use them."

Just when Napoleon was talking about an armistice and peace-making, he had resumed hostilities.
May 20 and 21 he fought the bloódy battle of Bautzen, in which he routed the Russians and the Prussians.   The enemy, who had lost eighteen thousand
men, but had inflicted a loss of twelve thousand on
the French, retreated in good order, burning their
material, laying the road waste, and making a stand
at every stream and gorge.   "What!" exclaimed
the Emperor, "after such butchery, no result! no
prisoners!   Those fellows won't leave me a pin!"

The Count of Montesquiou was charged to carry
the Empress the news of the victory of Bautzen.
She wrote to her father: " I think that I see that

this battle was very important. I can't tell you how happy this good news makes me. I was never better in my life."

At Paris, as at Vienna, every one believed in peace. The Emperor, it was said on all sides, was to show himself moderate, wise, disposed to peace. The death of Duroc, Grand Marshal of the Palace, who was killed the day after the battle of Bautzen, had doubtless filled him with sad and useful thoughts. This death was very sudden: a few moments before he was struck, two or three steps from his master, Duroc sadly said to Caulaincourt, " My friend, do you notice the Emperor? He has just won victories after defeats, and now would be the time to take advantage of the lessons of misfortune. But, you see, he is not changed. He is never satiated with fighting. The end of all this cannot fail to be bad." In fact, he was right. Napoleon ran up to his dying friend. Duroc pressed his hand, raised it to his lips, and said with a faint voice, " My whole life has been devoted to your service, and all I regret is that I can no longer be of use to you." " Duroc," answered the Emperor, " there is another life; there you will await me, and we shall meet some day." " Yes, Sire, but not for thirty years, when you shall have triumphed over your enemies and have fulfilled our country's hopes. I have lived as an honest man; I have nothing to reproach myself with. I leave a daughter; Your Majesty will be a father to her."

Thiers describes Napoleon leaving the hut where

he had just bidden farewell to his unhappy fellow-
soldier, and seating himself on some fascines near
the outposts: "There he sat, buried in thought, his
hands on his knees, his eyes wet with tears, scarcely
hearing the shots of the skirmishers, and not noticing
the caresses of a dog belonging to a regiment of the
Guards, which often galloped by the side of his horse,
and now stood before him, licking his hands. An
equerry came to rouse him from this revery; he
arose suddenly, hiding his tears, in order not to be
seen thus moved. Such is human nature, change-
able, mysterious in its various aspects, to be judged
fairly by God alone! This man thus moved by the
fate of one wounded man, had caused the mutilation
of more than eighty thousand men within a month,
of more than two millions in eighteen years, and was
yet to cause several hundred thousand more to be
torn by bullets."

Alas! no lesson was of use to the Emperor, not
even the Russian campaign. It was said that noth-
ing in the world could inspire him with the ideas of
moderation and wisdom, which were yet so necessary.
Austria sincerely desired that he should keep the
Kingdom of Westphalia for his brother Jerome; the
Kingdom of Naples for his brother-in-law Murat; the
Kingdom of Italy and the French Empire, that vast
Empire, not only with the frontier of the Rhine,
but also Belgium, Holland, Piedmont, Tuscany, the
Roman States, as French departments for himself. It
asked of him only to abandon three cities: Hamburg,

Bremen, and Lübeck; and to resign one title, that of Protector of the Confederation of the Rhine. It was through his unwillingness to make this slight concession that Napoleon ruined France and himself.

June 4, 1813, the Emperor signed the armistice, not to make peace, but to prepare a second campaign. He needed still two months to complete his armaments and to make war even with Austria. The fault of this fatal armistice, which saved the then desperate forces of the coalitions, and which Napoleon should not have accepted unless he sincerely desired peace, lay in his unwillingness to consent to the conditions imposed by the Cabinet of Vienna. But the news was received with joy by all Europe, except Prussia: Marie Louise fancied that she had come to the end of her trials, and believed that France and Austria would remain united forever. As soon as she heard of the armistice she wrote to her father: " I can truly say that no piece of news has ever given me greater pleasure. It dispels my anxieties and my fears. I see in it a proof of your kindness; this touches me, and I cannot be sufficiently grateful. I am sure that the Emperor will gladly accept this token of your friendship. The days I spent with you at Prague and at Dresden abound with touching memories. It was in this month, last year, that I had the happiness to see you and to assure you by word of mouth of my filial affection. I kiss your hand, dear father, and thank you for sending me a courier every fortnight." July 7, the Regent wrote again to her father: "I can give you good news of my husband. All my prayers are for a speedy peace. The armistice has already much improved my health. You know how anxiety affects me."

Napoleon, when he sent his army into their quarters, had decreed that a monument should be built on the summit of the Alps, with this inscription: "Napoleon to the French people, in memory of their generous efforts against the coalition of 1813."

These heroic efforts, this magnanimous struggle, these wonders of devotion and courage were to have for result the horrors of the invasion. The hopes that were felt were but a snare. The Congress of Prague was to be but an image; a ghost of a congress, and oceans of blood were, alas! yet to flow.

XIV.

NAPOLEON returned to Dresden June 10, 1813. Strange rumors had been circulating among the inhabitants of this city since Duroc's remains had passed through. Many thought that the Grand Marshal's coffin was really the Emperor's, who had been killed in the last battle, and whose body, they said, was in a room of the castle where one could see candles burning all night. When the Imperial carriage arrived, they maintained that it was not Napoleon whom they saw, but a stuffed figure. But when the next day the Emperor appeared on horseback in a field outside the city gates, they had to yield to the evidence and to acknowledge that the winner of so many battles was still alive. He established himself in the Marcolini Palace, a charming summer house in the Friedrichstadt suburb. A large, beautiful garden, the green fields of the Osterwiese, on the banks of the Elbe, and the most agreeable exposure rendered this spot in the month of June far more attractive than the winter palace where lived the King of Saxony. A large number of troops could be drilled on the river's edge, in Napoleon's sight. He arranged his life with military precision, and decided that in the morning he would hold a levee as he had done at the Tuileries; the middle of the day he would devote to drills and reviews; the evening to dinners, receptions, and theatrical performances.

The actors of the Comédie Française, among whom were Talma, Fleury, Saint Prix, Mademoiselle Georges, Mademoiselle Mars, and Mademoiselle Contat, were summoned from Paris, and reached Dresden June 19, 1813. Napoleon had written to Cambacérès : "It is well people should think that we are amusing ourselves here." The first performance took place in the Orangery of the Marcolini Palace, which had been turned into a little theatre, holding hardly more than two hundred persons. There was played in the first evening, the *Gageure imprévue* and the *Suite d'un bal masqué.* Comedies alone were given in this small room ; as for the tragedies, they were played in the great theatre of the city. It was M. de Bausset who acted as manager, in company with M. de Turenne. "A remarkable change," he tells us, "took place at this time in Napoleon's tastes, he previously having been fond of tragedy. Generally speaking, all men feel this effect of advancing years. In youth, in the age of passion, the masterpieces of tragedy carry us into an unknown conventional world. Then everything, to the language and the dresses, addresses our senses and our soul in a heroic way. That is the time when illusions delight and overcome us. Later this glow vanishes; we feel the need of drawing nearer to nature and real life; the society, the exact delineation of characters and manners interests and attracts us much more."

In 1813 tragedies seemed flat to the Emperor. His fate was the greatest of tragedies. Never was there a greater, a more thrilling piece, than that in which he took the leading part, and had for his support all the nations of Europe. Racine and Corneille sunk into insignificance before Napoleon. When he had reached the decisive point from which he had to rise higher or to fall into the abyss, the great actor felt that emotion, that combination of hope and anxiety, of joy and pain, which distinguishes the supreme moment.

War is the first of games. Battlefields are like huge green cloths on which genius and chance hold the cards. I have never read this passage from Lacordaire's *Conférences de Toulouse* without thinking of Napoleon: " Man has discovered amid the laws of numbers and movement combinations which express chances but not certainty; and chance has appeared as the sovereign happiness; for chance responded to one of his strongest needs, the dramatic need of his nature. He wishes to create for himself an action. . . . An action which moves him by its great interest, holds him in suspense by a complication independent of his will, and at last saves or fells him by a sudden turn. Every other drama is indifferent to

him. If he gazes at scenes from Sophocles or Corneille, he is not the victim or the hero; he weeps over
remote misfortunes which art evokes to move him.
But here he is himself, when he wishes, as he wishes,
to the extent that he chooses. Chance and cupidity
together make him the sport of a personal drama,
both terrifying and joyous, in which hope, fear, joy,
gloom, follow one another, or rather combine almost
at the same moment, and keep him panting in a fever
which grows to madness; for if we speak of the passion for drink, we speak of the fury of gambling."

To an honorable peace, which yet imposed upon his
pride a few sacrifices, Napoleon, that stubborn and
relentless gambler, preferred war with all Europe.
"It was doubtless," said Thiers, " madness for himself, a cruelty for the many victims doomed to perish
in the battlefield, a sort of treason against France."

· After having won fabulous sums, this hardiest of
players, lucky up to that day, lost suddenly a large
portion in the Russian campaign. He wished to take
his revenge, and found his old luck; his gains were
considerable : Lützen and Bautzen. Had he been
wise he would then have been satisfied; his losses
were almost made good. But no! that was not
enough; he wanted to go on playing. All or
nothing, was his motto. As foolish a motto as well
could be; for Fortune, who is a woman, finally tires
of her greatest favorites. Once more ! shouted Napoleon. No ! was Fortune's answer; and by wishing to regain the whole, he lost everything.

All Europe had its eyes fixed on Dresden. Except perhaps the Prussians, who were aroused to the highest excitement, and thought only of avenging Jena, every nation desired peace, and hoped that Napoleon's moderation would make this possible. Such, too, was Metternich's feeling when he reached the capital of Saxony to hold a decisive conference with the winner of Lützen.

We have no hesitation in saying that we always have a little distrust of narrations made from memory, especially when they deal with so long an interview as that which took place at the Marcolini Palace, June 26, 1813, between Napoleon and Metternich, as is recorded by the Austrian statesman with the minutest detail. Reading the report of this famous conversation, which began at quarter to twelve, and lasted till half-past eight in the evening, one would imagine that a short-hand writer had been present, taking down every word. However wonderful a man's memory may be, it is incapable of such a feat. Doubtless the account is in the main accurate; but the form cannot be literally given, and many of the sentences appear to us to belong more to fiction than to history. The two principal accounts are those of Prince Metternich and of Thiers, who received his information from the Prince; yet the two reports are far from being absolutely identical. Thiers took care to say that this famous interview is the most difficult of all those in which Napoleon took part to reproduce, from the lack of satisfactory documents. He says, speaking of this: "For Napoleon's other interviews, already recorded in this history, there existed numerous documents, either in our own diplomatic archives, or in those of other nations; but for this one, however, inasmuch as Napoleon transmitted no account of it to his Ministers, we are without one of the surest means of information. He contented himself with speaking about it to M. de Bassano, who was later the author of different versions that were published by writers with whom he was intimate. This memorable interview would then be nearly lost, if M. de Metternich had not written it down at great length and in full detail, in good season. He kindly favored me with a copy of this record, which seemed to me too severe to Napoleon, though generally accurate, and I have preserved everything which seemed to me incontestable." Evidently such an arbitrary selection can only approximate the truth. The interview lasted more than eight hours. At its close, the two interlocutors who had begun their conversation before noon, were in the dark. No one had dared to come into the room with a light. It would require almost a volume to give a faithful report of so long a conversation. Prince Metternich confines himself to a few pages. Consequently he has suppressed a good deal, and what he puts down in his Memoirs, I repeat, does not appear to me absolutely authoritative.

Half an hour after the interview the Minister contented himself with sending to Emperor Francis a short despatch, accompanied by a very brief docu-

ment labelled: "Condensed report of a conversation
with the Emperor Napoleon."

"This long interview," he wrote, "has been a
confused medley of the most curious sort, a series
of protestations of friendship mingled with the most
violent outbreaks. . . . 'It depends on Your Majesty,' I said to the Emperor Napoleon, 'to give peace
to the world, to establish your government on the
surest foundation, on a feeling of universal gratitude;
if Your Majesty lets this opportunity escape, what
limit can there be to the confusion?' The Emperor
replied that he was willing to make peace, but that
he would die before he would make a dishonorable
one. I made answer that no dishonorable proposition
could ever enter the Emperor Francis's calculations.
'Well! What do you mean by a peace?' the Emperor
interrupted. 'What are your conditions? Do you
wish to despoil me? Do you want Italy, Brabant,
Lorraine? I shall not give up an inch of territory;
I will make peace on the basis of *statu quo ante
bellum*. I will even give Russia a part of the Duchy
of Warsaw; I will give you nothing, because you
have not beaten me; I will give nothing to Prussia,
because she has played me false. If you want West-
ern Calicia, if Prussia wants part of her former
possessions, that may be arranged; but there must
be some compensations. In that case you will have
to indemnify my allies. The conquest of Illyria cost
me three hundred thousand men; if you want to
have it, you must give an equal number of men.'

After this first outbreak, I replied: 'I am not called upon to discuss here the conditions of future peace, but simply to insist on the speediest opening of negotiations through Austria, or else on the Emperor's refusal to negotiate through its mediation. Let the negotiators meet, and nothing can stand in the way of a discussion of the conditions of peace; in this important juncture Austria will perform its duty as mediator with absolute impartiality.'"

This document, written half an hour after the interview, bears the ear-mark of indisputable authenticity. It is a summary in which, to our thinking, the respective situation of the interlocutors is clearly and exactly expressed. As for the fuller report in Prince Metternich's Memoirs, it is very impressive on account of its dramatic character; but on certain points it seems that it should be accepted with reserve. Is it, for example, probable, that Napoleon, who up to that time had reason only to praise Marie Louise, and who openly congratulated himself on the way she performed her duties as Regent, should have said to Metternich: "Three times I have re-established the Emperor Francis on his throne; I promised to remain at peace with him as long as I lived; I married his daughter. I said to myself then: 'You are doing a foolish thing'; but it's done; I am sorry for it now"? Is it likely that Napoleon would have said a second time: "Yes, I did a very stupid thing in marrying the Archduchess"; and that Metternich should have answered: "Since Your Majesty desires to know my opinion, I will tell him very frankly that Napoleon the *Conqueror* made a blunder"?

Is it probable that the Emperor, returning for the third time to the expression of the same regret, should again say: "Yes, everything confirms me in the opinion that I committed an unpardonable blunder; by marrying the Archduchess I hoped to unite the present and the past, Gothic prejudices, and the institutions of my time; I made a mistake, and I now see all the consequences of my error; it may cost me my throne, but I shall bury the world beneath its ruins"?

Is it probable that Napoleon could have carried his boasting so far as to say: "How many allies are you? Four, five, six, twenty? The more numerous you are, the calmer I shall be"? Is it probable that he should have used this figure: "I have grown up on battlefields, and a man like me cares little for the life of a million men. . . . The French can't complain of me; to spare them I sacrificed the Germans and the Poles I lost three hundred thousand men in the Russian campaign, but in that number there were not more than thirty thousand Frenchmen"?

Prince Metternich thus describes the end of the interview: "It was dark. No one had dared to enter the room. Not a moment of silence interrupted the hot discussion. Six different times my words were equivalent to a declaration of war. . . . When Napoleon dismissed me, he had become calm and gentle. I could not see his face. He went with me

to the door of the anteroom; as he laid his hand on
the door-knob, he said to me:

"'We shall meet again, I hope.'

"'I am at your orders, Sire,' I replied; 'but I have
no hope of attaining the object of my mission.'

"'Well,' resumed Napoleon, laying his hand on
my shoulder, 'do you know what will happen? You
will not make war against me.'

"'You are a ruined man, Sire,' I exclaimed warmly;
'I had a presentiment of it when I came here; now
I am sure of it.'"

All this seems to us very improbable. On the
morrow of Lützen and Bautzen, no one spoke in that
way to Napoleon. We are inclined to think that
Metternich rather expressed regret.

The Baron of Bausset says in his Memoirs that
during the whole interview the King of Saxony and
the King of Naples waited to know the result, in
either the anteroom or the garden. "When he left,"
he says, "M. de Metternich seemed to me excited.
He waited silently at the palace door until the
Emperor, who had left the room at the same time
with him, had got on his horse. I silently studied
M. de Metternich's face, as I had long known him;
he took my hand mechanically, pressed it warmly,
and held it for a few minutes without saying a word.
This silent, almost convulsive parting, troubled me,
and seemed to express all the fate of the Empire."

June 30 Metternich again saw Napoleon and found
him perfectly serene. What the Emperor especially

desired was the prolongation of the armistice, in
order to complete his armaments. He was amiable,
familiar, courteous, with the Austrian Minister. " So
you insist," he said to him, laughing, " on threatening
us ? " The Convention was signed without difficulty,
and Metternich, who was treated with the utmost
courtesy, returned to the Emperor Francis. At
Prague he saw the Count of Narbonne, and frankly
exposed the situation to him. " The limit of August
10 once reached, there will not be a word said about
peace, and war will be declared. We shall not be
neutral ; the Emperor Napoleon need not flatter himself. . . . I give you my word and my Sovereign's
that we have made no engagements with any one.
But I also give you my word that at midnight of
August 10 we shall have some with every one except
you, and that on the morning of the 17th you will
have three hundred thousand Austrians more on your
hands. It is not lightly, not without pain, for he is
a father and he loves his daughter, that the Emperor
has formed this resolution ; but he owes it to his
people, to himself, to Europe, to restore tranquillity,
since he has the power, and since, besides, the only
alternative is some day in the future to fall beneath
your blows, in a condition of dependency worse than
that into which you have put Prussia. Don't come
telling us after the event that we have deceived you.
Up to midnight, August 10, everything is possible,
even at the last hour; the 10th of August passed,
not a day's, not a moment's respite; war, war with
every one, even with us ! "

In 1808, at Erfurt, Napoleon was conversing with
Goethe. The hero of Austerlitz and the author of
Faust discussed ancient tragedy and the notion of
fate. "What have we to do with fatality nowa-
days?" Napoleon broke out; "fatality is politics."
Yes, it is politics, that, at certain, solemn, historical
moments, — in 1813, in 1870, for example, — with a
certain fascination, leads sovereigns to an abyss which
they see but cannot avoid. Presentiments, flashes of
wisdom light up here and there the blackness of the
night into which they have voluntarily plunged; but
they are sure to deaden that importunate light with
their own hands, and to march with bowed head,
amid the gloom, towards the gulf.

XV.

B EFORE resuming the conflict, Napoleon wished
to take advantage of the armistice to spend a
few days with Marie Louise, and he asked her to join
him at Mayence. He still loved her sincerely, and
thought that she might be of some use to him. He
fancied that the regard with which he treated her
might make a good impression in Vienna, and
although he knew that the Prague Congress would
be barren of result, he wanted peace to be thought
probable, and he pretended that he himself hoped
for it. To the Archchancellor he wrote this letter, to
arrange for the Empress's journey: —

"Dresden, July 16, 1813. MY COUSIN: This letter
leaves the 16th, and will reach you on the 20th. I
wish the Empress to leave on the 22d, so that she
may be at Mayence on the 24th. She will bring the
Duchess of Montebello, two ladies in waiting, two
Eastern women, two negresses, a Prefect of the Palace, two chamberlains, two equerries, of whom one
shall start twenty-four hours in advance for Metz, so
that they may divide the journey between them; four

pages, to be distributed along the way, in order to make the trip less fatiguing for the young fellows; her private secretary, if he is well, and her physician. Moreover, she will bring servants and a dinner service so that her table may be well served; for I shall not take any one with me, and it is possible that several German Kings and Princes may call on her. Still she need not bring the silver-gilt service. Count Caffarelli will accompany the Empress to look after the escorts. The Empress will spend the first night at Châlons, at the Prefecture; the second at Metz, at the Prefecture; the third at Mayence. Her trip will be announced in these three cities so that due honors may be paid her. There will be four carriages in the first set, four in the second, four in the third: twelve carriages in all. So far as possible, the military commandant will supply escorts. The gens d'armes along the route will be under arms, in full uniform. All the prescribed ceremonial will be observed. The general commanding each division will accompany her in the territory of his division.

"The day of the Empress's departure you will have inserted in the *Moniteur* an article running thus: 'Her Majesty the Empress, Queen, and Regent, has left to spend a week at Mayence, in the hope of meeting His Majesty the Emperor there. Her Majesty will sleep the 22d at Châlons, the 23d at Metz, and the 24th at Mayence. Her Majesty will return early in August.'

"You will send me word by telegraph when the

Empress leaves Saint Cloud and when she is to reach Mayence; I shall arrange my departure accordingly. If any Ministers have anything important to say to me, and desire to come to confer with me, they can avail themselves of my stay at Mayence and visit me between July 24 and August 1. And now I pray God to have you in his holy keeping."

Marie Louise started from Saint Cloud July 23, and slept at Châlons and at Metz, where she received the principal authorities, and reached Mayence the 26th, at four in the morning, in wretched weather. She feared that the Emperor might have got there before her; but he did not arrive till the same day, at eleven in the evening. He was in good health. His complexion was brightened and sunburnt by the campaign. He embraced his wife tenderly and expressed the utmost confidence in the future. The next morning he watched the troops parade, and started the squadrons and battalions which were passing the Rhine to join the army. The Grand Duke and the Grand Duchess of Baden, the Prince Primate, the Prince of Nassau, the Grand Duke of Hesse-Darmstadt, came to pay their court.

The Prefect of Mayence, the chief town of the department of Mont Tonnerre, happened to be a former member of the Convention, and of the Committee of Public Safety, by name Jean Bon Saint André. He was a tireless worker, an admirable administrator, of simple tastes and austere appearance, with the bearing and tastes of a peasant of the Dan-

ube ; in a word, the old Revolutionary had preserved
the Republican airs of his youth after he had become
an Imperial functionary.   Count Beugnot, who at
that time governed the Grand Duchy of Berg, as
Minister of the Emperor, and who had come from
Düsseldorf to Mayence to pay his respects to his
sovereign, has drawn in his Memoirs a very curious
portrait of the former member of the Convention,
then a Prefect of the Empire, who, dressed partly in
uniform, partly, including his cravat, in black, greatly
disturbed the gilded band of courtiers.   He replied
to their remarks somewhat as follows: "Indeed, I
greatly admire your courage in busying yourself
about my dress and the color of my stockings, when
I am going to dine with the Emperor and Empress.
You don't express everything; you are scandalized
at seeing me invited to such a dinner, and as soon as
I have turned my back you will say: 'In fact, its inconceivable that the Emperor should invite to dine
with the Empress, the new Empress, a member of
the Convention, a "voter," a colleague of Robespierre
on the Committee of Public Safety, who is rank with
Jacobinism.'"

"Oh! M. Jean Bon, how can you put such stupidity into our mouths!   We respect you too much
to allow ourselves —"

"Not at all, gentlemen; that is not stupidity, but
the pure truth.   I will confess that Europe had then
conspired against France, as it has to-day.   It had
drawn an iron girdle about us.   Treachery had

already surrendered some important cities, and it was spreading. Well! the Kings were beaten. We recovered our own territory and carried into theirs the invasion which they had begun against us. We conquered Belgium and the left bank of the Rhine which we joined then to ourselves, although at the beginning of the war they forbade the division. We extended our preponderance and compelled those same Kings to sue for peace. Do you know what government secured and prepared those results? A government consisting of members of the Convention, of furious Jacobins, wearing red caps, rough woollen, and sabots, living on coarse bread and bad beer, who flung themselves on mattresses laid on the floor of the place where they held their meetings when they were worn out by extreme fatigue and long watchings. Those were the men who saved France. I was one of them, gentlemen; and here, as well as in the Emperor's apartments which I am about to enter, I am proud of it. . . . Besides, let us wait a little. Fortune is fickle; she has raised France very high; sooner or later, who knows, she may cast her down as low as she was in 1793. Then we shall see if she will be saved by soothing measures, and what will be the good of decorations, embroideries, feathers, and especially white silk stockings."

After thus speaking to the courtiers, Jean Bon dined with Napoleon and Marie Louise. The Emperor's brow was dark and he seemed buried in thought. He ate but little. Two or three times he

spoke to the Prince of Nassau without listening to
his answers, so that the two seemed to be at cross
purposes. The Empress had an opportunity to utter
a few words, which she did very modestly.

Count Beugnot, who was one of the guests, says that
before the dinner the Emperor had wished to take a
little sail on the Rhine, to try a little boat which the
Prince of Nassau had just given him. He went from
the Palace of the Teutonic Order to the river bank,
and got into the boat with the Prince of Nassau, M.
Jean Bon Saint André, M. Beugnot, two aides, an
adjutant of the Palace, and his Mameluke Rustan.
Through a field-glass he examined a fine vineyard on
the right bank of the Rhine, in the middle of which
rose the Castle of Biberich. While the Emperor
stood at one side of the boat, near the edge, lost in
contemplation, Jean Bon Saint André said to Count
Beugnot: "What a singular thing! The fate of the
world hangs on a single kick, more or less." "In
Heaven's name, hush!" exclaimed Count Beugnot in
terror. "Don't distress yourself," the old member of
the Convention went on, "resolute men are rare."
When the sail was over, the dialogue between the
administrator of the Grand Duchy of Berg and the
Prefect of Mayence continued on the steps of the
grand staircase of the Palace of the Teutonic Order:
"Do you know that you gave me a real scare?"
"Of course I know it. I am surprised you recovered
the use of your legs enough to walk; but you can
be sure that we shall lament with tears of blood

MAYENCE.

231

that this trip to-day was not his last." "You are a madman!" "And you, saving the respect I owe Your Excellency, are a fool!"

Meanwhile, Napoleon appeared even more formidable. There was no breach of order throughout his immense Empire. From Rome to Hamburg perfect obedience prevailed. The young army, as well as the Old Guard, displayed enthusiastic bravery. The Princes of the Confederation of the Rhine conducted themselves like faithful vassals. It was not known that the Emperor of Austria intended to abandon the French alliance, and no one imagined that he was working to overthrow his daughter's throne. It was said that Napoleon's power would suffer some slight diminution, but no one believed that he would be ruined. The Bourbons were never mentioned. They were almost unknown in France, and kindled sympathy at the courts of Vienna, Berlin, or Saint Petersburg. At Mayence, the hero of Lützen and Bautzen received as much homage as in his most brilliant days. The Imperial star still shone in sight of every one, like a setting sun.

Marie Louise, who more than anything dreaded a rupture between her husband and her father, had moments of uneasiness. Napoleon did his best to reassure her, and talked continually of peace, even when he was perfectly determined on war. He was much touched by the attachment with which he seemed to inspire the daughter of the Cæsars of Germany, and he expressed the utmost regard for her, as much from motives of policy as from affection; for he wished to encourage the Emperor Francis to remain a good father, by remaining a good husband. The Empress, ever tranquil and majestic, gave no outward sign of her gloomy forebodings, and drove out every day in a barouche through the country about Mayence. The weather had become very fine, and the clear sky made a marked contrast with the vain agitations of men.

August 1 Napoleon left Mayence after bidding farewell to Marie Louise, whom he kissed in presence of the whole court. This time she could not control her emotion, and burst into tears. August 4, after stopping at Würzburg, Bamberg, and Bayreuth, to hold reviews, he was back in Dresden, more confident, more eager for war than ever. In vain had Caulaincourt written to him: " Every sacrifice now made in behalf of peace will render you, Sire, more powerful than your victories have done, and you will be the idol of your people." He remained deaf to the words of his most faithful servants, and appeared more determined than ever to risk everything on a single throw.

As for the Empress, she left Mayence August 2, and embarked upon the Rhine in the yacht which the Prince of Nassau had put at her disposition. Her suite consisted of the Duchess of Montebello, the Count of Beauharnais, Mesdames de Lauriston and de Talhonet, General Caffarelli, two chamberlains, a Prefect of the Palace, and the Baron of Méneval.

Between Mayence and Cologne she admired the banks of the picturesque and poetic river, with its fertile fields, its cliffs, and its castles of the Middle Ages. At Coblenz, where she arrived August 3, she was greeted by the ringing of bells, artillery salutes, and flourishes of trumpets; and she appeared much touched by this brilliant reception, which she had not expected. At Cologne she left the yacht, and continued her journey by post. August 5 she was at Aix-la-Chapelle, where she visited the cathedral. Then she passed through Liège, Namur, Soissons, Compiègne. August 9, at seven in the evening, she was back at Saint Cloud, where she met her son as she alighted from her carriage, and she pressed him tenderly in her arms.

XVI.

WHEN Marie Louise had returned to Saint Cloud and was no longer within reach of her husband's cheering words, she became profoundly melancholy. Her only consolation was the sight of her son, a superb boy, whose strength and intelligence were developing most remarkably. The Queen of Naples had made him a present of a little gilded carriage, to which the skilful riding-master Franconi had harnessed two trained sheep, like horses. Whenever the infant King was seen driving in this pretty carriage, under the venerable trees in the gardens of Saint Cloud, he inspired tender admiration. Marie Louise was proud of her son; but the more she loved him, the more anxious she felt as to the lot reserved for this child whose cradle had been saluted with so much applause and homage. The letters she wrote at that time to the Emperor Francis were marked by a melancholy akin to discouragement. " I am in a painful uncertainty about the issue of the negotiations," she wrote to him, August 12, 1813. " Heaven grant that there may be no war! The

234

thought of it horribly alarms me. If war breaks out, I hope you will not be mixed up in it, for I cannot bear to think of its consequences. I found the Emperor very well at Mayence. He has gained flesh. Unfortunately I saw him for only six days. On my return I found my son very well and very gay. He already talks, and is very amiable. The Emperor sends me to Cherbourg for the inauguration of the basin."

What the Empress most feared, a war between her father and her husband, became imminent. The Count of Narbonne's prophecies came true. He had written: "No defection is more certain than one that is involuntary; which is not determined some morning out of calculation or passion, but which grows from day to day. . . . The Emperor Napoleon counts too much on family ties. The titles of son-in-law and father-in-law seem to him like indissoluble bonds. It is true that, according to an old diplomatic saying, Austria re-establishes itself by marriages; but there is also truth in the Italian proverb, 'When the storm is over, the saint is laughed at.'"

Throughout Austria the war-feeling was at its height. War was demanded as a means of recovering lost fame. Prince Schwarzenberg, who was appointed Commander-in-Chief, tried to wipe out the memory of his former zeal for the French alliance. The last convention had prolonged the armistice until the 10th of August, with a delay of six days between the denunciation of the armistice and the renewal of hostilities. Consequently the war would be resumed August 17, unless the Prague Congress should establish immediate peace. After much backing and filling, and many delays, which were ascribed to Napoleon, the Congress at last met, July 29; France was represented by the Duke of Vicenza and the Count of Narbonne; Austria by Metternich; Russia by M. d'Anstett; Prussia by the Baron von Humboldt. Their deliberations were a mere matter of form.

The Duke of Bassano, Minister of Foreign Affairs, had written to the Count of Narbonne: "I send you more powers than power; you will have your hands tied, but your legs and mouth free for walking and dining." Napoleon's infatuation had reached such a height that he imagined that he could not make any concession to Austria. The Duke of Bassano had written to the Duke of Vicenza, July 21: "The Emperor's intention is to negotiate with Russia and to make a glorious peace for that power; a peace that shall punish Austria for her bad faith in breaking the alliance of 1812, by depriving her of her influence in Europe, and shall also draw Russia and France nearer together. The Emperor intends to arrange matters in a way that will not force him some day to disentangle complications with Russia. If Russia secures an advantageous peace, she will have purchased it by the devastation of her provinces, by the loss of her capital, and by two years of terrible warfare, misfortunes from which she will long suffer.

Austria, on the other hand, has made no sacrifices, and has deserved nothing. If she derives any profit from her present intrigues, she would foster others in order to obtain new advantages. The aims of her demands on France are infinite. One concession would encourage her to urge another. It is hence for the interest of France that she do not acquire a single village."

The Duke of Vicenza, a clear-sighted man, received these imprudent instructions with regret. On his arrival at Prague, he wrote to the Minister, July 28: " We are already on a volcano; the minutes are numbered; our delays have produced a bad impression. Everything I hear makes me doubly regret that the Emperor should have bound your hands and mine more tightly than he promised." Metternich continually said to the French plenipotentiaries that up to August 10 matters were not desperate, but that after that date, if peace was not concluded, Austria's mission as a mediatorial power would be at an end. This date of August 10 was to be fatal to the Empire, as it had been twenty-one years before to royalty.

August 3, Metternich said to the Duke of Vicenza: " There can no longer be any doubt about your Sovereign's intentions. The Emperor Napoleon has merely tried to gain time. The armistice is entirely to his advantage; it is injurious to the allies. They sincerely desire peace, and a moderate peace; it would be made if the Emperor, your master, had wished it. Probably it is now too late."

The same day Napoleon sent from Dresden to the Duke of Vicenza a despatch, all of which he dictated himself; in it he said: "The Emperor commands you, by an extra-ministerial channel, to do as follows, without the knowledge of the Count of Narbonne. This step has for its object to ascertain in what way Austria judges that peace can be made, and whether, in case the Emperor adheres to his propositions, Austria would make common cause with us, or would remain neutral. There is no question of negotiations, but of an absolutely confidential overture, which rests on such obvious feelings that it would be a renunciation of the aim which Austria says that she desires, if she should not answer without reserve. This step will always remain secret, and as soon as the Emperor Napoleon shall be certain of Austria's last word, he will give instructions in consequence to his plenipotentiaries. The simplicity of this step carries with it the mark of the man who makes it, and of his firmness. M. de Metternich, then, must see that it is necessary for him to set his lowest terms, and propose nothing dishonorable for the Emperor Napoleon. M. de Metternich will probably require twenty-four hours; twenty-four hours will be granted him, and the conditions will be written down at his dictation. Our answer will be given in three days, and thereby all the embarrassments of the Congress and all the difficulties that beset it will be dispelled. The Emperor Napoleon is more thoroughly prepared for war than he can ever expect to be ; but inasmuch as he is consistent in his policy, before abandoning his alliance with Austria and destroying a system which the two powers had regarded as the foundation of their common security, which they liked to establish on personal feelings, he desires this question answered, and to weigh carefully the advantages and disadvantages. Before you make this overture, you will ask M. de Metternich not to repeat to the Emperor of Austria what you may say, and not to transmit it to any of the allied powers. Likewise you will give your word that everything said in this interview will be kept profoundly secret by yourself."

Thus, M. de Narbonne himself, this favorite Ambassador, this trusted agent, was not admitted to this secret. This was a singular diplomacy by which a sovereign kept from his own plenipotentiary the most important point of the negotiations.

August 6 the Duke of Vicenza had a very secret interview with Metternich, in which he informed him of Napoleon's confidential overtures. The Austrian Minister appeared much surprised. He thought the step was taken very late, and declared once more that the negotiations could not be prolonged beyond August 10, the date irrevocably fixed. Nevertheless, he went to Brandeiss where the Emperor Francis was, to receive his sovereign's orders. After some hesitation the Emperor consented to dictate to his Minister a despatch which was Austria's final word, its ultimatum. The conditions which it set for peace were as follows: "Dissolution of the Duchy of War-

saw, which shall be divided between Russia, Austria,
and Prussia. Dantzic shall be restored to Prussia.
Restoration of Hamburg and Lübeck to their conditions as free Hanseatic cities, and a later arrangement, connected with the general peace, regarding
the other parts of the 32d Military Division. The
renunciation of the Protectorate of the Confederation
of the Rhine, so that the independence of the reigning sovereigns of Germany shall be placed under
the guaranty of the great powers. Reconstruction
of Prussia, with a suitable frontier on the Elbe.
Cession of the Illyrian provinces to Austria. Re-
ciprocal guaranty of the state of things established
by the treaty of peace."

This ultimatum had as corollary the following lines
dictated by the Emperor Francis to his Minister:
" I expect a *yes* or *no* in the course of the 10th. I
am determined to declare on the 11th, as will be done
by Russia and Prussia, that the Congress is dissolved,
and then I shall not take into account these conditions, which shall be decided by war."

The Austrian ultimatum, which was communicated
to the Duke of Vicenza August 8, was not placed
before Napoleon until three o'clock in the afternoon of
the 9th. At the same time the Emperor received a
letter, in which the Duke of Vicenza said to him:
" Your Majesty will observe in the ultimatum of the
Emperor of Austria a few sacrifices of his pride; but
France is not asked to make any real ones; no diminution of your real glory is demanded. I pray you, Sire,

to put into the scales with peace all the chances of war. Consider the general irritation, the state in which Germany will be as soon as Austria shall have spoken; the lassitude of France, its noble devotion, and its sacrifices after the Russian disasters; listen to all the prayers uttered in France for peace; to those of your devoted servants, true Frenchmen, who, like me, are forced to tell you that it is necessary to allay the feverishness of Europe, to loosen this coalition by peace; and, whatever may be your projects, to await in the future what the greatest successes cannot give you to-day. Such a peace, made after our army has recovered its honor in several battles, can only be an honorable one. After so much time has been lost, the hours are numbered; one of the objects of this letter is to remind Your Majesty of this. There are too many passions urging war to allow of any delay in making peace. I repeat it, because such is my strong conviction; may Your Majesty thus decide; and be sure that in speaking to him as I do, I think less of the honor of signing it, than of the happiness of my country, and of that which Your Majesty will find in the certainty of having done something wise in policy, and worthy of his great character."

Austria left Napoleon only forty-eight hours to receive its ultimatum, to consider it, and to decide. If he accepted, it had to be done at once, and he had no opportunity to alter a single word. At the most, he had still time enough to accept everything and to send word to his plenipotentiaries. But he made the

mistake of supposing, in spite of what Metternich
said, that August 10 was not an absolutely final
date, and that negotiations might be still prolonged
to the 17th, the day set for the resumption of hostilities. Hence he thought it possible to send a proposition of his own to Prague. According to this,
Dantzic was to become a free city; the King of
Saxony be indemnified by territorial concessions for
the loss of the Grand Duchy of Warsaw; Austria
should acquire Illyria, but neither Istria nor Trieste;
the King of Denmark should have the integrity of
his states guaranteed; Napoleon was to continue to
hold the Hanseatic cities and the Protectorate of the
Confederation of the Rhine. The day and night of
August 9 were devoted to the preparation and drawing up of this document which could not be sent off
till too late, that is to say till the night of August
10.

This decisive and fatal 10th of August was a
holiday. In all Germany from the North Sea to the
frontiers of Bohemia, the French army was noisily
celebrating the Emperor's birthday a few days in
advance, Napoleon having preferred the earlier date,
the 10th, instead of the 15th, in view of the resumption of hostilities on the 17th, lest the rejoicings
should be too near the approaching bloodshed. The
15th would be taken up with thoughts of battles;
the 10th was to be devoted to the enjoyment of life,
— that life which so many brave men were soon to
lose. Away with gloomy forebodings! Everything

was alive with joy and merry-making. In every camp there were banquets in honor of Napoleon, and paid for by him. He dined with the marshals; the soldiers feasted together at tables set in the open air. They pledged France and the Emperor, drinking their glasses merrily, forgetful of dangers past, indifferent to those before them. Never had the soldiers been more confident of their invincibility. The conscripts who had left their villages but a few weeks before, already had the air of veterans. At Hamburg, Marshal Davout gave a dinner at which the Prince of Hesse, Commander-in-Chief of the Danish troops, was present, and in the evening there were fire-works in the Alster basin.

While the whole army was revelling, one brave soldier, a skilled diplomatist and great patriot, General Caulaincourt, the Duke of Vicenza, that sturdy hero who had never known fear on any battle-field, was trembling with anxiety. He had told the truth to his master with the noblest frankness. See-ing the gulf open before him, he awaited with pain-ful anxiety the despatch which might yet save everything. But the hours passed and nothing came. The day was terrible, but the night was still worse. Nine o'clock, ten o'clock, eleven o'clock, not a word! The fatal hour drew near. The old clocks of Prague struck twelve. Metternich had not deceived Napoleon; he had always told him that at midnight the die would be cast. The Russians and Prussians were sighing for that hour which in their thought

would be that of the deliverance of Europe. Up to
the last minute they had feared a reconciliation between the son-in-law and the father-in-law. They
knew that without Austria they were powerless, and
with Austria, capable of everything. It struck midnight: they did not lose a minute in announcing the
rupture of the armistice. Fires, the agreed signals,
were lit on mountains between Prague and Trachen-
berg. The Russian army, under the command of
Barclay de Tolly, broke camp and entered Bohemia.

It was not till the morning of August 11 that the
Duke of Vicenza was able to communicate to Metternich Napoleon's propositions. This tardy step was
without success, although the Austrian Minister gave
a faint hope that there might be a direct arrangement
with the Emperor Alexander who was to be at Prague
August 15. The Duke of Vicenza, uncertain whether
he ought to stay or leave, asked on the 11th for new
instructions, and particularly for full powers. He
declared, however, that Austria would not yield in
the matter of Trieste or the Hanseatic cities, or of
the territorial indemnity asked for Saxony. He
wrote on the 12th that if the Emperor Napoleon
would not insist on these three points, matters were
not yet desperate. The Emperor received this despatch on the 13th, and on the same day the Duke of
Bassano wrote at his dictation to the Duke of Vicenza:
" We refuse Trieste, because Trieste is Istria, and
for us Istria does not mean Istria but Venice. It is
a matter of honor for France to require suitable

indemnities for the King of Saxony. We demand that nothing shall be said about Hamburg or Lübeck. You may request communication to M. de Metternich of His Majesty's ultimatum. We send you the necessary powers for signing everything within two hours. . . . As soon as you are sure that there remains no possibility of agreement, you will depart at once; His Majesty is ·unwilling that you should remain to grace the Emperor Alexander's triumph at Prague. You will leave the city before his arrival. Moreover, His Majesty is determined not to lend his aid to the prolongation of the armistice, and he is quite as anxious for war as is Austria. He desires that you start from the principle that we are not sorry that this power should be in a state of war with us. The secret joy that His Majesty feels in a situation worthy of his genius, has not escaped the perception of M. de Bubna. He knows that we have on our side the advantage given by possessing all the pieces on the board. He recognizes, with all Europe, that we have all the power of genius. His Majesty, trusting in Providence, sees the vast designs it entrusts to him. He sees about him only grounds for confidence."

On the receipt of this despatch, monumental proof of that spirit of imprudence and error of which the poet speaks, the Duke of Vicenza was seized with deep melancholy. He wrote at once to the Duke of Bassano: " I confess that I had hoped for greater freedom; when one desires anything, one must desire also the means of doing it; I hope for another despatch to-night; if I have no other reason to go to M. de Metternich I have but faint hopes; I shall have all the inconvenience, and yet shall not be at fault. How many tears to-morrow may wipe away or call forth ! "

The Duke of Vicenza, whose patriotic anguish was at its height, wished to make one final appeal to his master, and in the night of August 15 he wrote to him this eloquent letter: " Weigh well in the balance, Sire, the real interests of France, those of your dynasty, those finally of a wise policy. Throw these into the same scales with the glory of war and its chances, and Your Majesty will make peace. Deign to persuade yourself, Sire, that this war is not like those that have preceded it. Every one has seen the faults, and, what is more, has calculated the risks of the course he has taken. Austria has not prepared for the removal of its archives from Vienna, and made other preparations, without foreseeing reverses in this general conflict. Russia runs no further risk, fighting as she does in the territory of others. Prussia is engaged in a life or death struggle in spite of herself. As for Germany, it will follow Austria, which feels only too well that its cause will be without appeal if the signal is once given. England defends herself in Spain ; but when the first cannon is fired, she will command everywhere, and Your Majesty will not be everywhere. If your armies meet with the slightest defeat, if even the battles, like the last ones, are without great results, who can foresee the consequences of this general reaction and assign a limit to this coalition?

" Confound your enemies, Sire, frustrate their plans, make peace, if only to let the storm pass by. This will calm them, and prevent their using the same means to excite enthusiasm. No sacrifice is asked of French honor, because nothing is asked of France. . . . France and the world ask peace of you. The peace which is proposed to you will be of more service to you than the happiest war. Deign, Sire, to listen to this prayer for peace, and permit a good Frenchman, a man who loves your true glory as much as his country, to present it to you."

Whether it was that these noble words had touched Napoleon's heart, or that he wished to assume an air of moderation because he knew that Prussia and Austria would not accept his last offer, the Emperor sent to the Duke of Vicenza full powers with a despatch conceding all Austria's demands. This despatch reached Prague August 15, at one in the morning. Five days sooner, it would have saved everything. The 15th, Metternich said to the Duke of Vicenza, " The propositions made by France to-day would have made peace on the 10th, because then Austria would have used all the force of its authority against the allies, if they had not accepted them. I repeat it, the 10th, the Emperor Napoleon might have given the world peace. . . . To-day we have one hundred and fifty thousand Russians among us, and we

have made agreements with them. The Russians
and Prussians have made a treaty with Sweden. We
have none yet with those two powers, and, on the
10th, we had none with any one. It is not our fault,
if you were unwilling to speak when we asked you
so to do." The Austrian Minister promised to communicate the French propositions to the allies, but
without any illusion as to the possibility of agreement. The same day, August 15, the Emperor of
Russia entered Prague, and the. Duke of Vicenza
withdrew to the castle of Königsraal, near the city.
The next day he learned that the Czar and the King
of Prussia had rejected the conditions proposed by
the Emperor Napoleon as inadmissible. Negotiations
were definitely broken off, and war was to decide
everything.

Meanwhile, what was going on in Paris? The
Emperor's birthday had been celebrated, August
15, with the customary festivities. The Empress-
Regent, preceded and followed by her lady of honor,
and the ladies and gentlemen in waiting, went to the
Throne Room, in the Tuileries. The Grand Chamberlain there presented the Princes, the Cardinals, the
High Officers of the Crown, the Grand Eagles of the
Legion of Honor, the Princes of the Confederation
of the Rhine, and all those who had the right of
admission. The Grand Master of Ceremonies then
introduced the Diplomatic Body and all went to the
chapel to hear mass and the singing of a *Te Deum.*
Then there was a great audience in the Emperor's

apartments, and in the evening the second act of the Opera *Dido* was given in the palace theatre. After the performance, Marie Louise appeared on a balcony, amid the applause of the crowd, and listened to a concert given on the terrace and looked at some fireworks which were set off in the Place de la Concorde. The Empress spent the night at Saint Cloud. The populace, who had no idea of what was going on at Prague, and still hoped for an early peace, celebrated the Emperor's birthday with great rejoicing; but it was for the last time.

August 25, Marie Louise's birthday, was celebrated with great splendor. Napoleon had wished her to go to Cherbourg to preside at the opening of the grand basin. Her journey thither was one succession of ovations. She entered Caen August 24 amid the roar of cannon and the ringing of bells. The town was decked as for a rustic festival; every house was adorned with leaves and garlands. In the morning of the 25th, the Empress passed beneath a triumphal arch raised at the crossing of the roads from Paris to Cherbourg, and from Bordeaux to Rouen. At nine in the evening, she reached Cherbourg. The next morning, the 26th, at eleven o'clock, she visited the Port Napoleon. Fifty young girls, dressed in white, threw rose-leaves beneath her feet; they were headed by the daughter of the sub-prefect of Cherbourg. This girl gave the Empress a basket containing several pieces of lace made in that region, and recited some verses composed for the occasion, which all her companions repeated in chorus.

The Empress, accompanied by the Minister of the Navy, went down into the basin, to admire the work before the waters of the ocean should be admitted for all time. Meanwhile, two English men-of-war were tacking to and fro at a distance of about four leagues. The new moon and the springtide determined the destruction of the dam for the next day. The sailors and a great number of workmen were employed in making three openings in the dam, through which the water, as it rose, should enter the basin. The 27th more than forty thousand persons filled all the neighboring approaches, and crowded the elevations, whence, as from the rising seats of an amphitheatre, they could witness the whole ceremony. Near the dam there had been set up a pavilion for the use of the Empress. She entered it at six in the evening, just as the sea began to enter the basin. All the cannon on the platforms about the Port Napoleon were set off, and rapturous applause broke out. The Bishop of Constance, with all his clergy, received the Empress with an address; then turning towards the further port, he recited the usual prayers and blessings. The sea rose majestically, and gradually filled the basin through the three openings. At nine in the evening the crash occurred, the dam gave way with a loud roar, and the basin was filled to the level of the sea.

During this grand festivity, Marie Louise seemed depressed. She had reached Cherbourg tired by the bad roads beyond Carentan, suffocated by the dust,

and with a bad cold on her chest. At Cherbourg
she heard of the resumption of hostilities. The
honors that met her were no consolation. September 5, at one in the morning, she was back at Saint
Cloud, and the memory of the ovations she had
received had not dispelled her uneasiness and her
gloom.

XVII

THE RESUMPTION OF HOSTILITIES.

THE war had begun again under formidable conditions. At the very moment when Marie Louise was presiding at the inauguration of the basin at Cherbourg, Napoleon was fighting the battle of Dresden, which lasted two days, August 26 and 27, 1813. After the first day he returned at midnight to the castle of the King of Saxony, and spent the whole night in dictating orders. At dawn he got on his horse again in vile weather; rain and blood were equally abundant. Moreau, forgetful of his laurels at Hohenlinden, had just taken service in the Russian army, and had had his two legs carried away by the side of the Emperor Alexander. That evening Napoleon returned victorious to Dresden, wet to the skin, as if he had fallen into the river. The King of Saxony, his staunch ally, kissed him tenderly, greeting him as his preserver. The battalion of the Guard, who had surrounded him during the battle, and had escorted him to the Saxon capital, was under arms the next morning, in the courtyard, in as good trim as at a review in the Place du

Carrousel. These brave soldiers, instead of resting after all their fatigues and perils, had spent the night cleaning and drying their uniforms about large fires. A word from the Emperor was their reward.

Marie Louise heard of the victory of Dresden before leaving Cherbourg. She wrote to the Baron of Méneval: "My health would be excellent were it not for my cough, which is very fatiguing; I shall not do anything for it until I get back to Paris. Besides, the good news I have heard to-day does me more good than any medicine. I hope this great victory will soon bring back the Emperor and, with him, peace."

This was fortune's last smile. Napoleon, intoxicated with his success, had no suspicion of the disasters that awaited him. The allies had retreated in disorder through all the roads of the mountains, which were cumbered with wounded and baggage. The conqueror, who had them pursued, counted, for the completion of their defeat, on General Vandamme's army corps, while he himself, by the fatigues and exposure of the battle, was compelled to return to Dresden. But August 30, at Culm, General Vandamme met with defeat, wherewith began the series of misfortunes which brought about the successive defections of Bavaria, Würtemberg, of all the Princes of the Confederation of the Rhine, and culminated in the catastrophe of Leipsic.

Napoleon spent the whole month of September in manœuvring in turn against the Prussian army of

Silesia and against the Austrian army of Bohemia, both of which declined battle. If he advanced against Blücher, the Austrians descended into Saxony; if he advanced against Schwarzenberg, the Prussians threatened Dresden. Meanwhile, Würtemberg was in open insurrection; the Cossacks had captured Cassel; the Saxons and Würtembergers were worked upon by secret societies, and the King of Bavaria, under the compulsion of his people, gave notice to the Emperor that he should be obliged to join the coalition. " My star grew dim," said Napoleon, speaking of this period at Saint Helena; " I felt the reins slipping through my fingers, and I was powerless. Nothing but a miracle could have saved us, and every day by one fatality after another our chances diminished. Ill will began to appear among us; fatigue and discouragement overcame the majority; my lieutenants became lax, awkward, careless, and consequently unsuccessful; they were no longer the men of the beginning of the Revolution, nor those of my successful days. The superior generals were tired; I had granted them too much respect, too many honors, too much wealth. They had tasted the cup of pleasure, and were anxious for ease at any price. The holy fire burned dim."

What discouraged all thinking men, soldiers as well as civilians, was the entry of Austria into the coalition. France might have been able to resist all its other enemies together; but to fight against their armies and the Austrian armies as well, was too much,

even for the bravest troops; even for a general like
Napoleon. His father-in-law had become the most
dangerous of his enemies, and yet, even when at war,
he wrote to him in the most courteous way, as in the
happiest days of the alliance. September 6, 1813, the
Emperor Francis replied thus: —

"MY BROTHER AND VERY DEAR SON-IN-LAW: I
have received the letter which Your Imperial Majesty
wrote to me August 29 last. The assurance it contains of the excellence of your health gives me the
keenest pleasure. My own is no less good, and I take
this opportunity to beg Your Imperial Majesty to
forward to my daughter, the Empress, the enclosed
letter, which I cannot entrust to better hands than
those of Your Imperial Majesty. I beg you to
receive the assurance of the high regard and of the
sincere personal attachment which I invariably feel
for you. Your Imperial Majesty's kind brother and
father-in-law,   FRANCIS."

A sad and curious contrast: these two sovereigns
styling each other brothers, congratulating each other
on their good health, while their people were cutting
one another's throats.

"Quidquid delirant reges, plectuntur Achivi."

September 11, 1813, between the battles of Dresden
and of Leipsic, Napoleon wrote to the Duke of Bassano: "The desire for news is so eager in Paris that
you must not lose a moment in sending it. Make
everything as moderate as possible, and admit nothing personal against the Emperor or Metternich."

Marie Louise, who adored her father, was very glad to receive a letter from him. " I cannot tell you," she wrote to him, September 23, " what happiness I felt when I found your letter in one from the Emperor. I was deeply touched by this attention. I had expected not to hear from you so long as the war lasted. This silence was very painful for me. . . . Every day I pray God to put an end to hostilities, for then I should be calm, and my feelings would no longer be divided. . . . The Emperor has promised to be careful to forward all my letters. I shall write as often as possible, for you know, dear father, that that is one of my greatest pleasures. I often think of you, and I am much touched by your satisfaction with my feelings. You see, dear father, that I do my best to follow the principles I have learned from your example." Marie Louise was mistaken when she hoped to be able to write to her father; she was not free to do this until the second half of November.

Meanwhile, however, the Emperor Francis wrote again to his son-in-law. From Töplitz, September 28, 1813, he wrote to him this letter: —

"MY BROTHER AND VERY DEAR SON-IN-LAW: I have received Your Imperial Majesty's letter dated September 25. Since Zamosz was not besieged by my troops, I could not interfere with the terms of surrender, which had to be agreed upon by the respective commanders. Your Majesty can have no doubt of my desire for peace. Out of my reign of twenty-one years, ten have been lost for the happiness of my nation. The paper which the Duke of Bassano sent August 18 to Count Metternich seems to prove that Your Majesty shares my conviction, which is also that of my allies, that Europe can no longer be wholly pacified, and that it would be better to take all the risks of the present war than to bring it to an end, while preserving the fear of new and inevitable disturbances. Simultaneously with the Emperor of Russia and the King of Prussia, I have forwarded to England Your Majesty's overtures. I expect shortly the answer of the Prince-Regent, and I shall speedly communicate it to Your Imperial Majesty. You are quite right in mentioning to me, among the motives that make peace desirable, the misfortunes of France. The welfare of the country in which my daughter is established will never be indifferent to me; and doubtless France has, no less than Austria and the rest of Europe, need of peace. If Your Majesty's intentions favor conditions which can make this general, France will owe to you its happiness, and Europe its tranquillity. Your Imperial and Royal Majesty's kind brother and father-in-law,

"FRANCIS."

Thus, then, at the very height of the war, the Emperor of Austria manifested regard for his son-in-law, and addressed him in almost friendly terms. We are convinced that at this moment he had no thought of the Bourbons, and that the idea of dethroning his daughter had not crossed his mind. Napoleon, whose chances were dwindling from day

to day, might yet have saved his crown. Doubtless
the integrity of his vast Empire was forever compro-
mised; but yet, we think he could have saved for
France its natural frontiers, and have prevented the
soil of the great nation from being profaned by
foreigners. At this time his father-in-law had not
become his irreconcilable enemy.

Marie Louise did not despair of a reconciliation
between her father, whom she adored, and her husband, to whom she was sincerely attached. It would
not be easy to suppose that the German ideas and
feelings, in which she had been brought up since her
tenderest infancy, had not left traces. But these she
carefully concealed; and possibly she did not confess
to herself anything like sympathy for the national
movement of Germany; at any rate, she discharged
her duties as Empress-Regent in the most irreproach-
able way, and no one in France, or elsewhere, ever
suspected her of placing filial duty above her duties
as wife and mother.

It was Marie Louise herself whom Napoleon
charged with making a solemn appeal to French
patriotism. October 8, 1813, she went in a great
procession to the Palace of the Senate. Preceded
by the heralds at arms, the masters of ceremonies,
the councillors of state, the grand eagles, the high
officers of the Empire, the Ministers, the ladies of
the bed-chamber, the ladies of the palace, the
Knight of Honor, the High Chamberlain, the Grand
Master of Ceremonies, the Princes holding high

positions, she drove from the Tuileries to the Luxembourg in the Coronation carriage, in which were also the Lady of Honor, the Duke of Conegliano, who discharged the duties of Colonel General, and Count Caffarelli, the Emperor's aide, Commander of the Guard. The equerries were on horseback about the carriage; troops escorted her, and salutes were fired. The high officers of the Senate and twenty-four Senators received the Empress at the outer door of the palace. The Empress, after resting in the apartments arranged for her reception, went to the hall where the Senate met, at the head of the procession. At her arrival all the Senators rose. She ascended the throne which was to the left of the Emperor's. One step lower to the right and left of the throne sat on chairs the Princes; to the right and left, on the steps, the Ministers and High Officers; before and behind the throne, on stools, sat the Chamberlain and the Grand Master of Ceremonies. Behind Marie Louise stood the Lady of Honor, the Duke of Conegliano, Count Caffarelli, the Knight of Honor, the First Equerry, the Lady of the Bed-chamber, the ladies of the palace, the Chamberlain and the equerries, the Master of Ceremonies; a little lower, the assistant masters of ceremonies, and the pages seated on the steps of the throne.

Amid a solemn silence the Empress-Regent read the following speech: "Senators: The principal powers of Europe, disgusted with the claims of

England, joined last year their armies with ours, to secure the peace of the world and the re-establishment of national rights. At the first chances of war slumbering passions awoke. England and Russia have drawn Prussia and Austria to their side. Our enemies desire to destroy our allies, to punish them for their fidelity. They wish to carry the war into our beautiful country to avenge the triumphs which bore our victorious eagles to the heart of their countries. I know better than any one, what our people would have to fear if they ever let themselves be conquered. Before ascending the throne, to which I was called by the choice of my august spouse, and by my father's wishes, I had the highest opinion of the courage and energy of this great people. This opinion has been daily strengthened by everything that I have seen. Sharing for four years my husband's most intimate thoughts, I know by what emotions he would be torn on a throne, disgraced, wearing a dishonored crown. Frenchmen, your Emperor, your country, your honor appeal to you!"

As soon as the Empress had stopped, warm applause broke out. Then the Count of Lacièpède arose and said: "Madame: Before proposing to the Senate measures regarding the decree of the Senate, I have the honor of begging Your Imperial Majesty to deign to allow me to offer her, in the name of my colleagues, the respectful homage of all the feelings with which we are inspired by seeing Your Majesty preside over the Senate, and by hearing the memor-

able words she has spoken from the throne. With
what gratitude, with what pious care we shall ever
guard their memory!"

The Archchancellor then received the Empress's
orders before giving the floor to the Minister of War,
and to Count Regnaud who presented the outline of
a decree of the Senate proposing a draft of two hundred and eighty thousand men, one hundred and
twenty thousand of the classes of 1814 and previous
years, in the departments which had not contributed
to the last draft of thirty thousand men, and one hundred and sixty thousand of the conscription of 1815.
Then the Empress returned to the Tuileries in great
pomp.

In official circles every means was tried to kindle
enthusiasm. October 17, after mass, Marie Louise
gave an audience, in the Hall of Mars, at the Palace
of Saint Cloud, to the Municipal Council of Paris.
The Prefect of the Seine read the following address:
" Madame : What Frenchman can remain deaf to the
voice of the Emperor, to the appeal of his country,
and of honor? The appeal which Your Majesty has
just made has found an echo in every heart; the
need is felt of manifesting those generous sentiments
which in all time have been the proudest possession
of France. This esteem which Your Majesty had
long since conceived for this great people, the love
she feels for it, the hopes to which she has given
birth, will not be deceived; the august daughter of
Maria Theresa cannot summon in vain the courage

and energy of her people; the French will have no
rivals in their love for their Sovereigns; they will
count no sacrifices, no efforts when honor commands;
they cannot live without glory, and their Emperor's
crown shall never be despoiled of a single laurel.
This is the unanimous oath sworn to to-day throughout the Empire; these are the feelings which the
good city of Paris expresses, in laying at Your
Majesty's feet the tribute of its respect and devotion.
Madame, it is by redoubling their zeal and affection, it
is by turning their eyes to this august throne, to
which Your Majesty has brought with every virtue,
the noble courage of her ancestress, that the inhabitants of the good city of Paris are inspired as faithful subjects, with all that they owe to their Prince
and to their country."

While Marie Louise was thus receiving the protestations of devotion which, in less than a year, were
to be repeated, not to her, but to the Bourbons, the
Emperor was fighting the bloodiest battle of modern
times, which the Germans call the Battle of Nations,
— the battle of Leipsic. It was fought from the 16th
to the 18th of October. Napoleon's army, consisting
of one hundred and forty thousand men, contended
heroically with a hostile force of three hundred thousand men. In the centre, and to the right, it maintained its position; but on the left treachery made it
lose ground. There, forty thousand men were crushed
by one hundred thousand men and three hundred cannon, commanded by Bernadotte — the former Mar-

shal of France, who, with the Emperor's permission, had become the Crown Prince of Sweden — when twelve thousand Saxons, forming nearly a third of the left, ran over to the Russians, entering their ranks, and at Bernadotte's request, discharged their artillery on the French, their fellow-soldiers whom they had just abandoned. Night put a stop to the carnage. Napoleon was beaten.

Retreat was imperative. This was such a cruel blow to the Emperor's pride that he was nearly prostrated. An enormous mass of wounded, cannons, baggage, and about ninety thousand men, still under arms, were hemmed in against the city of Leipsic, between two rivers with but one narrow bridge, beyond which ran a defile half a league long across deep marshes. To make the retreat sure, it was necessary to make many bridges, which could easily have been constructed in the night of October 19. Men and material were abundant; but Napoleon, although he was told that a vast and disorderly throng encumbered the approaches to the Elster bridge, took no precautions. At noon of the 19th he went to bid farewell to his unfortunate ally, the King of Saxony, who was in the middle of the city. Meanwhile, the suburbs were invaded on all sides. A new battle began on the ramparts, in the streets, from house to house. The crowd was so impenetrable that Napoleon, after leaving the King of Saxony, could not make his way out of Leipsic through the Lindenau gate. Compelled to retrace his steps, he went around the city along the boulevards, and thus got to the Elster bridge, where the crowd was so dense that his escort could only make their way through by violence. As soon as he had crossed the bridge, he alighted, and gave orders that it was not to be destroyed till after the passage of the army corps and of the artillery guarding the approach to it.

The Elster bridge was destined to be as fatal as that of the Beresina. When the defection of the Baden troops gave them command of the city, the allies hastened to the bridge. Then the French sappers who had charge of blowing it up, thought the time had come, and fired the mine.

The French rear-guard, consisting of fifteen thousand men, almost as many wounded, and with an immense quantity of wagons, thus saw itself cut off from the rest of the army which had already crossed, and they uttered a long, despairing cry. It was a terrible scene. One truly brave man, whom the Emperor the evening before had made marshal for his heroic conduct, Prince Poniatowski, plunged on horseback into the current of the Elster, to gain the other bank. He was drowned. It seemed as if the fortune of France and of Poland sank at the same time beneath the wave. The glorious death of the Polish hero made a deep impression, even then ; when, after such fearful slaughter, after a battle like that of Leipsic, where a hundred and ten thousand men were killed or wounded, death seemed a familiar story. A picture of Horace Vernet's and a song of Béranger's have combined to make of the noble victim plunging into the fatal waters of the Elster one of the most famous and most touching of legends.

This defeat at Leipsic was for Napoleon a combination of grief and surprise. Of all the battles he had fought, this was the first that he had lost. Up to that time he could boast that if he had been conquered by the elements, he had never been conquered by man; and now he was to know for himself the sufferings he had inflicted on others. He was to learn by personal experience the bitterness of defeat, the anguish of retreat, the desperation of useless bloodshed. War, which up to that time had been a source of gratification to his unparalleled pride, now showed to him its horrors, with its humiliations and inexpressible anguish. The hour had struck when he could make tardy reflections on the emptiness of genius and glory, on the intoxication of pride that had turned his head. He was obliged to acknowledge to himself that everything that his true friends, Caulaincourt, Otto, Narbonne, and many others had told him, was perfectly true. In his own heart, he knew that his boasted infallibility was a mere idle dream; that he had judged men and circumstances wrongly; that he had blundered as a soldier and a diplomatist; that at the Congress of Prague he had done wrong to refuse the generous conditions offered by Austria; that Metternich had predicted to him at Dresden what had just happened; that every needed warning had been given to him in due time, and that, in fact, he was alone to blame. For a character as proud and impetuous as that of the great Emperor, it is easy to imagine what such a confession, wrung from him by the course of events, must have cost him.

At certain moments the fallen giant seemed dazed and stupefied, unable to advance or to draw back. He awaited the issue with a sort of fatalism. He exposed himself like a simple soldier, as if he saw in death a solution, an escape. He was tortured by the thought of appearing defeated and humiliated, before his wife, his Ministers, and the Parisians. It seemed to him like descent from the capitol to the potters' field. So accustomed was he to victories and ovations that every road which did not pass under a triumphal arch appeared to him like one of shame. Without glory he could not breathe. He had as yet no experience of misfortune. He had so long been the favorite of Fortune that he was perhaps more surprised than grieved by finding her fickle. This struck him as something abnormal, inexplicable. The thought that with a little moderation he might have been spared his defeats, and that by giving up a little, he might have kept everything, distressed him beyond measure. His sole consolation was to say that he had been betrayed; but every one had predicted to him this treachery of Germany, of its diplomatists and its generals. In fact, he had been the architect of his own ruin.

October 19 he slept at the mill of Lindenau, where he stopped, utterly worn out, and was sound asleep when he was awakened by the news of the Elster disaster. At first he refused to believe it, but when he was convinced of it, he had to continue his humiliating retreat without delay. On his way he saw once more the battlefield of Lützen where he had gained that brilliant but barren victory. October 21 he passed, silent and morose, between the memories of Rossbach and Auerstadt. At Erfurt, the 23d, he recalled the memorable interview of 1808. According to General de Ségur it was noticed that while he was dictating his orders he turned his eyes away from the place where he had seen the Emperor Alexander bow before his fortune, proud of his friendship, and enthusiastic over his glory. The retreat continued amid unceasing obstacles. The troops, in greater and greater confusion, were harassed by hunger, fatigue, and sufferings of every sort. Napoleon narrowly escaped being prevented from crossing the Rhine. At the pass of Hanau, fifty thousand Austrians and Bavarians blocked his path; he thought that he was lost. He exposed himself recklessly to the shells bursting all about him, refusing to seek shelter. General Drouot's artillery saved him; he hurled the enemy back, and continued his journey. November 2 he was at Mayence. His whole army, now reduced to sixty thousand men, had crossed the Rhine.

" This memorable campaign," Napoleon said at Saint Helena, " will be famous as the triumph of the innate courage of the French youth, of the crafty

intrigues of English diplomacy, of the intelligence
of the Russians, of the shamelessness of the Austrian
Cabinet. It will mark the period of the disorganization of political societies, that of the severance
between sovereigns and their peoples, and finally of
the decay of the primary military virtues: fidelity,
loyalty, honor. . . . What is very remarkable is
that the kings, the soldiers, and the people had in
fact nothing to do with these infamies, which were
the work of a few military intriguers and political
desperadoes who, under the specious pretext of
removing the stranger's yoke and of recovering
national independence, simply sold and delivered
their rulers to rival and covetous cabinets. It was
the King of Saxony, the most honest man that ever
wielded a sceptre, who was robbed of half his province; it was the King of Denmark, so true to his
promises, who lost his crown. Yet that is the return
to morality, its triumph and distributive justice, in
this world! However, I take pleasure in repeating
for the honor of humanity, and even of thrones, that
amid all these infamies, there were also unequalled
virtues. Not for a moment did I have to complain
of a single one of the Princes, my allies. The good
King of Saxony remained faithful to me to the end;
the King of Bavaria loyally sent me word that he
was no longer master; the King of Würtemberg's
generosity was especially remarkable. The Prince of
Baden yielded only to force, and at the last moment.
All, I must say in justice, gave me warning in time,
in order that I might make ready for the storm."

This remark of Napoleon's is very striking. It is certain that the German Princes manifested less haste and shamelessness in their defection than did the French Senators.

The Princes of the Confederation of the Rhine had been anxious to keep their promises to the Emperor, but they were prevented by the action of the universities and by the popular uprising. " To the fervor of the *Tugendbund*," says General de Ségur, "everything seemed equally honorable : vile spying, heroic devotion, perfidious enticing, sublime poetry, infamous treachery; it inspired, lifted up, ennobled everything, and with glory or effrontery assumed every form." Professor Fichte in 1813 was lecturing on duty. He closed thus: " The course will be suspended until the end of the campaign. We shall then resume it when our country has become free once more, or we shall have died in trying to regain our liberty." A poet, transforming Queen Louisa of Prussia into a symbolic shade, said of her: " How sweetly she sleeps! Ah! may you sleep until the day when the people shall wash in blood the rust from its sword! Awake! Be the angel of liberty and of vengeance!" Körner composed at the bivouac the hymn of the *Lyre and the Sword* : —

" *The Cavalier.* Tell me, my good sword, sword of my side, why to-day your glance is so bright? You look at me with the eye of love, my good sword, you who make my joy; hurrah!

" *The Sword.* It is because a brave soldier carries me : that is why my glance is bright; it is because I am the strength of a free man, that I am joyous; hurrah!

"*The Cavalier.* Yes, my sword; yes, I am a free man; and I love you from the bottom of my heart; I love you like my betrothed; I love you like a dear mistress.

"*The Sword.* And I have given myself to you. To you I devote my life and my soul of steel! Ah! if we are betrothed, when will you say to me, 'Come, come, my beloved mistress'?"

As Chateaubriand said: "The man whose life was a dithyramb in action fell only when the poets of Germany had sung and drawn their sword against their rival, Napoleon, the armed poet."

Alas! what is more lamentable than this colossal struggle in which such a vast sum of heroism was spent on both sides, and so many brave young men, inspired by the purest and noblest sentiments of the human heart, succumbed in the flower of youth, at this beginning of the nineteenth century, of which they should have been the ornament and the honor! A German cannot withhold his admiration for these young French conscripts, who in a day acquired the intrepidity of the sturdiest veterans. Frenchmen, too, admire the young German students, soldiers, and poets, who so bravely left their universities for the camps. Such adversaries were made to esteem and understand one another, and they slew one another! Then if the blood that was shed had been fertile, if the conquerors had become free! But no; the sovereigns of the coalition were to forget the victory once gained, the liberal promises which they had lavished, and, in a word, it was the people who were to suffer for their kings!

XVIII.

THE END OF 1813.

WHEN Napoleon had once more crossed the Rhine and was once more within his Empire, at Mayence, November 2, 1813, he suffered from a despondency which he could hardly conceal. This was not one of the triumphant returns to which he had accustomed his people. The hero of so many battles had been defeated at Leipsic. He dreaded meeting his young wife, in whose eyes he had ceased to be the incarnation of success. Instead of hastening to Saint Cloud, he waited six days at Mayence, leaving it on the 8th, at one in the morning, without sending word to Marie Louise by telegraph.

The same day, a Sunday, the Empress was receiving at Saint Cloud, in the Hall of Mars, after mass, deputations from six cities. That from Antwerp said, " Your good city of Antwerp, the recipient of so many favors from the government, would, Madame, deem itself wanting in the solemn demands of gratitude if it did not hasten to lay before the throne the expression of the limitless devotion it feels for Your Majesty." The deputation from Brussels expressed

itself as follows, " The Belgians, united to the desti-
nies of this illustrious Empire, have not forgotten the
wars and the bloody revolutions to which their weakness had exposed them.   They know that they would
not have suffered these calamities if they had formed
part of this great people.   We, the mouth-pieces of
your good city of Brussels, come to-day to assure
Your Majesty that she will always find them ready
to shed their blood to preserve for the French name
the glory it owes to the Emperor's genius, and ready
to offer their fortunes in defence of the Empire against
those who dare to threaten it."   The deputation from
Ghent said, " Great prodigies ought to announce a
century, that posterity, which always begins early
for the founders of empires, already calls the century
of Napoleon.   The Belgian provinces, always proud
to be part of this glorious Empire, hasten to outdo
the sacrifices of the other provinces.   The good city
of Ghent which boasts of having been the birthplace
of Charles V., one of the most illustrious ancestors of
Your Imperial Majesty, proudly shows these glorious
feelings."   The deputation from Cologne said, " The
memorable words uttered by Your Majesty in the
Senate have deeply touched our hearts, and have
kindled the most ardent enthusiasm.   No, the country's hopes shall not be deceived, and the French
shall not have been called in vain to conquer the
enemies of the Empire, the enemies of peace.   Every
citizen will fly to the field of honor and, under the
banners of our august leader, will join the host of

brave men who fight for the glory and for the peace of the world." This, even at the end of 1813, was the language of the inhabitants of Belgium and of .the banks of the Rhine. Marie Louise, who only knew vaguely of the recent disasters, was still surrounded by courtiers and flatterers, who hid the truth from her and promised unflinching devotion.

Napoleon, although defeated, could not make up his mind to abandon the airs of a conqueror. He wanted his return, gloomy as it was, to wear a glorious appearance. The eve of his departure from Mayence, when Marie Louise was receiving at Saint Cloud the deputation of the good Belgian and Rhenish cities, an aide-de-camp of the Prince of Neufchâtel reached Paris with twenty battle-flags of the enemy which Napoleon sent to the Empress. The arrival of these flags had already been announced by the Emperor to Marie Louise in a letter from Frankfort, dated November 1, 1813. It ran as follows: —

"MADAME, AND MY VERY DEAR WIFE: I send you twenty flags captured by my armies at the battles of Wachau, Leipsic, and Hanau. This is a mark of respect which I like to pay to you. I hope you will see in it a token of my great satisfaction with your conduct during the regency which I entrusted to you."

Napoleon was anxious that the Parisians should learn at the same time from the *Moniteur* his return and the reception of the flags. Defeated or victorious, he always understood how to arrange picturesquely the events of his career.

November 9, at five in the afternoon, Marie Louise, who was quietly installed at Saint Cloud, where the utter calm presented a marked contrast to the distant rumors of war, had no idea of the moment when her husband would return, when suddenly two carriages were heard driving into the courtyard. It was Napoleon arriving. He had already ascended the staircase when he saw his wife before him. He kissed her affectionately; she burst into tears, trembling with emotion. Then the little King of Rome was brought, and his father greeted him most tenderly. Every one was moved by this pathetic spectacle. Napoleon said nothing about the way the campaign had turned out, and had not a word of blame for his father-in-law's desertion.

November 14 there arrived at Paris a messenger from the allies, bearing an important communication; a peace overture, which, in our opinion, still offered Napoleon a chance of safety. It was the Baron of Saint Aignan, the Emperor's Equerry, and his Minister Plenipotentiary at Weimar. At the entry of the allies into that city, M. de Saint Aignan had at first been treated like a prisoner of war; but then he was carried to Frankfort where all the principal Ministers of the sovereigns of the coalition were assembled, and after he had been treated with the utmost respect, he had been commissioned to carry to Napoleon a proposition leaving to France its natural frontiers. Was this a serious proposition or a feint? Opinion is divided on this question. "Being perfectly familiar with the state of mind of the French public," says Metternich in his Memoirs, " I was convinced that to avoid irritating it, to offer it rather an allurement which would be welcome to every one, it was better to flatter the national pride, and to speak of the Rhine, the Alps, and the Pyrenees as the natural boundaries of France. In the aim of still more isolating Napoleon, and at the same time of acting on the mind of the army, I proposed attaching the offer of immediate negotiations to the idea of natural boundaries. The Emperor Francis having approved of my project, I submitted it to the Emperor of Russia and to the King of Prussia. Both feared that Napoleon, confiding in the chances of the future, would take some prompt and energetic resolution, and refuse the proposition in order thus to determine the situation. I succeeded in inspiring the two sovereigns with my own conviction that Napoleon would never voluntarily adopt this course."

The Baron of Saint Aignan saw the Emperor at Saint Cloud, November 15. " This time at last," exclaimed Napoleon, " the English are willing to treat." At this moment the Czar, and especially the Emperor of Austria, did not desire the return of the Bourbons. France still overawed the allies. They dared cross neither the Pyrenees nor the Rhine. Ignorant that they were no longer faced by the France of 1792, full of ardor and enthusiasm, but a France wearied, exhausted, and discouraged, they were full of hesitation. The wisest of their generals

said that a peace in conformity with the Frankfort
propositions would be for the sovereigns of the coalition a confirmation at once honorable and prudent.
What strength Napoleon would have had, if, at once
acting on the propositions that had been made to him
he had accepted them unreservedly, and had immediately convoked the Legislative Body to announce
the good news! This would have secured for him
the approval of public opinion, not merely in France,
but in all Europe. Instead of that, what did he do?
He replied November 16, but his answer was evasive.
He designated Mannheim as the place for the meeting of the future Congress, but he threw no light on
the propositions that had been made. He feared to
show by a hasty agreement the impotence to which
he was reduced, and France, even with its natural
frontiers, seemed too narrow for him. The thought
of having squandered in vain so many human lives
beyond the Rhine, the Alps, and the Pyrenees, disturbed and tormented him like a feebleness, a humiliation, a remorse. He thought that there would
always be time enough for such a confession. Having been so long accustomed to be the master over
others, this haughty sovereign could not be satisfied
with being master at home. Hence he let slip through
his fingers the last moment of respite that fortune
granted him before leaving him forever; and when,
December 2, he at last decided to accept the Frankfort propositions, the allies, who had learned the true
state of affairs, declined to grant them. Traitors

within the Empire had informed them of the royalist intrigues, and had told them that France, divided against itself, must surely fall their prey. Napoleon, when he opened his eyes to the light and saw the necessity of peace, had wished to confide the portfolio of Foreign Affairs to Prince Talleyrand; but he declined it, because the Emperor wished him to cease being Vice-Grand Elector on resuming the Ministry. It was then by means of this petty detail of etiquette that a combination failed which might have altered many things. Desirous of giving Europe, and especially Russia, a pledge of peace, Napoleon, November 20, appointed the sagacious and peace-loving Duke of Vicenza Minister of Foreign Affairs; this was the man who had already given him many good counsels, and he was highly thought of by the Emperor Alexander. But it was too late; as at the Congress of Prague, he had let the opportunity slip by. The time for diplomacy had ended; nothing was left but a final appeal to arms. This terrible catastrophe, of which no one had thought for a long time, so improbable did it seem, the invasion so terrible for a conquering race, was now threatening.

Marie Louise, anxious and tormented, looked forward to the future with gloom. To the letter she had received from her father through the Baron of Saint Aignan, she replied: "Heaven grant that we may soon renew our intimate and regular correspondence; it would be a symptom of peace and calm; it would be the end of my uneasiness. You cannot imagine how much I am distressed by the thought that you and my husband are enemies, while you both have qualities which ought to bring you together. The Emperor is wonderfully well. I found him stouter and better than before he left for the war. . . . We are soon going into the city; I am sorry; for the air of Saint Cloud is better than that of Paris."

The etiquette was just the same; the manners of the courtiers continued as obsequious as ever; yet the Empress detected on their faces signs of uneasiness. The anniversary of the coronation and of the battle of Austerlitz was celebrated for the last time. Saturday, December 4, 1813, there were free performances in all the Paris theatres. Sunday, the 5th, a *Te Deum* was sung at Notre Dame, and the Parisians were invited to illuminate their houses in the evening. The tragedy of *Ninus II.* was given the same evening in the theatre at the Tuileries. The palace and the city were ablaze with countless lights, but they contrasted strikingly with the deep gloom that possessed nearly every one. All the activity of the police could scarcely prevent the expression of the general discontent. All were unanimous in blaming Napoleon for not making peace after the victories of Lützen and Bautzen. He was criticised as much as he had been previously praised. The officials were dejected, dispirited; and Marie Louise, alarmed for herself, for her husband, for her son, no longer spoke, but was always in tears.

December 19 Napoleon opened the Legislative
Body in person. He started from the Tuileries in
great pomp. The procession passed through the garden, the Place de la Concorde, and over the bridge.
He got out of his carriage at the foot of the steps,
but was not received with the usual enthusiastic
applause. The Empress, accompanied by Queen
Hortense and surrounded by the officers of her household, was already in the gallery, opposite her husband's throne. In the midst of a stony silence he
uttered a majestic but mournful speech, which was
more likely to discourage than to reassure his hearers.
" Brilliant victories," he said, " have adorned the
French arms in this campaign; unexampled defections have rendered these victories useless; everything has turned against us. France itself would be
in danger, were it not for the energy and the harmony of the French. . . . I have never lost my
head in prosperity, adversity would find me superior
to its assaults. I have often given peace to nations
that had lost everything. With a part of my con-
quests I have built thrones for kings who have abandoned me. I had conceived and carried out great
designs for the world's prosperity! . . . As monarch
and father, I feel that peace adds to the security of
thrones as well as to that of families. Negotiations
have begun with the united powers. I have consented
to the preliminary propositions which they presented.
I had hoped that before the opening of your session,
the Mannheim Congress would have assembled; but

new delays, for which France is not to blame, have retarded this moment, anxiously expected by the whole world." Napoleon closed with a phrase which was only too frequent in his speeches: "My people," he said, with a pride unbroken by misfortune, "cannot fear that their Emperor's policy will ever betray the national glory; for my part, I am confident that the French will ever be worthy of themselves and of me."

Two days after this speech was uttered, the invasion began. The allies crossed the Rhine, December 21, between Basle and Schaffhausen. The 31st the Army of Silesia, commanded by Blücher, also crossed it between Mannheim and Coblentz. In 1814 happened what was to happen in 1870; for, unfortunately, experience is vain. France, which had thought of nothing but an offensive war, was totally unprepared for a defensive. The idea that the foreigner could pollute the soil of the great nation, — the sacred soil, — had never crossed her mind. In 1870 our officers had all the maps of Germany; none had maps of France. In 1814 the fortresses on the Elbe and the Vistula had been thoroughly equipped, but no one had thought of the French fortresses. Magdeburg and Hamburg had been supplied with what should have been at Strasburg and Metz; Alessandria with what should have been at Grenoble.

General de Ségur describes the beginning of the invasion in this touching passage: "We passed," he says, "through the citadel of Phalsbourg as easily as if it had been a village; not a gun was in its place; not a sentinel was to be seen; not one ' Who goes there?' stopped us; as if there had been no ramparts, gates, or garrison. Enraged by this indifference, I bade the first drummer I met sound the alarm, announcing the enemy which was pursuing me. The commander at last woke up and closed the gates. He said he had been forgotten by the Minister, and had received no orders; that his garrison was insufficient, without food, without a single gun-carriage in proper condition." Then speaking of the spirit of the army, the brave general went on sadly : " What had become of the joyous, brilliant animation of our sturdy and victorious young men? What a change had come about! Their faces marked with wounds and vigils now appeared grave and careworn! Their once calm and confident brows were now bald, or their hair was bleached, not by age, but by the fatigues of distant wars; and all were now depressed by the pain of seeing our country, hitherto victorious, threatened in its turn by the disgrace and the horrors of conquest! There was the same difference in their talk: instead of merry stories, and voices loud with confidence, there were muttered phrases, full to be sure of jests, but these were forced, bitter, derisive even of ourselves, as if anticipating those of the enemy, at last our master, and ready doubtless to repay with usury all the humiliations that for more than fourteen years we had inflicted on them."

It was not the army alone that suffered from this depression; all France, worn out, exhausted by conscription and taxes, shared the same feeling. Never had there been seen so many mothers in mourning. Never had war — war hated by mothers (*bella matribus detestata*) — appeared in a more terrible light. It inspired the same horror as the guillotine in old times. No one desired it more. A committee, consisting of Messrs. Lainé, Raynouard, Gallois, Flaugergues, Maine de Biran, had been appointed to examine the diplomatic documents.

This committee felt the influence of public opinion. " Our evils are at their height," exclaimed M. Raynouard; "the country is threatened at every frontier; commerce is extinct; industry is at the point of death; conscription has become an odious blight; a cruel and aimless war periodically destroys the young men. It is time for thrones to strengthen themselves, and for France to escape the reproach of carrying everywhere revolutionary torches." Napoleon, impatient of opposition, was very indignant.

"Your committee," he said to the deputies, "has been guided by the spirit of the Girondists. Instead of assisting me, you aid the stranger. Instead of uniting, you divide us. Is this the moment to speak of abuses, when two hundred thousand Cossacks are crossing the frontiers? The question is not about individual liberty and safety, but about national independence. Were you not satisfied with the Constitution? You should have asked for another four years ago. . . . And in whose name do you speak? I alone am the real representative of the people; four times I have received the votes of five millions of citizens. An attack on me is an attack on the nation!"

And, December 31, he adjourned the Legislative Body indefinitely. The previous evening, its president, the Duke of Massa, had communicated to the questors this letter: —

"GENTLEMEN : The Master of Ceremonies on duty has the honor of informing you that Saturday next, January 1, at midday, His Majesty the Emperor and King will receive in the Throne Room, in the Palace of the Tuileries, the congratulations of the Legislative Body. Full dress will be worn. After this audience the Legislative Body will betake itself to the Diana Gallery to meet Her Majesty the Empress as she passes through, and to pay their respects to her."

XIX

THE BEGINNING OF 1814.

THE *Moniteur* of January 2, 1814, contained the
following lines: "To-day, January 1, before
mass, the Emperor being in the Throne Room, the
Master of Ceremonies on duty, assuming the functions of the Grand Master of Ceremonies, after receiving His Majesty's commands, introduced the Senate,
the Council of State, the Legislative Body, the Court
of Cassation, and the Municipal Council of Paris.
These different bodies were led by a Master of
Ceremonies and an aide, and were presented to His
Majesty: the Senate and the Legislative Body by the
Prince Vice-Grand Elector; the Court of Cassation
and the Municipal Council of Paris by the Prince
Archchancellor of the Empire. On leaving the
Throne Room, these bodies went to the Diana Gallery, to form in line for the Empress to pass through,
and to present their respects to Her Majesty."

The *Moniteur* made no mention of the address, at
once familiar and alarming, with which the Emperor
had received them. "What do you want?" he burst
forth, assuming a fury which, in fact, he did not feel,

for he was perfectly master of himself. "What do you want? To take possession of the power? But what would you do with it? What one of you could exercise it? Have you forgotten the Constituent Assembly, the Legislative Assembly, the Convention? Should you be any more fortunate than they? Would not all of you perish on the scaffold like Guadet, Vergniaud, Danton? And besides, what does France need at this moment? Not an Assembly, not orators, but a general. Is there one among you? And then where is your commission? France knows me. Does it know you? . . . The throne is not merely a combination of four pieces of gilded wood, covered with velvet. The throne is a man, and I am that man, with my will, my character, and my renown. . . . You wanted to throw mud in my face. I am, you must know, a man who may be killed, but who cannot be insulted. . . . Besides, I don't defy you all. Eleven-twelfths of you are good men; but they let themselves be led by mischiefmakers. Go back to your departments, tell France that, whatever may be said, it is against her that war is made as much as against me, and that she must defend, not my person, but her own national existence."

When he had returned to his apartments the Emperor summoned the Archchancellor Cambacérès, the Duke of Bassano, and the Duke of Rovigo. The last-named says in his Memoirs: "He was not at all angry with the Legislative Body; he only complained

in a general way that it was impossible to form an
Assembly which should proceed freely in the same
direction as the government which it always looked
on as an enemy; and he pointed out that it was while
showing the best intentions that King Louis XVI.
had been gradually led to the scaffold."

At heart the Emperor was rather saddened than
enraged. " I need two months," he said ; " if I had had
them, the enemy would not have crossed the Rhine.
This may become serious, but I can do nothing about
it alone. If I receive no help, I shall succumb. Then
they will see whether it is with me that they are
angry." When the Senators who were sent to the
various provinces as extraordinary commissioners, to
arouse the zeal and enthusiasm of the populace, came
to take leave of him, he spoke to them with touching
pathos, laying aside his pride to confess his faults at
last. " I have been too fond of war," Louis XIV.
had said on his deathbed. " I have made war too
much," said Napoleon. " I had formed vast projects;
I wished to secure for France the control of the world.
I was mistaken; these projects were not in propor-
tion to the numerical strength of the population. I
must expiate the mistake of relying too much on my
good-fortune, and I shall expiate it. I shall make
peace, such as the circumstances command, and this
peace will not be mortifying for me. I, who made
the mistake, must suffer, and not France. She has
made no blunders ; she has lavished her blood for
me ; she has refused me no sacrifice. Let her then

have all the glory of my undertakings! I leave it to her. As for me, I reserve for myself the honor of showing a difficult courage, that of renouncing the greatest ambition in the world."

It is easy to understand what a man like Napoleon must have suffered in making such avowals, which, it should be said, were not made public. At the Tuileries, etiquette went on as smoothly as ever; but to those who examined it closely, it was evident that the machinery was only moving by the momentum it had acquired. Like France, the court was overwhelmed by a lassitude, both moral and physical. Enthusiasm was dead, except in the soul of some brave veterans and fiery youths who deserved to fight under better conditions. In vain was the attempt made to rekindle the sacred fire, by recalling the enthusiasm of 1792, by reviving patriotic songs, and by having played on the organs in the streets the air of the *Marseillaise,* to which had been adapted words in honor of Napoleon. But as Count Miot de Mélito says: " The grand ideas of liberty and equality which had moved the body of the nation were extinct. The affection for the throne, the love of the sovereign which previously filled their place, did not exist in behalf of a recent dynasty. The government alone spoke, and there was no response. Languor pervaded every heart; the conscription had exhausted the strength of the nation. What could be done with such elements? Even those who employed them knew the general powerlessness, and the officials sent into the departments could not inspire a confidence which they did not feel themselves. The army alone remained devoted and faithful to its leader; its defeats had not affected its affection; but the generals began to make claims, and to manifest discontent."

Napoleon distrusted his brothers, his Ministers, his generals. He had a foreboding of speedy defections. Death on the field of battle did not seem to him the worst solution. What he most feared was the humiliation of France. The thought that he might leave it smaller than he had received it from the hands of the Directory troubled him like a horrible nightmare. He could not think of it for fear that he might go mad with shame and grief. He suffered cruelly; but, respecting his young wife's peace of mind, he kept from her all his mental anguish. He avoided speaking to her about the Emperor Francis and Austria. In her presence, he was calm and majestic, as in the days of his supremacy. He even tried to be gentler, more attentive than usual. He regarded it as a point of honor to lose no jot of his coolness and dignity. As Count Mollien, Minister of the Treasury in 1814, remarked, he alone did not change when everything about him changed; amid the many ruins which foretold his own, he continued impassible, trying to impress others with the confidence which he endeavored to assume himself. He let no one suspect that one day he might be abandoned by his wife. He liked to have others believe, and possibly to believe himself, that she

would always be a model of virtue and fidelity.
He proceeded without the slightest hesitation to in-
vest her with the duties of Regent. Regarding her
as forever a Frenchwoman, he preferred her to his
own brothers, and treated her as if there had been
no change in the Austrian policy.

For her part, it never occurred to Marie Louise to
distinguish between her cause and her husband's.
She was, we are sure, determined to perform all her
duties as Empress, wife, mother, and to observe most
scrupulously the oath which she was about to take
as Regent to the Empire. She was told, besides,
that the Duke of Vicenza was resuming diplomatic
negotiations with the allies; that the Napoleonic
dynasty was immovable; that France would certainly
preserve its natural frontiers; and that a reconciliation between her father and her husband was imminent. This hope was her consolation.

Marie Louise had written an affectionate and
respectful letter to the Emperor Francis, to send him
her good wishes for the new year; to which he at
once sent the following answer: —

"December 26, 1813. Dear Louise: I received
yesterday your letter of December 12, and I am glad
to hear that you are well. I thank you for your
kind wishes for the new year; they are very precious
to me, because I know you. I send you mine with
all my heart. As to peace, be sure that I desire it
no less than you do, than France does, and, I hope,
than your husband does. In peace alone can happi-

ness and security be found. My views are moderate. I desire everything that can make peace lasting; but in this world wishes are not enough. I have solemn duties to perform with respect to my allies, and unfortunately, the question of the future and, I hope, speedy peace, is very complicated. Your country has turned all ideas upside down. In approaching this question, it is necessary to face just complaints or prejudices. Still this is no less the most ardent desire of my heart, and I trust that soon we shall be able to reconcile our nations. In England there is no ill will, but great preparations are making. Necessarily this causes some delay until things get fairly under way; then, please God, all will go smoothly. The news you send me of your son gives me great pleasure. Your brothers and sisters were, at last accounts, very well, and so was my wife. I, too, am in good health. Believe me as ever your loving father, FRANCIS."

At the beginning of 1814 Marie Louise, who heard much more talk about armaments than about nego- tiations for peace, wrote to her father a letter which contained this sentence, full of alarm: "Since your troops are at the French frontier, the whole nation is arming. I am afraid that the Emperor will leave soon for the army, and will leave me in the middle of this city, which is preparing for the combat." Far from her husband, the young Empress was to feel lonely and anxious. Her principal counsellor was to be Joseph, whom she scarcely knew, and who, in deep distress at losing the Spanish crown, had only within a few days recovered Napoleon's good graces.

At the end of 1813 Napoleon was on bad terms with his four brothers. His quarrel with Lucien still continued. He forbade Jerome to come to Paris, and the unhappy monarch, inconsolable for the loss of his Westphalian kingdom, was wandering with his shadow of a court, from Coblentz to Cologne, from Cologne to Aix-la-Chapelle. Louis's heart was full of bitterness, and though he submitted, it was only conditionally. " So long as Holland is occupied by the enemy," he wrote to Caulaincourt, "I do not claim the title of king, and it is a matter of indifference to me whether I am given another. I come simply as a Frenchman to share the dangers of the moment, and to be as useful as I can. If Holland falls again into the Emperor's power, and he does not restore it to me, my conscience as King would prevent my remaining in France, and I should again depart. If, on the other hand, at the peace, Holland should be ceded to any other monarch than the Emperor, and my abdication were necessary for sanctioning the treaty, I should not refuse it."

As for Joseph, he looked upon himself as a victim ; and at the end of 1813 he was still denouncing Napoleon from his castle of Morfontaine, where he lived surrounded by a little court which Count Miot de Mélito thus describes: " The assemblage of persons at Morfontaine presented a curious sight. There was to be seen a King of Spain without an inch of territory in that country ; a wife of a French general who had been raised to the rank of Prince and had become our mortal enemy; a Princess, the daughter of the King of Würtemberg, who had been given in marriage to a brother of Napoleon, and who was to join a league formed to overthrow the Emperor's power; Spanish, German, and French courtiers, who had no more court to pay ; and to crown all, the Patriarch of the Indies, Grand Inquisitor of Spain, said mass to us from time to time. Hunting, fishing, picnics, meals, the card table, brought together the crowd who were surprised to find themselves together. We were all simply amusing ourselves until the tempest that was roaring at a distance should break upon us and scatter us."

To Joseph's great despair, Napoleon, who saw at last that his brother's cause in Spain was absolutely desperate, had secretly negotiated with Ferdinand VII., who was still a prisoner in the Castle of Valençay. Then a treaty had been drawn up, December 11, 1813, containing the following conditions: The restoration of Ferdinand VII. to the throne, the return of the French garrisons, the withdrawal of the Spanish and English armies beyond the Pyrenees, and a general amnesty. If this treaty had been signed a few weeks earlier, it would have saved the Empire, by adding to Napoleon's army all the French troops in Spain. But it was too late. The Spanish Regency threw delays in the way of the recognition of the treaty, and Wellington continued his march.

When Joseph heard that the treaty of Valençay had been signed, he was profoundly mortified. He regarded himself as tricked, insulted, betrayed by his brother; and no sovereign by divine right was ever more furious at the loss of his crown. The King of Spain, after he was dispossessed, imagined that he could obtain another kingdom, as if Napoleon still had thrones at his disposition. A long and painful negotiation was to ensue between the two brothers before Joseph could resign himself to being simply a French Prince, still bearing the title of King. December 29, 1813, he wrote to the Emperor: —

"SIRE: The violation of Swiss territory has opened France to the enemy. In such circumstances I desire that Your Majesty should be convinced that my heart is wholly French. Having been brought back to France by events, I should be happy to be of any use to you, and am ready to undertake anything to attest my devotion. I also know, Sire, what I owe to Spain; I see my duty, and I desire to do it thoroughly. As to my rights I am anxious only to sacrifice them in behalf of the general good of humanity, happy if, by this sacrifice, I may be able to contribute to the pacification of Europe. I hope that Your Majesty will consent to appoint one of his Ministers to come to an understanding on this subject with the Duke of Santa Fé, my Minister of Foreign Affairs."

The Emperor replied: —

"MY BROTHER: I have received your letter of December 29. It contains too much wit for the posi-

tion in which I am placed. In two words the case
stands thus: France is invaded, all Europe is in arms
against France, and especially against me. You are
no longer King of Spain. I do not desire Spain for
myself, and I am not desirous of disposing of it; I
do not care to interfere any further with the affairs
of that country than to live in peace with it and to
be able to make use of my army. What do you mean
to do? Do you desire to side with the throne like a
French Prince? You have my friendship, your suite,
and will be my subject, as a Prince of the blood.
Then you must, like me, announce your position; you
must write me a plain letter which I can have printed,
receive all the authorities, and show yourself zealous
for me and for the King of Rome, and favorable to
the Regency of the Empress. Do you not find that
possible? Have you not enough good sense for that?
If not, you must withdraw to a distance of forty
leagues from Paris to some obscure provincial castle.
There you will live quietly if I live; you will be killed
or arrested if I die. You will be of no use to me, to
the family, to your daughters, to France; but you
will not be dangerous to me, and will not annoy me.
Choose promptly, and decide."

Joseph had to submit, and this he did. January 7,
1814, he wrote to his brother: —

"SIRE: I have received Your Majesty's letter.
You speak to me of friendship, and I confess that I
had not expected this. I respect Your Majesty too
highly, and I set too much store by your friendship,

not to accept it as heartily as before. The first proof
of it that Your Majesty can give me is to appoint M.
de Santa Fé, or any one else, to superintend the dis-
tribution of aid to the excellent families that have
followed me from Spain. The second is to approve
my retaining the Spanish and French officers whom,
after their showing me such remarkable devotion, I
cannot abandon without becoming the most ungrate-
ful and neglectful of men."

The reconciliation between the two brothers was
complete. January 10, 1814, Napoleon sent this
letter to Joseph: —

"My Brother: I have it published in an order of
the palace, that henceforth you are to be announced
as King Joseph, and the Queen as Queen Julia, with
the honors and formalities employed for French
Princes. . . . I authorize you to wear the uniform
of the grenadiers of my Guard, such as I wear myself. I think it would be well for you not to wear
any foreign orders, but simply a French decoration.
Send me a list of the persons you would like to have
form your household, as well as the Queen's household, and tell me what day you would like to receive
the court and the authorities."

King Joseph established himself at the Luxembourg. The palace resumed the appearance it had
worn eight years before, when Joseph lived in it as
a French Prince and Grand Elector. January 16,
1814, the Senators and high officers of the Empire
called upon him there to pay their formal respects.

At the very moment when Napoleon was becoming
reconciled with King Joseph, he heard of the defection of King Murat. Curiously enough, there were
at that time two Queens of the Two Sicilies, one by
divine right, the other by right of Napoleon's con-
quests; both were named Caroline. One was a sister
of Marie Antoinette, the other the sister of the Emperor Napoleon. Well, of these two Queens, the
one of whom the Emperor had reason to approve
was the sister of Marie Antoinette. While Caroline,
Murat's wife, was already thinking of siding with
Austria, against her own brother, the other Caroline
took pains to send Napoleon word in good season.
June 8, 1813, the Count of Narbonne, the French
Ambassador at Vienna, had written to the Duke of
Bassano, at that time Minister of Foreign Affairs:
" I must inform you of the arrival of an agent of the
former Queen of Naples, the mother-in-law of the
Emperor of Austria. He has orders to come to an
understanding with the French Ambassador, and is
to give me a memorandum of everything that he has
seen, of everything with which he is charged. . . .
This man, who brings, as it were, credentials from
the Queen, talks of nothing but the hate of the English in Sicily and Malta, of the ways of driving them
out, and forces me, by everything that he says, to
recall to your attention what I had the honor of laying before you with regard to Prince Cariati." This
Prince was aide-de-camp of King Murat; he had
aroused the suspicions of the Count of Narbonne,

who wrote about him thus: "Prince Cariati, who has come here under the pretext of buying horses, holds himself aloof from me more and more every day, and lives on most friendly terms with our enemies. Of whom, of what is he the agent?" So it was a Princess of Bourbon, a Hapsburg by birth, who tried to open Napoleon's eyes to the approaching defection of the husband of a Princess Bonaparte! And it was this same sister of Queen Marie Antoinette who was soon to reproach the Empress Marie Louise with having abandoned the Emperor in his misfortune! That was certainly one of the strangest occurrences in a period fertile in contrasts and all sorts of surprises.

The anticipations of the sister of Marie Antoinette were soon verified. King Joseph wrote, January 14, 1813, to his brother-in-law, King Murat: "I have just had a long interview with the Emperor, and I am convinced that he is sincerely desirous of peace. If you can contribute to that in any way, it will only be by siding as your heart and your duties direct, with the party that sincerely desires peace. You cannot forget that your political duty is to-day in harmony with the demands of honor, which require you to make every effort to procure peace for France that she may consolidate the present political institutions. I do not think I am wrong in thus stating to you my opinion. I am convinced that the misfortunes of France will sooner or later bring about your own. A prompt peace will save everything; you

ought then to aid it in every way, and to be sure that
this peace will be of more service to you than anything which the allies may now promise you.   Their
promises are evidently fallacious; the day when you
shall give yourself up to them will have no morrow
for you, because then they will have no interest in
sparing you, and they will covet for themselves or for
their families the possession of the most beautiful
country in Europe.   Your existence, my dear brother,
is certainly bound up with the Imperial dynasty of
France.   If the Bourbons could reappear in France,
do you think that you would long retain Naples?
However, fortune has changed, and the allies are now
the stronger; but if all the Princes of the Emperor's
family, if all Frenchmen follow my example, the
balance will soon be restored, peace will be made, and
the different States consolidated.   This requires that
you reject every other feeling, and that you throw
yourself, with the noble enthusiasm for the right that
distinguishes you, on the side of duty, of honor."

Alas! why did not Murat, the champion of the
Revolution, the first cavalry officer in Europe, the
embodiment of bravery, the hero of legend, listen to
the patriotic advice of Joseph?   He might have
united his forces with those of Prince Eugene and
have attacked the invasion in the rear; he would have
saved the Empire and France; he would have died
on the throne, covered with glory, instead of being
shot!   But what did he do?   He joined with Austria, and declared war against France; he invaded the

Roman States which then formed a French department, the Department of the Tiber, and became one of the principal members of the coalition.

On hearing this Napoleon sent Monseigneur de Beaumont, the Archbishop of Bourges, to Fontainebleau, bearing this letter to the Pope : —

"VERY HOLY FATHER: I turn to Your Holiness to inform you that inasmuch as the King of Naples has formed an alliance with the coalition, of which one object seems to be the eventual reunion of Rome with its States, His Majesty the Emperor and King has judged it in conformity with the true policy of his Empire and the interests of the Roman people to restore the Roman States to Your Holiness. He prefers seeing them in your hands to seeing them in the hands of any other Sovereign whatsoever. Consequently, I am authorized to sign a treaty re-establishing peace between the Emperor and the Pope. The temporal power of Your Holiness will be recognized, and the Roman States, so far as they have been added to the French Empire, will be restored, together with the fortresses, to the hands of Your Holiness, or of his agents; this Convention will relate only to temporal matters and to the Pope as Sovereign of Rome." This letter was given to the Pope January 20, 1814.

Count d'Haussonville, in his fine and dignified studies on the Church of Rome and the First Empire, has observed : "Strangely enough it was the Emperor who voluntarily offered the Pope, not merely liberty, not merely the restoration of part of his States, but

the complete re-establishment of his temporal sovereignty as it had existed before all the wars, which,
ever since the Revolution, had changed the whole
face of Europe.   Stranger still, by a curious exchange
of positions, which almost seemed like a punishment, it was now Napoleon, who after violently
wringing from the Pope so many sacrifices, was reduced to wondering whether the Pope would receive
this present from his hand.   He was justified in his
doubts, for Pius VII. refused it."

The Holy Father received M. de Beaumont with
his usual kindliness, but told him that he could not
enter into any negotiations, because the restoration
of his States, being a mere act of justice, could not
become the subject of any treaty, and that besides,
whatever he should do outside of his own States
would seem the result of violence, and would be an
occasion for offence for the Catholic world.   "All
that I ask," he went on, "is to return to Rome as
soon as possible.   I have need of nothing, and Providence alone will lead me back.   It is possible that
my sins make me unworthy of seeing Rome again,
but you may be sure that my successors will recover
all the States that belong to them."

What had been the upshot of the conqueror's attempts on the Eternal City?   He had succeeded no
better in Rome than in Spain.   This hardy gamester,
who had been so successful at the beginning of his
career, failed at every point the moment that his luck
left him.   The construction that he had reared at

the cost of so much blood fell like card-houses. The earth crumbled before him. Betrayed by fortune, suspicious of his own family, regretting the short-lived crowns he had given to his brothers and his brother-in-law, perceiving only too late that the main cause of his disasters was that he had set a fruitless family ambition above the great principle of nation-ality, Napoleon, dissatisfied with himself and with others, did not like to see his brothers dethroned; they were a living reproach to him. This principle of nationality, the programme of which he announced only at Saint Helena — the application of which, tim-idly and incompletely tried by his successor, was to be so fatal to France — the principle which he had failed to recognize throughout his reign, in Holland, Germany, Spain, and Italy, created against the win-ner of countless battles a coalition of peoples far more to be feared than a coalition of kings.

Ferdinand VII. was to leave Valençay too late, and Pius VII., Fontainebleau too late. If the Holy Father had been restored to his temporal sovereignty a few weeks earlier, he would have prevented Murat's invasion of the Roman States, he would have pre-vented the defection which that brave monarch, when he returned in the following year to a feeling of his duties towards France and the Emperor, was to atone for most heroically.

Napoleon, when he was about to take an eternal farewell of his wife and son, was overwhelmed with the gloomiest thoughts. To whatever side he turned his eyes, he saw on the horizon nothing but clouds as black as night, or red as blood. About his tottering throne he perceived an air rank with a fatal taint of decay and treachery. Doubtful of everything, no longer forming illusions, he vowed to throw the final cast, to conquer or die; but Providence was not to consent, and he would have smiled pitifully if any one had predicted to him that he would survive the catastrophes and humiliations concealed in the immediate future. It was through his pride that the great man had sinned, and it was in his pride that he was to be punished.

XX.

WHEN Napoleon was on the point of setting out for the war, he consoled himself for all his cares and sorrows with seeing his son. But this sight brought anguish as well as comfort. What future did Providence reserve for the boy? Would he be Emperor or an exile? Would his first steps be guided by his father, or would he become a prisoner of the foreigners? Would he wield the sceptre of the new Charlemagne, or suffer the fate of Astyanax? It was a cruel uncertainty, an enigma of fate! Then the conqueror, knowing by experience what a father's love is, possibly repented the barren sacrifice of so many young men upon the battlefield. Then he was moved by a retrospective pity, and the voice of humanity made him quiver. His own suffering taught him what others had suffered, and reminded him of the anguish he had brought on other parents, who had known the torture of surviving their children. He no longer loved war, which before had been the object of his ardent passion. Instead of preparing new slaughter, he would have preferred to dry the tears and to heal the wounds, making himself loved and blessed. But it was too late. The untiring warrior became peaceable when peace was no longer possible. There was no other solution than bloodshed, and always more bloodshed. He who had taken the sword was to perish by the sword. Meanwhile his eyes, still full of gloomy visions, which had gazed on burning Moscow, on the snowfields of Russia, the struggle on the Elster bridge, were resting gently on the fair head of the boy who looked like an angel. His ears, so long fatigued by the roar of shells and muskets, now found delight in listening to the first stammering words of infancy. He, sated with glory, tired of all the grandeur and the misery of the world, sick of the smell of incense, already suspected that after all their adulation, his courtiers would hurl mud in his face, and depressed by all this ingratitude, apostasy, and treachery, he became disgusted with human nature, and found his only pleasure in the contemplation of innocence.

The King of Rome was nearly three years old. His charming disposition and his precocious intelligence were much admired. Madame de Montesquiou, his governess, said that he was " proud and sensitive." " Proud and sensitive," repeated Napoleon; " that is very well. That is the way I like to have him." Amid the numberless cares besieging him during the troubled days preceding the fatal campaign of 1814, the Emperor, in spite of the manifold afflictions that tormented him, found time to play with his son.

M. de Méneval says : " Whether he was busy reading
an important report, or was sitting at his desk, which
was hollowed in the middle, with two shelves, like
wings, on the sides, and was always covered deep
with papers, when he was signing a despatch, every
word of which had to be weighed, his son, seated on
his knees or held against his breast, never left him.
Being endowed with a wonderful power of concen-
trating his attention, he knew how to give his attention to the most serious matters while humoring his
son's whims. Sometimes he would lay aside his
great thoughts and lie down on the floor by the side
of his son, playing with him like another child, eager
to amuse him and to spare him every annoyance."

Napoleon never grew tired of looking at the little
King of Rome. A vague foreboding warned him
that he had not long to see him, and he was softened,
and he wished to inspire others with his own feelings ; he hoped that the appeals of his paternal heart
would find echoes in others' hearts. Sunday, January 24, 1814, he assembled at the Tuileries, in the
Hall of the Marshals, the officers of the National
Guard which was to defend Paris, and prepared one
of those moving, pathetic, as well as somewhat
theatrical scenes, of which he possessed the secret ;
for no man in the world understood better how to
strike the imagination and to place himself majestically before, not merely his contemporaries, but also
posterity.

The officers of the National Guard, to the number

of seven or eight hundred, all in uniform, formed in a circle around the Hall of the Marshals. At noon the Emperor passed through this hall on his way to the chapel, according to his habit on Sundays, and he was warmly greeted. He did not stop, but pushed on to the mass. That over, he returned, and took up his place in the middle of the hall where the officers of the twelve legions of the National Guard of Paris had remained. A few moments later, the Empress appeared accompanied by Madame de Montesquiou, who held the King of Rome in her arms. No one expected this; and the reason of this sudden entrance was unknown to all. Napoleon had the little King put down; then, holding him by one hand while his mother held him by the other, he made his way to the midst of the group of officers of the National Guard who lined the Hall of the Marshals; then, with a warmth and an emotion which deeply moved his hearers, he uttered these solemn words: "Officers of the National Guard, I am glad to see you gathered about me. I am starting to take my place at the head of my army. As I leave the capital I confide to your protection my wife and my son on whom so many hopes rest. I owed you this proof of my confidence in return for all those that you have never ceased to give me at the most important moments of my career. I shall leave without anxiety, since they will be under your faithful guard. I leave in your care what is, next to France, the dearest thing I have in the world. It may happen that during the coming campaign the enemy may find an opportunity to approach your walls. If this takes place, remember it can be an affair of no more than a few days, and that I shall soon come to your aid. I beg of you to remain united and to withstand all attempts to divide you. Every means will be employed to detach you from the faithful performance of your duties; but I count on your rejection of these perfidious temptations." Then Napoleon stopped for a moment; he fixed his eyes on Marie Louise and on the King of Rome whom the Empress had taken in her arms and showing the Assembly the child whose expressive face seemed to correspond with the solemnity of the occasion, he exclaimed, with a voice full of emotion, " I entrust her to you, gentlemen; I entrust her to the affection of my faithful city of Paris."

At these words their enthusiasm reached its height; tears filled every eye. In the hall there was not a single man who did not seem ready to shed the last drop of his blood in behalf of the Imperial family.

The very men who, the evening before, had been harshly criticising the Emperor, forgot their griefs in a moment. They condemned the monarch; they had pity for the father. What he had lost as Emperor he regained as a man. Politics gave way to humanity. Marie Louise, generally cold and self-possessed, was overcome by the general emotion and nearly fainted. This foreigner was for a moment the living image, the symbol of France harassed and distressed. Napoleon, seeing that he was still loved and admired, had a momentary return of confidence in himself and his star. He fancied himself capable of wonders, as in the heroic days of his marvellous career. His genius arose to its full height. He dreamed of a brilliant revenge, of ovations, and of a real apotheosis. He promised himself a return under triumphal arches.

The Emperor received the high officials after the officers of the National Guard. " What struck me most," says Count Miot de Mélito, " was the language of the Senators. Never had they been more obsequious. Among others M. de Laplace, who came up to me, spoke of the state of affairs with such keen interest, of his devotion to the Emperor, and of his confidence in him with such deep emotion, and especially of the current rumor of the proclamation at Bordeaux in favor of the Bourbons with such indignation, that I might have thought that the former royal dynasty had no greater enemy, and our Emperor no greater friend than he. Could I indeed have ever supposed from his language that, as has since been affirmed, he had never ceased to love the Bourbons in his heart ! "

Miot de Mélito said, speaking of this same reception, January 23, 1814 : " The Emperor received the officials, to whom he uttered assurances of devotion which were soon contradicted. But it was his fate to nourish illusions up to the last, and to take for sincere protestations of loyalty what were really artificial utterances begotten by long practice in servility.

As for me, I soon discerned, in all I saw and heard, the change that had taken place in this court, at once so magnificent and so humble. I recalled the brilliant days after the birth of the King of Rome, and compared them with those I was witnessing. Where was the herd of Ambassadors from every nation, the Princes, the Kings, the courtiers, who, in other and different days, crowded this place, and saluted the throne, now so insecure? All that pomp had vanished. Of the crowd of foreigners there remained only a few Senators, a handful of German or Italian Councillors of State, summoned from the departments annexed to France."

Touching as was the scene of the morning, that of the evening was profoundly gloomy. Count Mollien, Minister of the Treasury, thus describes it: "When the Empress had gone away, the Emperor detained the Ministers, to whom, he said, he wished to announce his final preparations. His first words, in fact, had all the solemnity of the reading of a will; but after he had spoken briefly of the insufficiency of the means at his disposal, in spite of the exertions of his Ministers, to whom he rendered perfect justice, his eye, as if falling by chance on those present, lighted up, and as if suddenly inspired, he added that he knew very well that he was leaving in Paris other enemies than those with whom he was going to fight, and that his absence left the field free for them. These insinuations were veiled, but there was no possibility of mistaking them. He grew more violent when he noticed that this official coolly continued his conversation with King Joseph in a corner of the room. Count Mollien then spoke to the Emperor of the financial condition, and proposed measures to prevent an absolute deficit. 'My dear man,' said Napoleon, 'if the enemy reaches the gates of Paris, the Empire will have ceased to exist.'"

The same day, Sunday, January 23, 1814, Pope Pius VII. left Fontainebleau. He had refused to treat with Napoleon, but he had said to the prelate charged with proposing the arrangement to him: "Assure the Emperor that I am not his enemy. I love France, and when I get to Rome, you will see that I shall do everything that is proper." Since Cossack bands had already appeared in the neighborhood of Montereau, Napoleon did not care to leave his venerable adversary within reach of a sudden attack. But, instead of letting him depart alone and free, he had entrusted him to the care of Lagorse, the commander of the gens d'armes, who, while seeming to carry him back to Rome, was really charged with leading him slowly, by a devious route, to Savona, where a credit had already been deposited with the Receiver General of the Department of Montenotte, providing twelve thousand francs a month for the support of the Pope.

The Pope was then still a prisoner. As M. Veuillot has said: "It was well that the Roman pontiff, timid and captive, should nevertheless appear before the eyes of the whole world as the only sovereign whom Napoleon could not force to abandon his duty. When England invented so many lies and purchased so much treachery, when haughty Austria gave the hand of an Archduchess to the divorced husband of Josephine, this dethroned monarch, this poor priest, gazing at his crucifix, after listening to the Imperial messages of human omnipotence, replied, ' No; I will not give up my conscience to recover my crown! *Non possumus.*' The world had need of this lesson, at once haughty and humble."

At the moment of leaving Fontainebleau, Pius VII., who had just heard mass, summoned all the Cardinals present in the palace, and spoke to them these words : " On the point of leaving you, without knowing our destination, even without knowing whether we shall have the consolation of seeing you again gathered about us, we have desired to call you together to express our feelings and our intentions. We have the firm conviction — and could we think otherwise ? — that your conduct, whether you remain together or are again scattered, will conform to your position and your character. Still, we recommend you all, wherever you may be transferred, to act in such a way that your attitude and all your actions shall express the just grief you feel for the sufferings of the church and for the captivity of its head. . . . We expressly recommend to you to close your ears to any proposition relating to a treaty about spiritual and temporal affairs ; for this is our absolute and firm wish." The Cardinals were touched, and promised obedience. Then the Holy Father, after a short prayer, went down into the courtyard by the grand staircase, by which Napoleon was to come down a few weeks later to bid his memorable farewell to the Imperial Guard. The venerable old man, calm and serene, quietly entered the carriage which was to carry him to his unknown destination ; and extending his arms through the window, gave a last blessing to the few spectators who stood mourning his departure.

It was when Pius VII. was leaving Fontainebleau that Napoleon was signing the letters patent conferring the regency upon the Empress. Marie Louise took her oath before her husband, at a council composed of the French Princes, the high officials, and the Ministers. At that time she was determined to remain faithful to this oath as sovereign, wife, and mother. It must be acknowledged that up to the fall of the Empire she did nothing blameworthy, and that, though she left Paris, it was with great regret and in obedience to her husband's formal command. At this time her attitude was absolutely correct, and in none of the contemporary Memoirs do we find a word of criticism of her conduct up to the time of her husband's abdication.

Later she displayed ingratitude, and a lack of the devotion which her duty required; but it would be unjust to hold her responsible for the sufferings of

France. Her leave-taking from the Emperor, which took place at the Tuileries, January 25, 1814, at seven in the morning, was very touching. She wept profusely. Thiers says about this farewell: "Napoleon, when he left, unconscious that he was embracing them for the last time, hugged tenderly his wife and his son. His wife was in tears, and feared she would never see him again. She was in fact fated never to see him, although the enemy's bullets were not to kill him. She would certainly have been much surprised if she had been told that this husband, then the object of all her care, was to die on a distant island, in the middle of the ocean, the prisoner of Europe, and forgotten by her. As for him, no prediction would have astonished him, — whether the cruelest desertion, the most ardent devotion, — for he expected anything from men; he knew them to the core, though he treated them as if he did not know what they really were."

Laying aside his sceptre and his gala dress to put on his uniform and his sword, the Emperor became a soldier. As Lamartine said: "The most prejudiced historian finds him great in this final effort to grasp his fleeting fortune. He seemed ten years younger. His soul, which had been benumbed by the throne, triumphed over the languor of his body." The trumpet-call aroused the hero of countless battles. He seemed back in the days of Arcole and Castiglione. But if he had the genius of that time, he lacked the good fortune. As admirable a tactician in the campaign of 1814 as at any period of his career, he was to accomplish miracles, but fruitless miracles; and his superhuman efforts proved power-less against implacable fate.

INDEX.

316   *INDEX.*

Typography by J. S. Cushing & Co., Boston.

Presswork by Berwick & Smith, Boston.

FAMOUS WOMEN OF THE FRENCH COURT.

CHARLES SCRIBNER's SONS, PUBLISHERS.

WITHIN the past few years M. Imbert de Saint-
Amand has written a series of volumes which
have made him one of the most popular authors of
France. Each has for its nucleus some portion of the
life of one of the eminent women who have presided
over or figured at the French court, either at Versailles or the Tuileries. But though thus largely
biographical and possessing the interest inseparable
from personality, the volumes are equally pictures of
the times they describe. He is himself saturated with
the literature and history of the period, and what
mainly distinguishes his books is the fact that they
are in considerable part made up of contemporary
letters and memoirs, so that the reader hears the
characters themselves speak, and is brought into the
closest imaginary contact with them. Moreover, the
complexion of the mosaic thus cleverly mortised is
familiar rather than heroic. The historian is not
above gossip in its good sense, and the way in which
the life of the time and of its distinguished personages is depicted is extremely intimate as well as vivid
and truthful.

The first volumes to appear, rendered into particularly idiomatic English by Mr. Thomas Sergeant
Perry, whose accomplishments as a translator are well
known, relate to Marie Antoinette, Josephine as wife
of the First Consul, and Marie Louise. They give a
vivid representation of the momentous times immediately before, during, and after the epoch of the
Revolution. Probably no times in any country were

ever so picturesque, so crowded with events, and so peopled with striking characters. The characteristics of the ancient régime, the occupations of the courtiers at Versailles and other incidents of the old order of things tottering to its fall, are grouped effectively around the sympathetic figure of Louis Sixteenth's queen. Josephine is taken as the centre of the new society that issued from the disorganization wrought by the Revolution, and in "The Happy Days of the Empress Marie Louise," we are led behind the scenes and shown the domestic life as well as the splendid court pomp of the world's Conqueror at the acme of his career.

THE WIFE OF THE FIRST CONSUL. By IMBERT DE SAINT-AMAND. Translated by THOMAS SERGEANT PERRY.

THE HAPPY DAYS OF THE EMPRESS MARIE LOUISE. By the same.

MARIE ANTOINETTE AND THE END OF THE OLD RÉGIME. By the same

CITIZENESS BONAPARTE.

MARIE LOUISE AND THE DECADENCE OF THE EMPIRE.

THE COURT OF THE EMPRESS JOSEPHINE.

Each with Portrait. 12mo. $1.25 per volume.

CHARLES SCRIBNER'S SONS,

PUBLISHERS,

743-745 BROADWAY, NEW YORK

THE FIRST AMERICAN EDITION

MEMOIRS OF

NAPOLEON BONAPARTE

By LOUIS ANTOINE FAUVELET DE BOURRIENNE

His Private Secretary

With 34 Full-page Portraits and Other Illustrations

EDITED BY COL. R. W. PHIPPS. NEW AND REVISED EDITION

The Set, 4 Vols., 12mo, Cloth, in a Box, $5.00

Characteristic bindings in Half Morocco and Half Calf, specially designed
for this work, can now be supplied

The Set, 4 Vols., in a box, Half Morocco, gilt top, . . . $8.00
  "   "   "   Half Calf,   " . . .   10.00

CHARLES SCRIBNER'S SONS, Publishers

NEW YORK

FOR sixty years Bourrienne's "Memoirs of Napoleon"
has been a standard authority to which every one
has turned for a graphic, entertaining picture of
the man as he appeared to his intimate friend and Secretary. Bourrienne, who had been the friend and com-
panion of Napoleon at school, became his Secretary in
1797 and remained in this confidential position till 1802.
His "Memoirs" has heretofore been accessible only in
the English editions. It is now proposed to publish
immediately in a popular Library Edition, in four 12mo
volumes, an exact reprint of the latest English edition.
This American edition will contain the thirty-four portraits and other illustrations of the original, together with
all the other features that give distinction to the work—
the chronology of Napoleon's life, the prefaces to the

several editions, the author's introduction, and the additional matter which supplements Bourrienne's work, an account of the important events of the Hundred Days, of Napoleon's surrender to the English, and of his residence and death at St. Helena, with anecdotes and illustrative extracts from contemporary Memoirs. The personality of one of the greatest figures in history is placed before the reader with remarkable fidelity and dramatic power by one who was the Emperor's confidant and the sharer of his thoughts and fortunes. The picture of the man Napoleon is of fascinating interest. Besides this, the book is full of the most interesting anecdotes, *bon mots*, character sketches, dramatic incidents, and the gossip of court and camp at one of the most stirring epochs of history, taken from contemporary Memoirs and incorporated in the work by the editors of the different editions.

LIST OF PORTRAITS, ETC.

NAPOLEON I.
LETITIA RAMOLINO
THE EMPRÈSS JOSEPHINE
EUGÈNE BEAUHARNAIS
GENERAL KLÉBER
MARSHAL LANNES
TALLEYRAND
GENERAL DUROC
MURAT, KING OF NAPLES
GENERAL DESAIX
GENERAL MOREAU
HORTENSE BEAUHARNAIS
THE EMPRESS JOSEPHINE
NAPOLEON I.

THE DUC D'ENGHIEN
GENERAL PICHEGRU
MARSHAL NEY
CAULAINCOURT, DUKE OF VICENZA
MARSHAL DAVOUST
CHARGE OF THE CUIRASSIERS AT EYLAU
GENERAL JUNOT
MARSHAL SOULT
THE EMPRESS MARIA LOUISA
GENERAL LASALLE
COLORED MAP SHOWING NAPOLEON'S DOMINION
THE EMPRESS MARIA LOUISA

MARSHAL MASSÉNA
MARSHAL MACDONALD
FAC-SIMILE OF THE EMPEROR'S ABDICATION IN 1814
NAPOLEON I.
MARSHAL SOUCHET
THE DUKE OF WELLINGTON
PLANS OF BATTLE OF WATERLOO
MARSHAL BLUCHER
MARSHAL GOUVION ST. CYR
MARSHAL NEY
THE KING OF ROME
GENERAL BESSIÈRES

"*If you want something to read, both interesting and amusing, get the Mémoires de Bourrienne. These are the only authentic Memoirs of Napoleon which have yet appeared. The style is not brilliant, but that only makes them the more trustworthy.*"—PRINCE METTERNICH.

"The writer was a man of uncommon penetration, and he enjoyed opportunities for intimate knowledge of Napoleon's life and character such as no other person possessed; and the liveliness of his style renders the Memoirs interesting reading from the first page to the last. The volumes are enriched with a large number of excellent portraits." —*The Academy.*

"It is a brilliant picture of Napoleon as he appeared in his daily life to one who held the unique position of friend, Minister and Secretary, depicting the personality of the Emperor with extraordinary vividness and truthfulness. It is impossible not to recognize the great value of these Memoirs."—*New York Times.*

"*M. de Bourrienne shows us the hero of Marengo and Austerlitz in his night-gown and slippers—with a* trait de plume *he, in a hundred instances, places the real man before us, with all of his personal habits and peculiarities of manner, temper and conversation.*"—FROM THE PREFACE.

THE SET, 4 VOLS., 12MO, IN A BOX, $5.00.

www.ingramcontent.com/pod-product-compliance
Lightning Source LLC
Chambersburg PA
CBHW020936030726
47496CB00005B/1220